ARCO

FEDERAL CIVIL SERVICE JOBS

13TH EDITION

Hy Hammer

ARCO

TM

THOMSON LEARNING

Australia • Canada • Denmark • Japan • Mexico • New Zealand • Philippines
Puerto Rico • Singapore • South Africa • Spain • United Kingdom • United States

ARCO ™

THOMSON LEARNING

Thirteenth Edition

An ARCO Book

ARCO is a registered trademark of Thomson Learning, Inc., and is used herein under license by Peterson's.

About Peterson's

Founded in 1966, Peterson's, a division of Thomson Learning, is the nation's largest and most respected provider of lifelong learning online resources, software, reference guides, and books. The Education Supersite^{SM} at petersons.com—the Web's most heavily traveled education resource—has searchable databases and interactive tools for contacting U.S.-accredited institutions and programs. CollegeQuest^{SM} (CollegeQuest.com) offers a complete solution for every step of the college decision-making process. GradAdvantage™ (GradAdvantage.org), developed with Educational Testing Service, is the only electronic admissions service capable of sending official graduate test score reports with a candidate's online application. Peterson's serves more than 55 million education consumers annually.

Thomson Learning is among the world's leading providers of lifelong learning, serving the needs of individuals, learning institutions, and corporations with products and services for both traditional classrooms and for online learning. For more information about the products and services offered by Thomson Learning, please visit www.thomsonlearning.com. Headquartered in Stamford, Connecticut, with offices worldwide, Thomson Learning is part of The Thomson Corporation (www.thomson.com), a leading e-information and solutions company in the business, professional, and education marketplaces. The Corporation's common shares are listed on the Toronto and London stock exchanges.

For more information, contact Peterson's, 2000 Lenox Drive, Lawrenceville, NJ 08648; 800-338-3282; or find us on the World Wide Web at: www.petersons.com/about

ISBN 0-7645-6107-3

Printed in the United States of America

10 9 8 7 6 5 4 3 2 1   02 01 00

CONTENTS

PART THREE
Useful Information About Civil Service Tests

Examination Preparation   175

PART FOUR
Appendices

A Important Civil Service Employment Contacts   243

B Webliography of Federal Employment Web Sites   249

C Federal Occupations that Require Examinations   251

D Glossary of Civil Service Hiring Terminology   257

Introduction

The federal government is the employer of a far greater number of Americans than any other employer. A large percentage of these government employees are members of the military, but there are also millions of civilian federal employees. Many civilian federal employees are employed through the legislative branch—the Congress itself, the General Accounting Office, the Government Printing Office, and the Library of Congress, for example—and through the judicial branch—the Supreme Court and the U.S. Court system. But by far the greatest number of federal civilian employees are employees of the executive branch, executive departments, and independent agencies such as the U.S. Postal Service, the General Services Administration, the Smithsonian, the Environmental Protection Agency, and the Office of Personnel Administration itself, to name only a few.

The executive branch includes the Office of the President, the departments with cabinet representation, and a number of independent agencies, commissions, and boards. This branch is responsible for such activities as administering federal laws, handling international relations, conserving natural resources, treating and rehabilitating disabled veterans, conducting scientific research, maintaining the flow of supplies to the armed forces, and administering other programs to promote the health and welfare of the people.

The federal government employs about three million white-collar workers. Entrance requirements for white-collar jobs vary widely. Entrants into professional occupations are required to have highly specialized knowledge in a specified field, as evidenced by completion of a prescribed college course of study. Occupations typical of this group are attorney, physicist, and engineer.

Entrants into administrative and managerial occupations usually are not required to have specialized knowledge but rather they must indicate, by graduation from a four-year college or by responsible job experience, that they have the potential for future development. The entrant usually begins at a trainee level and learns the duties of the job after being hired. Typical jobs in this group are budget analyst, claims examiner, purchasing officer, administrative assistant, and personnel officer.

Technician, clerical, and aide/assistant jobs have entry-level positions that usually are filled by persons having a high-school diploma or the equivalent. For many of these positions, no prior experience or training is required. The entry-level position is usually that of trainee, where the duties of the job are learned and skill is improved. Persons with junior college or technical school training or those having specialized skills may enter these occupations at higher levels. Jobs typical of this group are engineering technician, supply clerk, clerk-typist, and nursing assistant.

Blue-collar jobs—service, craft, and manual labor—provide employment to over 600,000 workers. The majority of these workers are in establishments such as naval shipyards, arsenals, air bases, or army depots, or they work on construction, harbor, flood-control, irrigation, or reclamation projects.

The single largest group of blue-collar workers consists of mobile equipment operators and mechanics. Among these jobs are forklift operator, chauffeur, truck driver, and automobile mechanic. The next largest group is general laborers who perform a wide variety of manual jobs.

Many skilled occupations may be entered through apprenticeship programs. Experience normally is not required to qualify, but a test may be given to indicate whether an applicant has an aptitude for the occupation.

Federal employees are stationed in all parts of the United States and its territories and in many foreign countries. (Although most government departments and agencies have their headquarters in the Washington, D.C., metropolitan area, only 1 out of 11 federal workers was employed there at the beginning of this year.)

ONE

The Best Job for You in Government

CONTENTS

DECIDING IF A GOVERNMENT CAREER IS RIGHT FOR YOU

Getting hired by the federal government is like trying to ride an elephant. It can be a safe and rather comfortable ride—and once you're on, it's not easy to fall off. But, getting *on* the elephant? Now, that's another story.

To a job-seeker, the federal government can seem as large as an elephant—and as slow and ponderous in the way it responds. This will soon become apparent to you in the amount of information you'll be asked to provide when you apply for a government job—and the time it takes for the government to respond to your application. It's not like sending in your resume to an advertisement in the Sunday paper. In fact, many people find the process of applying for a government job so complicated, so frustrating, and so time-consuming that they often throw up their hands in disgust and decide: "This is nuts. Forget about it." This is a shame because, like riding an elephant, there are real advantages to a government career, as you'll see in the following sections. In fact, you may even decide that the best possible job for you is with the federal government.

When considering any job, you're likely to go through the advantages and disadvantages of the position. You compare not only the number of pros and cons on each side, but also each one's relative importance. Not every pro equals every con. For example, a particular job might have five points listed in the pro column and only one con. But, if that single con can't be overcome—say, the job requires moving and you absolutely can't move—then the one disadvantage outweighs all the advantages.

Other disadvantages may not be stumbling blocks so much as they are trade-offs. This is especially true when the job you're considering is a government job.

In considering government employment, go through the same process you would with any job, listing the advantages and disadvantages. Besides the obvious points on each side, keep in mind the intangibles. A government career brings with it a certain frame of mind, almost a lifestyle. For people who see this lifestyle as bringing peace of mind, this will be a definite plus; for those who see it as repetitive, bringing boredom, it will be a minus. Be honest when assessing the pros and cons and your own reactions to them.

The Advantages of Government Work

The pros are the easiest points to assess about any job. They are what you get excited about in the first place. Listed below are the most significant pros of government work.

THE GOVERNMENT IS AMERICA'S LARGEST EMPLOYER

Nearly three million Americans work for the U.S. government. That's a lot of people—and a lot of jobs. Now you can understand why the government is one employment opportunity that cannot be overlooked. With this size comes diversity. Almost every imaginable occupation has its place in government work. There's room for everyone from soldiers, spies, and politicians to auto mechanics, pipefitters, and carpenters. There's room for satellite watchers and map readers, secretaries and file clerks, accountants and auditors, purchasing agents and contract administrators, scientists and medical doctors, teachers and law enforcement officers—well, you get the picture. Almost anyone can find a suitable job at some level of government.

THE GOVERNMENT IS ALWAYS HIRING

Roughly 10 percent of all currently filled federal jobs will become vacant and open for rehiring in any given year. This is due to turnover—attrition due to retirement and to subsequent promotions up the ladder, as lower-graded employees apply for the jobs that higher-graded employees have just left. This makes for a continual process of hiring, rehiring, and promotion throughout the entire federal government. As a result, jobs are always being filled.

But what of government budget cuts?

Politicians can stand in front of the cameras and announce that they're "going to cut the bloated federal payroll," but this fact can't be changed: The government is always hiring people, even during so-called "hiring freezes." Government agencies have had more than 200 years to learn how to protect themselves from Washington politics and are very creative about protecting their payrolls. Plus, these agencies provide real services that, when cut, cause taxpayers to complain and to change their votes. This means that when push comes to shove, politicians back off.

While hiring freezes may be felt more on the lower levels, the state and municipal levels of government are also engaged in a continual process of hiring new people—and have also learned how to survive the political axe.

A GOVERNMENT JOB IS A SECURE JOB

Although it's difficult to get a government job, once you're "on the elephant," it's likely that no one will be able to get you off of it until you're good and ready. In other words, you can stay or leave, according to your own schedule. Reductions In Force (RIFs) happen infrequently, and when they do, most agencies achieve their goals through early retirements—often accompanied by $25,000 incentives—and by attrition (not filling the jobs left vacant by people who have taken on other careers or retired).

A GOVERNMENT JOB PROVIDES ROOM FOR MOVEMENT AND GROWTH

While you may start out in one particular position, once you're working for the government, you'll find that you have opportunities to move upward or sideways in your field—or to change fields entirely. Advancement may not be rapid, but if you do your work well, it is almost guaranteed, as good work is generally rewarded. In addition, the security of a government position allows you to make long-term career plans. In most cases, you'll know just how to earn a promotion—as well as a raise to the next pay grade. These procedures will be clearly defined.

GOVERNMENT JOBS PROVIDE STRONG SALARIES

All civil service jobs vary in expectations, requirements, and salary, but we can look at some specific levels of government salaries to get a good sense of the general pay scales.

As an example, below you'll find the pay schedule for most white-collar federal employees. They're covered by the General Schedule, which is established by the Federal Wage System. Wages for the General Schedule originate from recommendations by the Federal Prevailing Rate Advisory Committee, which is made up of management and labor unions. The committee surveys non-federal pay for similar jobs in the same location, then advises the Director of the Office of Personnel Management on pay policy.

GENERAL SCHEDULE BASIC PAY FOR 1999

GS-1	$13,362	GS-5	$20,588	GS-9	$31,195	GS-13	$53,793
GS-2	$15,023	GS-6	$22,948	GS-10	$34,353	GS-14	$63,567
GS-3	$16,362	GS-7	$25,501	GS-11	$37,744	GS-15	$74,773
GS-4	$18,401	GS-8	$28,242	GS-12	$45,236		

Here's how the General Schedule works:

There are 15 grades, with five steps in each pay grade, which increase at 4 percent intervals. At step 2 of each grade, compensation is based on the average going rate for private-sector employees performing the same job. So while the first step may fall below the average pay rate, it would certainly fall within the range of what an actual private-sector job might pay. At step 5 within each grade, however, federal employees are paid 12 percent above this average private-sector rate, which demonstrates the advantage in moving through the ranks of federal employment.

Federal employees not only receive wages comparable to the same job in the private sector, they also receive wages comparable to the same job in each particular location. This is important, as certain areas of the country have a higher cost of living and often pay employees higher salaries. This *locality pay* can be 5.6 to 12 percent higher than the regular General Schedule amount for jobs within the continental U.S.—and 10 to 25 percent higher for jobs outside the continental U.S.

In addition to locality pay, certain hard-to-fill jobs in specialized scientific, technical, and medical fields begin at higher starting rates. And, as in the private sector, employees who work the night shift are paid a night differential.

GOVERNMENT EMPLOYEES GET MANY SOLID BENEFITS

Would you like paid vacations? Comprehensive health-care insurance? A secure retirement pension? Of course you would.

With health-care costs rising—and health insurance premiums skyrocketing just as quickly—a strong benefits package is one of the most important advantages of working for the federal government. In addition, a secure retirement is another major concern for many people. As the stock market rises and falls (and private-sector pension plans crumble under administration costs and poor investments), federal employees have the comfort of knowing their retirement benefits are secure.

An added plus is that this solid package of benefits is available to *all* government workers, not just a selected few. This fact, combined with a sense of job security, is often enough to sway people to find a government career.

What kinds of benefits do government workers receive? Below is a chart of the benefits offered to federal employees.

FEDERAL BENEFITS

Type of Benefits	Who Is Covered	Available Options
Health: *Federal Employees Health Benefits (FEHB)*	Federal employees and retirees and their survivors. Coverage may include: • Self only; or • Family coverage for yourself, your spouse, and unmarried dependent children under age 22	• Managed Fee for Service Plans; • Point of Service (PPO) options; or • Health Maintenance Organizations (HMOs)

(continues)

FEDERAL BENEFITS (CONTINUED)

Type of Benefits	Who Is Covered	Available Options
Retirement: *Federal Employees Retirement System (FERS)*	Almost all new employees hired after 1983 are automatically covered. Employees who leave may still qualify for benefits. Builds on the Social Security Benefits employees may earn in the future, or may already have earned, from non-federal work.	FERS is a three-tiered retirement plan, consisting of these components: • Social Security benefits (available for those age 62 and retired) • Basic Benefits Plan (financed by a small contribution from the employee and the government) *A Special Retirement Supplement, for employees who meet the criteria, is paid as a monthly benefit until the employee reaches age 62.* • Thrift Savings Plan (tax-deferred retirement savings and investment plan; similar to 401(k) plans)
Life: The Federal Employees' Group Life Insurance Program (FEGLI)	Federal employees and retirees, as well as many of their family members are eligible for this group life insurance program.	Basic Insurance (automatic unless employee opts out; insured pays two-thirds of cost and the government pays one-third); plus Optional Insurance (not automatic; insured pays 100 percent of cost)

A GOVERNMENT CAREER IS A CAREER IN PUBLIC SERVICE

Working for the government can provide a level of satisfaction that few other careers offer. You are a public servant, in the best sense. As just a few examples, consider these important federal agencies: the Federal Emergency Management Administration (FEMA), the Federal Aviation Administration (FAA), the Federal Bureau of Investigations (FBI), the Small Business Administration (SBA), the Center for Disease Control (CDC), or the National Institutes of Health (NIH). Each one of these agencies—and every one of its employees—is contributing to the health and welfare of the American people. In many instances, mid-career professionals who have already succeeded in the private sector want to give something back, and will choose to work for the government, precisely for this reason.

A GOVERNMENT JOB OFFERS OPPORTUNITIES FOR ADVANCED PROFESSIONAL TRAINING

Not everyone who is hired by a government agency is fully trained to begin working their first day on the to effectively handle an increase in job responsibility. In response to this need, both federal and state agencies see to the full training of their people. As a result, multiple training and educational opportunities are available. These opportunities may include full or partial tuition reimbursement, as well as time off—sometimes with pay—to complete the programs. This is a *major* benefit, as such training helps you do your current job better and helps prepare you for future promotions.

THE GOVERNMENT HIRES PEOPLE AT ALL STAGES OF CAREER DEVELOPMENT

This is an important fact. You can be a high school graduate with virtually no work experience, or a recent college graduate, or a student still in college, or a veteran who is separating or retiring from the U.S. military, and the government will have positions for which you can successfully apply. You can be a Ph.D. or a high school dropout who went back to finish the GED degree, and the government will have opportunities for you. There is almost no situation imaginable for which the federal government does not have opportunities!

The Disadvantages of Government Work

In the previous section, you were presented with several reasons to consider working for the federal government. But what about the other side of the coin: the con side? There are some very important factors you need to consider before you can make an informed decision about a career in government service.

YOU WILL HAVE TO WORK IN A LARGE BUREAUCRACY

The government is a bureaucracy, an organization with a strict hierarchy. This means several things to you, the federal employee, with regards to your ability to make a decision. First, every move you make must be approved by a rigid chain of command. Second, every action you take must have a precedent. Third, every aspect of your employment will be regulated by pre-existing guidelines and procedures (outlined in your personnel manual). These regulations protect you from being fired and protect your job from being eliminated. However, these regulations also require you to do your work according to rules and requirements that may no longer make sense.

A bureaucracy the size of the United States government changes slowly because many of its regulations were written long ago. The situations they were to address may have changed, but the regulations and requirements remain. That's why the government is often referred to as a "dinosaur."

THE GOVERNMENT FAVORS BUREAUCRATS OVER RISK-TAKERS

A bureaucracy favors bureaucrats. It makes wonderful sense. However, if *you're* not a bureaucrat, this can become a challenge to your patience and persistence. If you're the kind of person who sees what needs to be done, wants to do it, and is accustomed to doing it on your own, you may find this aspect of government work intolerable. What *you* see as taking initiative, the bureaucracy may see as taking risks; after all, you're acting without precedent and without approval. Actions *you* think show you off as a self-starter may make you, in the bureaucracy's eyes, a loose cannon.

CHANGE IN MOST GOVERNMENT AGENCIES IS A SLOW PROCESS

It is a general rule that as an organization grows, it becomes more cumbersome. As a result, it becomes resistant to change. With an organization as large as the government, change comes about very slowly.

When we speak of the United States government, we're talking about a vast empire of agencies and departments—all of which are subject to regulation by the legislative and executive branches of our national government. These agencies may have huge budgets, but they are not fully their own bosses. They do "the will of the people," as expressed by Congress and the executive branch.

It all boils down to this: If you're a government worker and somewhere along the way you become dissatisfied with the status quo, you're in for a very long ride if you try to change things.

INCOMPETENCE IS EASILY HIDDEN IN LARGE ORGANIZATIONS

The larger the organization, the more dead weight it will carry. By *dead weight*, we are referring to those employees who simply go through the *motions* of working, but who actually accomplish very little. These individuals rely heavily on the work ethic of those dedicated to their careers to cover for them.

You should be aware of this, because although most government employees will be just as diligent as you are, you may be carrying the weight for other, less motivated, employees. And because of all the job security that led you to the government in the first place, you may be stuck with these employees for the duration.

IT MAY BE DIFFICULT TO LEAVE A DEPARTMENT ONCE YOU'RE IN

It may come to pass during your employment that you would like to transfer into another position, or even another agency. Be forewarned, however, that receiving a transfer within the federal government can be just as cumbersome as getting hired was. Every personnel-related action involves large amounts of paperwork and will probably take months to process. Few bosses are likely to volunteer eagerly to get involved in instigating these paper-shuffling procedures. You may get lucky and have your transfer approved right away. Or, you may have to wait until so-and-so in the department you want finally decides to retire and frees up a vacancy.

GOVERNMENT AGENCIES ARE SUBJECT TO INTENSE POLITICAL PRESSURES

Because government agencies have so many constituencies and audiences to please, decisions can be difficult to make. The pressures governing a given situation, combined with political and/or media pressure, often cloud facts and logic—and even the purpose for which an agency exists. The bottom line is always changing and, in many cases, doesn't make sense.

A GOVERNMENT POSITION ON THE FEDERAL LEVEL MAY REQUIRE YOU TO TRAVEL AS PART OF YOUR WORK

Federal agencies and departments administer programs throughout the U.S. and, in many cases, overseas. Agencies need many people to ensure that these programs are operating properly and that field offices are doing what they have been asked to do.

One of the questions on the federal application form (Form SF-171) is "Are you willing to travel?" The next question is "How frequently are you willing to travel: 1–5 nights a month, 5–12 nights a month, or more than that?" If your response is that you are unwilling to travel, you may be ruled out of consideration for the position you prefer.

The bottom line is this: *Someone* needs to travel in many of these jobs. Are you willing to let that someone be you?

YOU MAY HAVE TO WORK HARDER FOR LESS THAN YOU EXPECT

Many people have the mistaken idea that government work is easy. Their perception may be that there is very little to do, ample opportunity for paid vacation and holidays, and unbelievable benefits. This perception is a myth—and the truth can come as quite a shock.

Government employees, for the most part, work *very* hard. And while their salaries and benefits are very good, they are not fantastic. If you're motivated by money alone and want to reach incredible professional heights very quickly, government work is not for you.

Comparing Public and Private Sector Employment

The pros and cons considered in the previous section address government work in and of itself. However, a career in the public sector is an alternative to a career in the private sector. So, it's useful to also look at how government work—with its advantages and disadvantages—compares to private-sector work.

GOVERNMENT JOBS ARE MORE SECURE

Government work has always been secure. In the last decade, however, security has become a rare commodity in the private sector. As a result, job security must be considered when comparing public and private sector employment.

Do you wake up every morning worrying whether you still have a job? Do you anxiously listen to news reports and rumors about corporate takeovers? Most of the traditionally accepted ideas about job security have been destroyed. Even the terminology has changed: "Laying off" has become "downsizing" has become "rightsizing"—as if changing the language could disguise the nightmare of losing your job. In the private sector, job security no longer exists. Period. Even a Fortune 500 company can be acquired by another company. It can always suffer huge profit downturns. And cutting payroll is one of the easiest methods for companies to show a temporary economic gain.

On the other hand, the government doesn't have to show a profit to stockholders every three months. And no one is trying to buy out the Department of Agriculture.

Because of this, security is one of the largest advantages of government work. With government work, you no longer have to worry about basic economic survival. You can finally have peace of mind.

GOVERNMENT PAY AND BENEFITS ARE COMPARABLE TO MOST PRIVATE-SECTOR PAY AND BENEFITS

Government salaries, at least on the federal level, are legally required to be comparable to their private-sector counterparts. Government pay is determined by surveying the salaries in the private sector. In addition, the government has a locality-pay differential for areas of the country that have a higher cost of living, as well as a night differential for night shifts.

In addition, government health-care benefits are strong and consistent across all agencies and departments. This may not be the case with many private-sector jobs. Benefits in the private sector are subject to more frequent change than in civil service—or they may not exist at all.

Additionally, civil service retirement plans are very good—and they're guaranteed. Private-sector plans, on the other hand, often become uncertain when it's time to actually pay out. The private sector favors executives in both salaries and benefits, while the government offers the same benefits package to all.

As a quick example of these differences, take a look at something relatively simple: the number of paid holidays a company might offer. Let's begin with paid holidays offered to federal employees:

FEDERAL HOLIDAYS

New Year's Day	Labor Day
Martin Luther King, Jr.'s Birthday	Columbus Day
Washington's Birthday	Veterans Day
Memorial Day	Thanksgiving Day
Independence Day	Christmas Day

How does the private sector compare? There are wide differences. As an example, one Fortune 500 company gives employees 12 paid holidays. Six are called national holidays (New Year's Day, Memorial Day, Independence Day, Labor Day, Thanksgiving, and Christmas Day). In addition to these, three more paid holidays are decided upon by the employee's local branch, depending on what other companies in the area give. And still another three days are given as personal holidays, chosen by the employee, for a total of twelve. By contrast, a large national retail store has only six paid holidays—the same six listed above. And, being a retailer, this organization is open for two of those six days—Memorial Day and Labor Day. So even though an employee will be paid for the holiday, he or she may also have to work on it.

THE GOVERNMENT HAS LESS DISCRIMINATION THAN THE PRIVATE SECTOR

No one likes to talk openly about discrimination, such as sexism or racism, in the workplace. It exists in both the private and public sectors. However, because the process of hiring and promotion of government employees is ruled by precedent and regulations and is less vulnerable to individual likes and dislikes, there is less discrimination.

This is particularly true with regards to age. In the private sector, youth is prized because of its energy and enthusiasm, its up-to-date knowledge straight from college or grad school, and its lower pay ranges. Someone in his or her 50s may find it difficult to find a new position in the private sector.

In government, however, positions are graded in terms of their salaries—not in terms of age (unless a job has physical requirements). Thus, a federal agency may have a GS-13 position to fill for an accountant. Anyone with the requisite experience is eligible to apply. If you're 37, you won't be paid any more or any less than someone who is 53, as long as you both qualify for the job.

As a result of this leniency towards age, many older workers who are coming from 10 or 20 years in the private sector can begin a full second career in government. In addition, veterans who have completed a full 20-year career in the military can begin a second career as civilian employees of the government. That's much harder to do in the private sector.

GOVERNMENT WORK ALLOWS MORE FLEXIBLE JOB QUALIFICATIONS

How many times have you seen a job advertisement ask for X years of experience or a specific type of college degree? Such qualifications are standard for most private sector jobs.

In the government, however, the process of qualifying for jobs is much more flexible. Often, a vacancy announcement will indicate that X years of experience can be substituted for X years of college education, or even for a college degree. Because it is a public-sector employer paying salaries with public funds, the government has made a point—supported by laws and legislation—to protect the rights and career aspirations of all Americans. As a result, very few government positions require a specific type of college degree. Not even senior-level positions require a specific degree, and in many cases, they require no degree at all. In practice, this means that a person with no degree can become a top-level manager overseeing the work of Ph.D.s.

As long as you present your qualifications effectively on the application forms that you submit, you can qualify for many government jobs that might be out of reach in the private sector. The key, of course, is presenting your qualifications effectively. You'll learn that in the following chapters.

THE PRIVATE SECTOR VALUES "SUPERSTAR" EMPLOYEES, MORE SO THAN THE PUBLIC SECTOR

Working in a government bureaucracy is not about acting alone. Nor is it about taking chances based on sudden hunches, in hopes of taking center stage and getting applauded for your intuition and initiative. Unlike private companies, there are very few "superstars" in the federal government. Instead, there are endless committee meetings to keep people in the loop. Government work is not about being an all-star or a lone wolf. It's more about building a set of working relationships with professionals throughout government service, and using these contacts to advance your organization's agenda.

If you are someone who needs attention and recognition, you may well be better off in the private sector. If you don't mind working behind the scenes and don't care who gets the credit as long as the job gets done, you may do very well in a government career.

THE PRIVATE SECTOR OFFERS FASTER, GREATER REWARDS TO ITS EXECUTIVE WORKERS THAN THE PUBLIC SECTOR

Do you want to make a lot of money—and make it quickly? Depending on how important this is to you, the private sector may be the better place.

Top executives in the private sector make as much as five times more than public-sector executives who are managing programs of comparable size. Commissions, stock options, golden parachutes—none of these are available to civil service workers.

Deciding on the Best Job for You

There is no easy formula for comparing civil service jobs to those in the private sector. There are no numbers that result in a right or wrong answer to the question of where you should work. There are only advantages and disadvantages to consider, each of which has its own importance to your particular situation. Many of the advantages are practical: salary, health care, vacation, and pension benefits. Conversely, many of the disadvantages are more a matter of atmosphere, context, and your own personality.

The smart way to make the decision is to be absolutely honest about your needs, your family's needs, what motivates you, and even what drives you crazy. Ask yourself these tough questions:

- How much money is "enough"?
- How much job risk is tolerable?
- How much money does your family need?
- How much risk can your family tolerate?
- What are the health-benefit needs of you and your family?
- How well do you handle change?
- Do you require constant change?
- What type of work environment do you prefer? (Slow-paced versus fast-paced, and so on.)
- How well do you work with other people?
- Can you be a team player or must you be the star?
- How much frustration can you tolerate, in exchange for how much security?

You will have to choose which factors make the most sense for you and your personal situation. You'll also have to rely on a certain level of instinct and decide which feels right to you—or at least feels better.

LAUNCHING YOUR FEDERAL GOVERNMENT JOB SEARCH

The federal government is so huge and complicated that it may be difficult to envision yourself as a federal employee. You're familiar with civil service on the local level: You know your town or city's police and fire personnel, at least by sight, and you've probably had dealings with borough officials. You may even be somewhat familiar with civil service on the county level; perhaps you've had jury duty and have toured the county's court and jail system. But the *federal* government? Since we seldom think of Frank, our letter carrier, as a federal employee, trying to "break into Washington" may summon up the picture of ourselves knocking on the door of the White House.

But the federal government has innumerable offices throughout the country. Look in your county phone book for the government listings. The Veterans Administration, Social Security Administration, various divisions of the Armed Forces, Justice Department, Internal Revenue Service, Small Business Department, Department of Transportation, and others all likely have offices surprisingly close to where you live right now. And everyone in those offices is a federal employee. You could be, too.

General Job Categories and Programs Available at the Federal Level

As I said in the last chapter, the federal government is the country's largest employer. That means it has room for almost every imaginable occupation. It also has an enormous variety of special programs to encompass many different hiring situations. A quick look will show you just how many:

- **Professional occupations** require knowledge of a field that is usually gained through education or training equivalent to a bachelor's degree or higher, with major study in or pertinent to the specialized field—for example, engineer, accountant, biologist, or chemist.
- **Administrative occupations** usually require progressively responsible experience. More than a college education is required, although professional training and study may be involved—for example, personnel specialist or administrative officer.
- **Technical occupations** involve training and experience—for example, computer programmer, telecommunications specialist, or electronics technician.
- **Clerical occupations** generally involve structured work in support of office, business, or fiscal operations—for example, clerk-typist, mail clerk or file clerk.
- **Skilled trades** involve manual work that usually requires a "journeyman" status in fields such as plumbing, HVAC technician, electricians, carpenters, and machinists.

PART-TIME PROGRAMS

Part-time positions—that is, 16 to 32 hours per week—are available in agencies throughout the federal government. Flex time, job sharing, and nontraditional workday and workweek scheduling is also available in some positions. Inquire at personnel offices in agencies where you feel you may want to apply.

STUDENT PROGRAMS

The federal government has a number of programs in place specifically designed to provide employment for students. These programs include the following:

- **Summer employment** for high school, college, law, medical, and dental students is available. Applications are accepted for summer employment from December through April 15, and the jobs usually run from mid-May through September 30. Hiring is done by individual agencies. Some restrictions limit summer employment in the same agency where the applicant's parent also may be employed.
- **The Federal Student Career Program** is a work/study option for high school, vocational, or technical school, and college students enrolled in school at least half-time. This program offers employment in positions directly related to the student's course of study. Positions in this program can lead to permanent employment upon a student's graduation. Students interested in this option should contact their high school counselors, college employment coordinators, or the agency where they would like to work.
- **Student temporary employment** offers a part-time opportunity for students. These positions are not necessarily related to the professional careers for which these students are preparing themselves. This employment must end when a student is no longer enrolled in school at least half-time. The procedure for identifying and qualifying for this program is similar to the Federal Student Career Program experience.
- **The Presidential Management Interns (PMI) program** is targeted at graduate students in the last year of their advanced studies who intend to make a career in public service. Only graduate students who expect to receive their degrees by the next June should apply. These students enter the two-year PMI program at the GS-9 level and perform high-level work in their chosen fields. At the end of the two years, PMIs may continue in regular federal employment at the GS-12 level. Students interested in this program must be nominated by the dean of their college or university or by the chairman of their department or graduate program.

VETERAN PROGRAMS

U.S. military veterans are entitled to special consideration in federal hiring. In some cases, veterans are entitled to positions that are not open to the general public. In other cases, extra points are added to their exam scores, giving them a competitive advantage. The Veterans Employment Coordinator at the agency where you want to apply can give you additional information.

PROGRAMS FOR PERSONS WITH DISABILITIES

Persons with disabilities should contact the Selective Placement Coordinator at the agency of interest to explore special placement assistance that is available to candidates with physical, cognitive, or emotional disabilities. By law, the federal government—just as the private sector must—will make "reasonable workplace accommodations" for persons with disabilities; this means that the employer may adjust the duties of the job, the location where it's performed, or the methods in which it's performed.

PROGRAMS FOR RESIDENTS OUTSIDE THE CONTINENTAL U.S.

Alaska, Guam, Hawaii, Puerto Rico, and the Virgin Islands offer very limited federal employment possibilities. Local residents will receive first consideration for employment in these areas. Other candidates will be considered only when there are no qualified residents available.

How to Find Federal Jobs that Are Right for You

Matching your experience and background to a federal job is perhaps one of the most difficult aspects of getting federal work. Part of this difficulty results from the fact that you have to find the vacancies yourself. You can't simply send in a resume or application and say, "Hey, Washington—here's what I can do. Who wants to hire me?"

There's no centralized personnel department for the federal government. Years ago, the Office of Personnel Management (OPM) used to serve that function. However, with so many agencies and so many applicants, OPM would take months to identify candidates and send their applications to the agency with the opening. Agencies complained that it was almost impossible for them to hire the people they needed, *when* they needed them. Finally, OPM gave up its authority in this area and now each federal agency does its own hiring. The result, however, doesn't make it easier for applicants, for a number of reasons, many of which are discussed below.

YOU MUST LOOK BEYOND THE TITLE

Say you want to become a federal employee. You're open to a number of position types, but because of your background you look for jobs with titles similar to your current title. If you limit yourself to that, you might miss other openings for which you qualify. Instead of looking at a title and thinking, "I don't have the experience to do that," pick titles that make you think, "Gee, that sounds interesting." Then read the qualifications. You just might be eligible.

Also, some titles can be very deceptive. When looking for a federal position, for example, an administrative assistant rightfully may think the position of "secretary" could be appropriate, then discover that it's for a high-ranking executive (think "Secretary of State"). Or, a recent graduate might see impressive-sounding titles such as "Agriculture Science Research Technician" or "Airway Transportation Systems Specialist" and immediately assume these are higher-ranked jobs for people with years of experience. A look at the salary, however, shows jobs that these jobs start under $22,000—obviously positions for the newer employee. A few extra seconds of investigation can help you decipher the title to get a closer look at the job.

Additionally, don't dismiss federal work in general because the government just wouldn't hire "someone like you." The government needs more than just accountants, soldiers, mechanics, clerks, nuclear scientists, and so on. On a single recent day, there were openings for a graphic illustrator, a sports specialist, an archaeologist, a horticulturist, a manager for a community club, an outdoor-recreation planner, a leisure-travel arranger, and a religious education specialist. What's even more surprising than the variety is that all these jobs were for the same agency—the U.S. Army!

KEEP CHECKING THE ANNOUNCEMENTS

You must apply for a particular position in a particular agency, because you're really applying for a specific vacancy, not just a job title. Most agencies don't refer to past applications. They don't "keep your resume on file," which many private-sector companies do. Think of it like this: You're not just applying for, say, an accounting position. When accountant Pat Smith retires, it's Pat Smith's vacancy you're applying for. What this means in terms of legwork is a constant monitoring of openings.

For every opening, agencies must publish an announcement of the vacancy, if they're going to fill it. This means you must constantly watch the job vacancy announcements for the agency you're interested in—or keep track of vacancies for several agencies if you're focused more on the kind of job rather than the agency where you perform it.

APPLY SEPARATELY FOR EACH VACANCY

Each time you spot an appropriate vacancy, you usually have to fill out an application form. You can't ask Agency X to refer to the application you sent in last month to Agency Y—even though that application might have taken days to fill out and was two dozen pages long. Except for a few closely related jobs that might be open within the same agency, each position requires its own application.

TAILOR YOUR APPLICATION OR RESUME TO THE JOB

While you would do this in the private sector as well, there is simply no comparison to the depth of "tailoring" that's needed to get federal employment. The two-dozen page application mentioned above is not an exaggeration. Your application should mirror the language of the vacancy announcement, then provide details that prove you have the knowledge, skills, and abilities (abbreviated KSAs) to fill the opening. You learn more about KSAs later in this chapter.

WATCH OUT FOR CIVIL SERVICE JOB-HELP SCAMS

About now you may be asking yourself, "Can't anyone help me? Aren't there federal employment agencies?" And the answer is—beware! The government does not sign itself up with employment agencies the way a private-sector company might, so avoid any "employment agency" that promises that the government or a particular agency is its client and that it can help you—for a hefty fee—get the job you want.

Everything you need to get federal work can be had directly from the government, and it's readily available if you're willing to spend the time and do the legwork to find it. All the information is free, the forms and directions are free, and the process of applying is free. A person or agency that suggests otherwise is stealing from you as directly as a pickpocket. Also, beware of a person or agency that guarantees you a job, guarantees you a higher score, or says that there are "hidden" vacancies not listed in the announcements, but which *they* can reveal to you.

REMEMBER, YOU CAN DO IT YOURSELF

What's *legitimate* help? Your *Federal Civil Service Jobs* book and other guides on the topic are not only legitimate, they're often your best buy—giving you "the most bang for your buck." These guides can help you save time and effort, plus give you valuable proven tips you might not have discovered otherwise.

There are also personal coaches who will hold your hand step by step through the search-and-application process. They, too, are legitimate but sometimes provide simply the same information that's in a guide like this, only at higher cost because of the personalized, one-on-one nature of their service.

With the advent of the Internet also comes brand new legitimate help—search engines that automatically match up keywords in your experience or education with keywords in current vacancies. Some of the free government sites will do this. There are also private sites that provide this matching, as well as a range of other services, for varying prices—a monthly subscription cost in some cases, a flat fee per each service in others.

If you're interested in this type of help, however, try to stay with sites that appear as links on official government Web pages. These will be the most reputable. And check carefully. Some online sites have names that imply they're "official government sites" by tagging "U.S." or "American" or the like onto the site title—then burying the fee down where the information you want most is located. Private sites say right up front that they're a private source of information.

And speaking of sources of information leads to the next question on any job seeker's list: Since you can apply only for a specific opening, where do you find announcements about actual job vacancies?

Making Contact: How and Where to Track Down Actual Job Vacancies

Although the difficulty involved may convince you otherwise, the federal government *wants* you to work for it and, therefore, has many ways you can find out what openings are available in what agencies. The following sections discuss the many sources for federal employment information and job bank listings.

DIRECT CONTACT

If you know which agency or agencies you want to work for, you may contact them directly to learn what vacancies exist and how to apply for them. At some agencies, you may be able to prepare an application that will be kept on file for future vacancies. Other agencies accept applications only for current or projected openings. Ask, so you'll know whether the agency's openings need constant monitoring.

If a federal agency has an office in your area, you may find its telephone number under "U.S. Government" in the blue pages of the phone book. If the agency has no office in your area, place a call to Information in the District of Columbia, (202) 555-1212, and ask for the telephone number of the personnel office or employment office of the agency you want to reach. Calls to government offices must be made during business hours, so prepare your questions ahead of time to hold down your phone bill.

To get you started, Appendix A, "Important Civil Service Employment Contacts," lists phone numbers, addresses, and Web sites for the major federal agencies.

AUTOMATED PHONE CONTACT

Under the blue-page listing for "U.S. Government," there should also be numbers for the U.S. Office of Personnel Management or the nearest Federal Job Information Center. This number can give you automated job information about your own area or may direct you to a location where you can pick up printed materials or conduct a detailed search on a computer touch screen. Automated telephone systems can be accessed 24 hours a day by touch-tone phone. Because you may be on for quite a while searching job categories and geographical areas, you may want to place your call while less-expensive evening, night, or weekend phone rates apply. A complete listing of local numbers for automated telephone systems appears in Appendix A, "Important Civil Service Employment Contacts."

Another source of automated telephone information is the Career America Connection. This system provides current worldwide federal job announcements, salary and employee-benefits information, special recruitment messages, and so on. The system can also record your name and mailing address so you can be sent vacancy announcements and forms through the mail. You can contact Career America Connection by calling (912) 757-3000. For TDD service, call (912) 744-2299.

FAX ON DEMAND

Yet another way to receive information is through FEDFAX. This fax-on-demand service allows you to receive information on a variety of employment-related topics, as well as forms, by fax. The automated service may be accessed 24 hours a day, 7 days a week, by calling any of the following telephone numbers from a touch-tone phone or a fax machine:

Atlanta: (404) 331-5267

Denver: (303) 969-7764

Detroit: (313) 226-2593

San Francisco: (415) 744-7002

Washington, D.C.: (202) 606-2600

STATE EMPLOYMENT OFFICES

Some state employment offices carry federal job listings in print or on microfiche. Others maintain touch-screen computers, which have the listings of available federal jobs within those states. To see what services *your* state employment office offers, call it directly or check with your public library.

TOUCH-SCREEN COMPUTER KIOSKS

Federal job information touch-screen computer kiosks are located throughout the United States. These kiosks (small, open-sided buildings, like newsstands) provide current federal job opportunities available worldwide, online information, and more. The kiosks are generally open during normal business hours, Monday through Friday. Appendix A, "Important Civil Service Employment Contacts," contains a complete listing of locations for these kiosks across the United States.

THE INTERNET

The Internet is perhaps the single most valuable source of federal job information. Information on federal jobs available in your neighborhood is as easily accessed as information on jobs across the country—or around the world. You can also download application forms, check salaries and benefits, even research the geographic areas where particular jobs are located. The Net greatly reduces your legwork; now you can "let your fingers do the walking."

In Appendix B, "Webliography of Federal Employment Web Sites," you'll find listings of sites that are enormously useful in getting federal employment. Not all of them are official government sites, but even the private ones contain much helpful information and practical tips—for free.

The Anatomy of a Federal Job Announcement: What to Look For and How to Use It

Job announcements in the private sector are short and simple. A classified ad, whether in the paper or online, states that the ABC company wants to hire someone for an XYZ position. The requirements are summed up in a few words or, at most, a few sentences. An address or phone number is given to mail, e-mail, or fax your resume. You send in your cover letter and one- or two-page resume, and that's it—you've successfully applied for the job. Your resume generally goes to ABC's Human Resources Department and, if it passes the initial screening, is forwarded to the actual department with the opening.

In the federal government, however, this process is more complicated. Most federal vacancy announcements are between four and eight pages in length, single-spaced. That's just the job *announcement,* not the application document you submit for the job. The announcement may include descriptions of the position's duties and responsibilities, qualifications, experience desired, KSAs (knowledge, skills, and abilities) desired, whether competitive testing is required, and so on.

The key to surviving the application process and to being seriously considered (and thus, hired) begins with your understanding the job vacancy announcement. The vacancy announcement is filled with details that *must* be on your application or instructions that *must* be followed to keep your resume out of the trash bin. The announcement is also filled with clues that, if found and understood, tell you what *should* be on your application to get you called in for an interview.

THE MUSTS

You must make absolutely certain that you include each of the following items on your application:

- **The job's vacancy announcement number.** You already know that to qualify for a federal job, you must apply for an announced vacancy: a *specific* position with its own vacancy announcement number. This number must be put on your application; otherwise, the screening panel won't know which position you want to be considered for. Without this number—whether you apply by form or resume—your application is likely to be thrown out. The screening panel will *not* sift through all the available jobs to match up other hints from your application to the current vacancies: "Oh, he must have meant Job #XXXX." It won't happen.
- **The job's title, job classification series, and grade-level number.** When you refer to the vacancy in your application, in any correspondence or communication, even in a phone conversation, you must refer to the position you want by its official job title, job classification series, and grade-level number. For example, *Computer Specialist, GS-334-11* means that the job title is "Computer Specialist," its classification series is "334," and its pay-grade level is GS-11. *GS* refers to positions covered by the General Schedule; they go all the way up to GS-13, 14, and 15 management positions. If the grade level is preceded with SES instead of GS, it indicates the higher-rated Senior Executive Service positions, which range from SES-1 to SES-5 in terms of the salaries they pay.
- **The application deadline.** While the deadline date does not have to be entered on your application, it absolutely must be met. Check the announcement for the date. Some federal jobs are open until filled and some are continuously open, but this usually isn't the case. Most federal announcements will have a two- to four-week application period. Also, how to meet the deadline is different from announcement to announcement. Some require that the deadline date be the *postmark date;* others require that the deadline date be when applications must be *received.* Read carefully. Most announcements look the same, but they don't all read the same. If you submit your application after the closing date, it will not be considered.

- **The application procedure.** Most federal vacancies can be applied for by one of several methods—Form SF-171, Form OF-612, resume, or computer-scannable resume. However, some vacancies must be applied for in only one way, or a page limit will be given for the usually longer-is-better form or resume. Again, read carefully. Each announcement is explicit about what is required.

THE SHOULDS

Once you have the mandatory details straight, also check the announcement for hints on what *should* be on your form or resume. Here's a list of strong possibilities:

- **Language that mirrors the job announcement language.** The federal announcements are lengthy and detailed. Agencies know what they're looking for. Your application should echo the job announcement's language to show the agency that *you* are *exactly* what it seeks. Obviously, this doesn't mean you quote directly from the announcement or falsify your background, experience, or abilities—but do keep the announcement at hand when crafting your application or resume. Focus on what's important to the hiring agency.
- **KSAs or "ranking factors."** An application or resume is sometimes not required to include a description of the applicant's KSAs (knowledge, skills, and abilities) to be considered for a job—but it really should. If more than one applicant passes the initial screening, the KSAs are used to rank the qualified applicants. An application with no or inadequate KSAs will drop to the bottom of the list.

Making Your Way through the Application Maze

You've already heard so many references to different forms and resumes—SF-171, OF-612, federal resume, computer-scannable resume, Resumix, KSAs, ranking factors—that you may want to just give up. If you're not accustomed to writing in your current job, or if writing intimidates you, you may be even more tempted. "I'm a talker, not a writer," you may be thinking. "Interview me!"

Unfortunately for talkers, at this stage of the process, effective written presentation of your background and experience is critical. Unless you can prove some kind of disability that prevents you from preparing a written application, you must conform to the set procedures. And although it feels otherwise, fear is not considered a disabling factor.

Here are a few tips that will hopefully get you past your fear and through the maze of forms and procedures:

- **You don't need to do everything.** Some of the forms and resumes constantly being mentioned are simply alternative ways of applying. You really only need two things: The first is a Form SF-171 *or* a Form OF-612 *or* a federal resume *or* a computer-scannable resume. (Each of these is explained more in the next chapter.) The second thing you really need is a list of your KSAs. That's all. Each one should be detailed, true, but that's far better than needing all of them.
- **You can choose to do what's most comfortable.** Most jobs do not require you to use a particular form, so use the one you're most comfortable with. To discover which one that is, be willing to experiment. You may be afraid of the SF-171's length, for example, only to find out the detailed questions are like someone taking your hand and walking you step-by-step through the application, making sure you forget nothing. See what works for you.
- **Everyone else feels as intimidated as you.** No one looks at an SF-171—either to write it up or read the filled-in form—and says, "What luck! And there was nothing good on television tonight, either!"

Every applicant is nervous; every applicant is doing something unfamiliar. Think of your fear as a leveling factor and just get on with it.

- **Filling out the form is half the battle.** So many people never get past the application, you're immediately ahead of many competitors just by sitting down and filling it out. Patient persistence often wins over talent and luck. Plus, quitting now only exchanges possible rejection for certain rejection. For that's what you're doing if you yield to fear—rejecting yourself.
- **Chapter 3 of this book gives you line-by-line help filling out the form.** Your fastest guide to getting help with your application is right in your hands—in the next chapter.

And remember that when you're culling information from the vacancy announcement and adding all the necessary detail to your application, you must be familiar with the government's hiring terminology. Appendix D, "Glossary of Civil Service Hiring Terminology," has a complete listing of the most common terms you'll encounter, and how the government agencies use those terms.

Examinations for Federal Civil Service Jobs

You filled out the application, you made it through the first step of the screening process, you made it through the second step. Is it time to polish your shoes for the interview?

Not yet. Many of the positions also require the results of competitive testing. The test must be passed, and test grades also become part of the factors that determine how you compare to other competitors.

There are generally two types of competitive tests: *assembled exams* and *unassembled exams*. An assembled exam means that all the applicants assemble at the same time to take the test—whether it's a written test or a physical test of performance. An unassembled exam actually means there's no exam at all. The applicant is judged on the education and experience presented in the application; proof of achievement is usually required (diplomas, training certificates, and so on).

A written test is usually a paper-and-pen, multiple-choice format. The format of the performance test depends on the physical tasks that need to be measured. You'll receive a notice in the mail telling you of the test date and where it is to be held. If the test or the test location presents a problem to applicants with disabilities, they should call personnel at once to make other arrangements. Appendix C, "Federal Occupations that Require Examinations," contains a listing of more than 220 exam-dependent occupations and their grades, and the type of exam required for each position.

The results of the test also come in the mail, giving you your test score (70 is passing) and your place on the list of eligibles when ranked with the other applicants.

Remember that not every federal job applicant has to take a competitive exam. Some positions are by appointment rather than testing. And some groups of people *may* be eligible for appointment; in other words, they *may* be exempted from the requirement. These groups include the following:

- **Disabled veterans** who are 30 percent or more disabled
- **Persons with severe disabilities** who have either physical or mental impairments
- **Peace Corps or VISTA volunteers** who have left the service within the past year
- **Foreign Service employees*** who have been, whether presently or formerly, appointed under the Foreign Service Act of 1946
- **Overseas federal employees or family members*** who seek appointments within three years of their return to the U.S.
- **National Guard technicians*** who have been involuntarily separated from service within the last year

*There may be restrictions on certain members of these groups. See the hiring agency for details.

PUTTING TOGETHER YOUR FEDERAL JOB APPLICATION

Finding the right job with the federal government is a big step—but it's only the first of many. The federal government application and hiring procedures are very different from those of the private sector. You need to know how to "read" the federal job announcement—to pull out all the information you'll need in order to craft the best application. Then you must find and correctly complete the right application form.

The federal job application is the "make or break point" of aspiring federal employees, the place where dreams either *remain* dreams, or become reality. Some people never even get past the forms and give up before they apply; others don't put enough effort into their applications and never get called.

There's no getting around it: The process is difficult, but it is *not* impossible. It may just take more time and patience than you had anticipated.

Giving Yourself the Edge in the Federal Hiring Process

Remember that you can't approach the federal-employment hiring process the same way you would the private sector. To begin, you have to hustle more in the beginning—to track down job openings, to apply separately for each one, and to tailor your application or resume to the listed requirements. It's not like applying to one employer, but to dozens—as many agencies and departments as you are interested in.

Above all, you must follow procedure—no matter how brilliant or qualified you may be. In other words, even though you haven't yet been hired, it's time to start thinking like a bureaucrat: Fill out the entire application, answer all the questions, recognize that *more* paperwork is *better* paperwork.

If you approach your federal job search the same way you approach the job search in the private sector, you might be hurt on several different points. For example, you might assume—because it's true elsewhere—that brevity is the heart of a good presentation. When searching for a job with the government, however, this is the not the case. You might also assume that if anything crucial were missing from your application package, the hiring agency would call and ask for it. Another wrong assumption. If an agency does not have the required information to process your application, you could be taken out of consideration—without knowing it. In other words, what you don't know *can* hurt you.

Information is key to your success. Find out as much as you can beforehand about the particular job, the agency, the application process, and so on. Then give the agency as much information as you can in return. It's really a very influential factor. In your search, patience and persistence are as important as any of the special qualifications you may bring to the job.

Finally, think of the application as an example of the kind of work you normally do, a way to show the screening panel the neatness, accuracy, and thoroughness you normally bring to the job every day.

Federal Application Forms

With your selected job vacancy announcement in hand, you now begin the process of filling out an application form. There is a wide variety of applications you may use to apply for a job with the federal government. So which do you use?

Basically, you only need two forms. First, you will need what is called an *entry document*, which can be an SF-171, an OF-612, a federal resume, *or* a computer-scannable resume. Second, you will need a set of KSAs. Let's look at each of these in turn.

THE SF-171

This is the Everest of federal employment forms—the one that has traditionally intimidated applicants on a regular basis. A completed SF-171 form can be quite long. A good one can run anywhere from 7 to 15 pages. (There's an example of one later in this chapter.) And the form is tedious to fill out. You have to provide details about your academic and professional career that you may not have thought about for years. But if you don't provide these details, or at least respond to these questions in some way, chances are that a personnel clerk may review your SF-171, see that items are left blank, and throw it out. Then, no matter how qualified you may be, your application will receive no further consideration.

As a result, you should fill in *all* the blanks. If you don't know the answer to a question on the form, write "N/A." But make sure you write *something* in every blank.

One final piece of advice: Remember to sign the form. In fact, federal personnel specialists advise that you sign it in *blue* ink, rather than black. On a quick glance, black ink may look like a photocopy. Since your application must contain an *original* signature, it could get thrown out by mistake.

THE OF-612

This form, developed during the mid–1990s, was part of a well-intended effort by the U.S. Office of Personnel Management (OPM) to simplify the federal hiring process by having an alternative form. The OF-612 is less cluttered visually and doesn't squeeze in two columns of questions on the very first page the way the SF-171 does. It also skips a few of the SF-171's questions, such as availability, military service, and others. Simply put, OF-612 looks less intimidating and more user-friendly, which is probably what the OPM wanted in an alternative form.

Unfortunately, in trying to simplify the federal hiring process, they wound up making it more complicated because they did not drop the old form when they instituted the new one. Instead of just having one simpler form, OPM gave people a choice, and choices are always confusing. Which form should applicants fill out? Is one form better than the other? Do two forms mean they need to fill out both? And finally, many applicants think that because the OF-612 form is only two pages long and looks easier to fill out and to read, that their responses should be shorter.

That makes sense, but it's not true. When the OF-612 comes to the questions on describing your past work duties and your other qualifications, you should provide the same detail as you would on an SF-171. Don't hesitate to attach your own sheets of paper to the application so that you have room to explain in full. As with all federal job application documents, you'll do better if you write more, rather than less. Invariably, federal screening panels choose the strongest set of paperwork. As far as these screening panels are concerned, a good candidate equals a good set of paperwork. If you keep this in mind, you'll think more like the people who actually have a vote about your application, and that's a useful thing to do. Their vote is your ticket to a federal job. Try to put yourself in their shoes.

THE FEDERAL RESUME

Yet another alternative way of applying, the federal resume is probably the least understood, because it often gets confused with a private-sector resume. Unlike a private-sector resume, which is usually no more than one or two pages, a federal resume can be as long or short as you want it to be. Some federal resumes are as long as an SF-171.

In fact, the only significant difference between this type of resume and an SF-171 is that the federal resume is generated by you and therefore doesn't have the form's printed lines and boxes all over the page. In addition, some of the personal information requested on the SF-171 isn't needed on a federal resume: your date and place of birth, questions about whether you've ever been arrested, how many hours a week you're willing to work, and more. In short, a good federal resume provides as much information about the details of your work history as an SF-171 does. The higher-level the position you are applying for, the more detailed your federal resume should probably be. Federal resumes that run 6 to 12 pages are acceptable. In the private sector, job candidates would never turn in a 12-page resume unless they were applying for an upper-level academic or research position and had dozens of publications to their credit.

Warning: Don't be misled by the word "resume" on the vacancy announcement. The resume you're being asked to submit is a federal resume.

If the "How to Apply" section of a vacancy announcement states that you can submit "a resume, SF-171, or OF-612," the kind of resume you should submit is the federal resume. If you read the vacancy announcement carefully, you will often see a list of details that your resume needs to provide: names and phone numbers of your present and past job supervisors, salaries you earned in these positions, and similar information. On a private sector resume, this information is not expected. However, on a federal resume you are usually asked and expected to provide this information and more.

THE COMPUTER-SCANNABLE RESUME, OR RESUMIX™

The computer-scannable resume and Resumix™ are one in the same. Resumix™ is simply the name of the company that invented this form. This is an application document that several federal agencies have started to use.

Unlike the SF-171 or OF-612 (which are reviewed by actual people), the computer-scannable resume is fed into the database of a mainframe computer system. An artificial intelligence program then scans your material, looking for certain key words and phrases. As a result, in writing this kind of resume, you need to mirror the language contained in the vacancy announcement you are responding to, since that is the key to this process.

You also need to produce a document that is physically capable of being scanned—or, in some cases, e-mailed. Forget the different fonts and stylistic creativity that you hope make your private-sector resume stand out in the pile. Here are some simple tips to follow:

- Do not underline for emphasis.
- Do not use bold or italics for emphasis.
- Do not use forward or backward slashes, such as "supervised each employee in drawing up his/her professional goals."
- Do not use fancy or unusual fonts. Simple typefaces are recommended, such as Courier, Arial, or New Times Roman. No part of any letter must touch any part of any other letter.
- Do not use very small or very large type sizes. The standard is 10 pt. or 12 pt.
- As with every computer document, do not bend, fold, staple, tape, or mutilate your resume in any way.

The hiring agency that allows a Resumix™ may ask that you cover only specific points on it, so that it may end up being rather short (compared to an SF-171). However, in those cases, the agency will also give you a *supplemental data sheet* with a list of questions, to be submitted as a separate document. The supplemental data sheet solicits the other information usually asked for on the SF-171—such as your lowest acceptable pay grade, willingness to accept temporary or part-time work, military experience, and so on. All this is in addition to the computer-scannable resume and in addition to the KSAs.

THE KSAs OR RANKING FACTORS

Almost every federal vacancy lists criteria that the hiring agency feels is essential for strong job performance. These criteria are called different names by different federal agencies. Some agencies call these *ranking factors*, *selection criteria*, or *rating factors*. Some agencies actually call them "KSAs."

KSA stands for "knowledge, skill, and ability"—because these are the general criteria an agency expects a successful candidate to possess in order to do the job. Some typical KSAs are "ability to communicate orally and in writing," or "knowledge of the federal budgeting system," or "skill in negotiating contracts with vendors and suppliers." Usually there are four to six of these KSA factors for each vacancy announcement. Many KSAs repeat from one vacancy announcement to another. That means if you're applying for eight different positions as, say, an accounting technician, you'll probably find that all eight vacancy announcements are fairly similar and that the KSAs you wrote for the first one can be reused almost verbatim for the others.

You must respond in writing separately—apart from your entry document—to these KSAs in order to be selected for an interview. As a rule of thumb, if you are applying for a position at the GS-5 level or below, a half-page response is usually sufficient. But if you are applying at the GS-7 level or above, you should submit a full-page written response to each factor, detailing examples of times when you used the type of knowledge, skill, or ability referred to in the vacancy announcement.

These KSAs are quite important in the final selection process. Don't ignore or neglect them, as they are usually the difference between a decent application and a winning one.

WHICH FORM DO I CHOOSE?

On occasion, a hiring agency will state in the job announcement the format that it prefers you use. So, of course, in that instance, you will use the requested form. However, most agencies accept all of them and will say so in the announcement. From your point of view, it probably makes no difference. The questions that have been dropped from the SF-171 are relatively short anyway. In all cases, you should focus on describing your past duties and responsibilities; detailing the knowledge, skills, and abilities you developed; and quantifying or in some other way explicitly explaining what you did and the results.

Crafting Your Application to Match Career Area and Agency Standards

The federal government uses a two-stage screening process in selecting candidates to be interviewed and, ultimately, hired. The first stage involves the SF-171, OF-612, federal resume, or computer-scannable resume that has been asked for in the vacancy announcement. In the first stage, these documents are screened by a federal personnel clerk to weed out those that are unacceptable or incomplete. Then they're screened by a panel of federal mid- to senior-level managers to see who is eligible to compete for the vacancy at the level that was announced. So, for example, your application as a GS-13 budget analyst might be complete in all its parts, but the panel may determine that you have only enough experience for a GS-11 level—which is not the advertised opening. At that point, your application will be out of the running.

If your application makes it through the panel, you face the second step in the screening process, where the panel then compares you directly to all the other applicants that have made it that far. The panel does this by using your KSAs to rank the "survivors." So you see how providing a wealth of detail on your application helps. You don't get a second chance to explain yourself; there is no back-up plan. Both the application and the KSAs must be as complete as possible from the very beginning.

To develop an effective and competitive SF-171, OF-612, federal resume, or computer-scannable resume for a federal position, you will need to keep the following points in mind:

- **Remember to describe your professional experience, in detail.** You will have to provide more details than any private-sector job application ever requested. Some of the questions may seem obvious or repetitious. Complete them anyway.

- **Do more than redescribe your official job duties and job description.** Most competent employees do a lot more than their job descriptions, because most official job descriptions don't capture the true complexity of the work that has to be done. Unfortunately, instead of writing about what they *really* do in their jobs, many people just repeat the official job description.

- **Give yourself credit.** You've earned it with your good work. But you've got to let people know. Federal screening panels are quite literal in the way they review and score your application. They give you points for what is relevant in your paperwork. And remember, they *don't* give you any points for what is not included. So don't feel bashful! You don't have to sound conceited, but you *do* have to point out your accomplishments.

- **Use your federal resume, SF-171, OF-612, KSAs, and scannable resumes to narrate your professional victories.** One good way to point out your accomplishments is to describe your professional victories. These could be times when you've made solid decisions; times when you've dealt effectively with problems, special projects, or troubleshooting assignments; or times when you've really demonstrated your value to the organizations for which you've worked. Properly described, these stories are like money in the bank. They make you and your abilities come alive to the screening panel and have impact, rather than be disguised by the verbiage of official job descriptions.

- **Highlight your professional skills by using an action/result presentation.** Show your skills actually being used. Most actions have a result, especially if your actions were effective. Don't shortchange yourself. If things you have done have generated bottom-line results for your employers, then say so. Did your innovative idea save them money? Did your initiative and persistence make them money? Say so—and how much. Describe what happened. There's nothing more convincing to a skeptical screening panel than to see the word "result" appear again and again throughout your application. It lets them know that *you* know where the bottom line is—and how to get there. *That's* what they are looking for in an employee.

- **Stop scaring yourself.** Writing an effective SF-171 or set of KSAs depends on your attitude, more than on your writing skills. Filling out these forms is unpleasant, but don't let that discourage you. The task is certainly within your abilities. And remember, the application is not a test. There are no right or wrong answers. There are only other competitors like yourself, who find the process just as difficult as you do. If you compete with these applicants effectively, you stand a good chance of winning.

And remember: *Someone's* going to be selected for these positions—it might as well be *you*.

"Before" and "After" Examples Taken from Federal Job Applications

What does a good 171 or KSA look like? The easiest way to learn how to write a good federal job application is to see the difference between some bad examples from several different fields—contrasted against actual job-winning entries. Note that the bad examples won't really seem dreadful, just rather ordinary when seen next to the good entries.

DESCRIPTIONS OF MAJOR DUTIES

Bad:

Coordinated complex civil cases. Developed detailed reviews and analyses. Researched and prepared comprehensive legal memoranda.

Now see how much detail has been added to the job-winning version:

Good:

Coordinated complex civil cases with various departments or divisions within FDIC. Developed detailed reviews and analyses, in preparation for counseling client representatives to improve their request for legal services.

Researched and prepared comprehensive legal memoranda for clients, drawing on my extensive knowledge and experience litigating various issues under the FDI Act, FIRREA, the FDIC Improvement Act, commercial law, real estate law, and the Bankruptcy Code.

Here is another example:

Bad:

Served as a contracting officer and contract administrator. Performed pre-award, award, and contract administration duties. Headed evaluation teams reviewing potential contractors. Prepared lease agreements.

The added details in the following show how the applicant's duties were much more responsible and varied:

Good:

Served as contracting officer and contract administrator for multimillion dollar supplies and services, construction, and architectural and engineering contracts. Possessed a contracting officer's warrant. Performed pre-award, award, and contract administration duties. Prepared *Commerce Business Daily* synopses and advertisements, developed and reviewed technical specifications, and issued solicitations and Requests for Proposals (RFPs). Headed evaluation teams reviewing potential contractors' financial data. Prepared lease agreements for properties where contractors performed construction work.

DESCRIPTIONS OF ADVANCED TRAINING

Bad:

FBI/RTC Bank Failure School (December 7–10, 1993); Basic Examination School for Attorneys (January 1998).

Good:

FBI/RTC Bank Failure School (December 7–10, 1993). This was a highly intensive course focusing on the aspects of fraud involving financial institutions, covering such topics as Fraud Detection and Investigation, Forensic Accounting Approach, Prosecution of Financial Institution Fraud Cases, and The Importance of CPAs to Bank Examiners and Criminal Investigations.

Basic Examination School for Attorneys (January 1998). This was a week-long concentrated course focusing on fundamentals of bank supervision, basic report analysis, bank accrual accounting, loan classifications, and financial analysis.

DESCRIPTIONS OF KSAs OR RANKING FACTORS (FOR AN UPPER-LEVEL POSITION)

Bad:

Knowledge of materiel life-cycle management functions, programs, and systems used to provide logistical support: Gained valuable understanding of military facilities planning while serving as Acting Chief of the Facilities Management Office. Responsible for issuing policy pertaining to the total acquisition life-cycle baseline parameters. Strong working knowledge of PPBES. Broad experience writing, revising, and implementing policy.

Obviously the applicant didn't know that, at this job level, he or she should include a full page for each KSA, explaining how and when the knowledge, skills, or ability was demonstrated. The paragraph above works as a bare-bones outline for the detailed job-winning entry below.

Good:

Knowledge of material life cycle management functions, programs, and systems used to provide logistical support.

My current job includes a very substantial degree of life-cycle management responsibility. For example, I currently run the policy operation of Acquisition Life Cycle management. In this capacity, the information related to guidance addressing Army's Acquisition Program Baselines (APBs) for Army Acquisition Category (ACAT) I, II, and some representative III programs. Examples of my strong working knowledge in this area include the following:

Analyze the content of the APBs and ensure that APBs adequately address program requirements.

Result:

I recently issued APB policy that now requires APBs to address "total life-cycle costs," which by definition includes operating and support (O&S) costs.

Keep Army and OSD leadership informed regarding how the Army executes their cost, schedule, and performance parameters within their respective APBs.

Result:

Maintain close ties and frequent contacts with officials at all levels in the Army and DoD as well as the respective PEOs and PMs and Command Groups. Any known logistical support requirements would also be captured within the respective APBs.

I have gained substantial working knowledge and hands-on experience through interacting with officials in the Comptroller and Acquisition communities related to acquisition life-cycle subject matter contained within APBs, SARs and DAES reports, as well as through managing these processes.

Result:

My effort to include O&S costs within APBs is unique. To this point, the other military services have not yet followed suit but will likely do so soon, since it is DoD policy to make Program Managers responsible for "total life-cycle management." If and when this happens, these Program Managers would have total "cradle-to-grave" program responsibility—as well as operational control of the budget dollars to make sure that this level of responsibility is discharged fully and effectively.

The job-winning applicants might well have phrased their experience, background, and abilities as in the "bad" examples. If these had been private-sector resumes, that might have been enough. But the procedure for applying for a federal job is very different.

Samples of Completed Application Forms

Now let's see the results when this kind of attention to detail is applied to the entire form. Following are full-length, filled-in samples of actual job-winning application tools: a filled-in SF-171, a filled-in OF-612, a federal resume, a Resumix or computer-scannable resume, and a KSA list.

A COMPLETED SF-171

Application for Federal Employment–SF 171

Read the instructions before you complete this application. *Type or print clearly in dark ink*

Form Approved
OMB No. 3206-0012

GENERAL INFORMATION

1 What kind of job are you applying for? Give title and announcement no. (if any)

2 Social Security Number
000-00-0000

3 Sex
[X] Male [ ] Female

4 Birth Date *(Month, Day, Year)*
2-4-53

5 Birthplace *(City and State or County)*
XXXXXXXX,

6 Name *(Last, First, Middle)*
XXXX, XXXXXXX

Mailing address *(include apartment number, if any)*
000000 XXXXXX Street

City	State	ZIP Code
Mission Viejo	C A	9 2 6 9 2

7 Other names ever used *(e.g., maiden name, nickname, etc.)*
N/A

8 Home Phone
Area Code 714 Number 000-0000

9 Work Phone
Area Code 714 Number 000-0000 Extension

10 Were you employed as a civilian by the Federal Government? If "NO", go to item 11. If "YES", mark each type of job you held with an "X".
[ ] Temporary [ ] Career Conditional [X] Career [ ] Excepted
What is your highest grade, classification series and job title?
GG-905-15/6, Counsel
Dates at highest grade: FROM 6/96 TO present

AVAILABILITY

11 When can you start work? *(Month and year)*
Within 2-4 weeks from notification

12 What is the lowest pay you will accept? *(You will not be considered for jobs which pay less than you indicate.)*
Pay $ ___ per ___ OR Grade 15/6

13 In what geographic area(s) are you willing to work?
Per announcement; no geographic restriction

14 Are you willing to work:	YES	NO
A. 40 hours per week *(full time)*?	X	
B. 25-30 hours per week *(part time)*		X
C. 17-24 hours per week *(part time)*?		X
D. 16 or fewer hours per week *(part time)*?		X
E. An intermittent job *(on call/seasonal)*?		X
F. Weekends, shifts, or rotating shifts?		X

15 Are you willing to take a temporary job lasting:		
A. 5-12 months *(sometimes longer)*?		X
B. 1-4 months?		X
C. Less than 1 month?		X

16 Are you willing to travel away from home for:		
A. 1-5 nights each month?	X	
B. 6-10 nights each month?	X	
C. 11 or more nights each month?	X	

MILITARY SERVICE AND VETERAN PREFERENCE

17 Have you served in the United States Military Service? If your only active duty was training in the Reserves or National Guard, answer "NO". If "NO" go to item 22.	YES	NO
		X

18 Did you or will you retire above the rank of major or lieutenant commander		

FOR USE OF EXAMINING OFFICE ONLY

Date entered register

Form reviewed:
Form approved:

Option	Grade	Earned Rating	Veteran Preference	Augmented Rating
			[ ] No Preference Claimed	
			[ ] 5 Points *(Tentative)*	
			[ ] 10 Pts. *(30% Or More Comp. Dis.)*	
			[ ] 10 Pts. *(Less Than 30% Comp. Dis)*	
			[ ] Other 10 Points	
			[ ] Disallowed	[ ] Being Investigated

FOR USE OF APPOINTING OFFICE ONLY

Preference has been verified through proof that the separation was under honorable conditions, and other proof as required.

[ ] 5 Point [ ] 10-Point—30% or More Compensable Disability [ ] 10-Point—Less Than 30% Compensable Disability [ ] 10-Point— Other

Signature and Title

Agency

Date

MILITARY SERVICE AND VETERAN PREFERENCE

19 Were you discharged from the military service under honorable conditions? *(If your discharge was changed to "honorable" or "general" by a Discharge Review Board answer "YES". If you received a clemency discharge, answer "NO".)*	YES	NO

Discharge Date *(Month, Day, Year)*	Type of Discharge

20 List the dates (Month, Day, Year), and branch for all active duty military service.

From	To	Branch of Service

21 If all your active military duty was after October 14, 1976, list the full names and dates of all campaign badges or expeditionary medals you received or were entitled to receive.

22 Read the instructions that came with this form before completing this item. When you have determined your eligibility for veteran preference from the instructions, place an "X" in the box next to your veteran preference claim.

[X] NO PREFERENCE

[ ] 5-POINT PREFERENCE—You must show proof when you are hired

[ ] 10 POINT PREFERENCE—If you claim 10-point preference, place an "X" in the box below next to the basis for your claim. To receive 10-point preference you must also complete a Standard Form 15, Application for 10-point Veteran Preference, which is available from any Federal Job Information Center. ATTACH THE COMPLETED SF 15 AND REQUESTED PROOF TO THIS APPLICATION.

[ ] Non-compensably disabled Purple Heart recipient

[ ] Compensably disabled, less than 30 percent

[ ] Spouse, widow(er), or mother of a deceased or disabled veteran

[ ] Compensably disabled, 30 percent or more.

THE FEDERAL GOVERNMENT IS AN EQUAL OPPORTUNITY EMPLOYER
PREVIOUS EDITION USABLE UNTIL 12-31-90
Page 1

NSN 7540-00-935-7150   171-110

Standard Form 171 (Rev. 6-88)
U.S. Office of Personnel Management
FPM Chapter 295

WORK EXPERIENCE If you have no work experience write "NONE" in A below and go to 25 on page 3

23 May we ask you present employer about your character, qualifications and work record? A "NO" will not affect our review of your qualifications. If you answer "NO" and we need to contact your present employer before we can offer you a job, we will contact you first ....

YES	NO
X	

24 WORK EXPERIENCE

A	Name and address of employer's organization (include ZIP Code, if known)	Dates employed (give month and year)	Average number of hours per week
	Federal Deposit Insurance Corporation (FDIC) 4 Park Plaza Irvine, CA 92714	From: 1/96 To: present	40
		Salary or earnings	Place of employment
		Starting $ GS-15 per year	City Irvine,
		Ending $ GS-15 per year	State CA

Exact title of your job COUNSEL, CLIENT SERVICE GROUP	Your immediate supervisor Name XXXX XXXXXX	Area Code 714 Telephone Number 000-0000	Number and job titles of any employees you supervise(d) N/A
Kind of business or organization *(manufacturing, accounting, social service, etc.)* US Government	If Federal Employment (civilian or military) list services, grade or rank and the date of your last promotion GG-905-15/6, 6/96		Your reason for wanting to leave Career advancement; office is being closed.

Description of work: Describe your specific duties, responsibilities and accomplishments in this job. If you describe more than one type of work (for example, carpentry and painting or personnel and budget), write the appropriate percentage of time you spent doing each.

OVERVIEW
- **Client Services Group Attorney** for the Major Asset Group.
- **Provide in-depth legal advice and counsel** to senior management on litigation and bankruptcy strategies affecting the disposition of assets from the Client's $1.1 Billion asset portfolio.

KEY ACTIVITIES

Coordinate complex civil cases with various departments or divisions within FDIC. Developed detailed reviews and analyses, in preparation for counseling Client representatives to improve the Client's requests for legal services. Research and prepare comprehensive legal memoranda for Clients, drawing on my extensive knowledge and experience litigating various issues under the FDI Act, FIRREA, the FDIC Improvement Act, commercial law, real estate law and the Bankruptcy Code.

RESULT:
- Initiated major civil fraud investigation of FDIC judgment debtor, who fraudulently transferred assets in anticipation of entry of FDIC's judgments, including use of asset freeze provisions pursuant to Crime Control Act.
- Successfully coordinated FDIC's efforts to obtain $11 Million restitution order in U.S.A. v. Charles W. Knapp case.
- Initiated and coordinated FDIC's efforts to collect on reserved fraud claims involving $10 Million golf course formerly owned by Great American Bank and its wholly owned subsidiary.
- Researched and developed best foreclosure practices for environmentally contaminated real estate for Client's use in Western Service Center in Irvine.

EVALUATION OF PERFORMANCE

"Has demonstrated a very high degree of analytical ability. Particularly, Mr. Xxxx has been involved in providing background information and assistance to the Washington DC Appellate Litigation Section regarding the ACC/Lincoln Savings Securities Litigation and the RTC v. Keating, et. al. Mr. Xxxx's contributions have been relied upon by the Appellate Section in their representation of the FDIC."
(from Evaluation, 1996)

For Agency Use (skill codes, etc.

Standard Form 171-A—*Continuation Sheet for SF 171*

•Attach all SF 171-A's to your application at the top of page 3.

1. Name (Last, First, Middle Initial)	2. Social Security Number
XXXX, XXXXX	000-00-0000

3. Job Title or Announcement Number You Are Applying For	4. Date Completed

ADDITIONAL WORK EXPERIENCE BLOCKS IF NEEDED

B

Name and address of employer's organization (include ZIP Code, if known)	Dates employed *(give month and year)*	Number of hours per week
Resolution Trust Corporation (RTC) 4000 MacArthur Boulevard - 5th floor Newport Beach, CA 92660-2516	From: 6/92 To: 12/95	40

	Salary or earnings	Place of Employment
	Starting $ 70,656 per year Ending $ 82,209 per year	City Newport Beach, State CA

Exact title of your job	Your immediate supervisor			Number and job titles of any employees you supervised
COUNSEL / SECTION CHIEF, PROF'L LIABILITY SECTION	Name XXXXXXXX	Area Code 202	Telephone Number 000-0000	14: legal / support staff

Kind of business or organization *(marketing, accounting, social service, etc.)*	If Federal Employment (civilian or military) list series grade rank and the date of your last promotion	Your reason for wanting to leave.
US Government	GG-905-15/4 3/95	Office was closed; career advancement

Description of work: Describe your specific duties, responsibilities and accomplishments in this job. If you describe more than one type of work (for example, carpentry and painting or personnel and budget), write the appropriate percentage of time you spent doing each.

OVERVIEW

<u>MANAGERIAL:</u> **Directed and managed a 14-person staff,** including five attorneys and a support staff of nine paralegals and legal technicians. Assigned, managed, and evaluated the staff's work performance. Planned and coordinated work assignments within both the PLS unit and the Investigations Department.

<u>TECHNICAL:</u> **Reviewed and recommended the initiation of litigation** against directors, officers, shareholders, other insiders, employees, borrowers, accountants, attorneys, or other persons employed by failed financial institutions or any affiliate, underwriters, or any party causing a loss to a failed financial institution.

KEY ACTIVITIES   <u>MANAGERIAL</u>

Employed proactive and consultative management techniques to motivate and unify professional staff to achieve RTC's PLS program objectives. Developed methods to increase cross-communication between PLS and the Investigations Department. Conducted extensive in-house meetings with staff to determine the staff's training needs and to identify various ways to increase staff morale and productivity.

<u>RESULT:</u>
- Created a cohesive, unified working group of professional staff from what had been a fragmented and demoralized staff following RTC's reorganization in 1992.

- Significantly improved working relationship and communication between PLS and RTC's Investigations Department which later served as a model for national policy statement on the Roles and Responsibilities between the two departments.

- Successfully downsized PLS for RTC's 12/31/95 sunset without adverse actions from affected employees.

- Advocated and developed a national civil fraud training program including written materials to improve RTC's national civil fraud program.

For Agency Use (skill codes, etc.

Standard Form 171 (Rev. 6-88)
U.S. Office of Personnel Management
FPM Chapter 295

XXXXXX XXXX
SSN 569-76-5020

#24-B, continued – KEY ACTIVITIES:

MANAGERIAL

Developed outreach initiatives to generate a greater degree of active participation by women-owned and minority law firms in PLS cases.

    RESULT: • Recognized by RTC's Minority and Woman's Program Office for efforts to increase the participation of minority and women law firms in PLS cases.

EVALUATION OF PERFORMANCE

"A highly effective manager. Mr. Xxxx has organized the work of his section effectively and manages the work skillfully notwithstanding the high level of controversial high profile matters that cross his desk on a daily basis. He has been instrumental in establishing and fostering excellent working arrangements with the US Department of Justice and the US Attorney's Office. He has a natural maturity and confidence and has been a strong contributor to the California Legal Division Management Team."   *(from Evaluation, 1995)*

TECHNICAL

Investigated 62 failed thrifts and prosecuted civil claims from 34 thrift institutions. Advised and conferred with immediate supervisors regarding significant developments affecting legal cases and/or personnel matters.

    RESULT: • Generated cash recoveries of $88,149,523, as of 12/31/95.

                 • Maintained a 5-to-1 recovery to cost ratio. The total cost of collection, exclusive of in-house salaries and overhead, was $16,172,374.

                 • Issued more than 577 administrative subpoenas prior to initiation of Authority to Sue Memos developing thorough factual and financial investigations of potential targets.

                 • Authored comprehensive memo for Assistant General Counsel analyzing the potential impact that the Senate's proposed D'Oench reform legislation would have on future parallel proceeding cases such as Lincoln Savings & Loan.

Cooperated with U. S. Attorneys Office in San Diego in civil forfeiture of 2,000 acres of undeveloped land involved in a sham joint venture between a subsidiary of HomeFed Bank and a developer.

    RESULT: • The forfeiture has resulted in cash recoveries of $13.6 million and the elimination of contractual obligations of at least $9.8 million.

SEE NEXT PAGE

XXXXX XXXXX
SSN 000-00-0000

#24-B, continued – KEY ACTIVITIES:

TECHNICAL

In addition to duties as PLS Section Chief, **I continued to work on the resolution of Lincoln Savings & Loan's outstanding professional liability matters,** which were not finished when I began my tenure in California with PLS in June of 1992.

RESULT:
- Generated civil settlements totaling approximately $295 Million.

- Generated cash recoveries totaling in excess of $248 Million, and nondischargeable judgments totaling approximately $1.4 Billion.

- Successfully argued an entry of summary judgment against Keating for an amount in excess of $4.3 Billion.

- Successfully argued for Federal criminal convictions of Keating on 77 federal felony counts; and of his son, Charles H. Keating, on 64 felony counts for bank fraud, wire fraud, securities fraud, bankruptcy fraud, and racketeering.

- Successfully obtained Federal criminal indictments against eight Keating confederates and resulting felony pleas by Judy Wischer, Ray Fidel, Andrew Ligget, Robert Wurzelbacher, Mark Sauter, Bruce Dickson, Robin Symes, and Ernie Garcia.

- Obtained criminal forfeitures, including Charles H. Keating's for $122 Million, in excess of $265 Million.

EVALUATION OF PERFORMANCE
"Has outstanding analytical and problem solving skills that he has applied to virtually every kind of legal problem arising from failed financial institutions.
"His high level of cognition and his ability to analyze difficult legal scenarios are evident on a day-to-day basis. A dedicated professional...consistently performs at a high level. Very creative and original in his work."
(from Evaluation, 1995)

Standard Form 171—*Continuation Sheet for SF 171*

•Attach all SF 171-A's to your application at the top of page 3.

1. Name (Last, First, Middle Initial)	2. Social Security Number
XXXX, XXXXXX	000-00-0000

3. Job Title or Announcement Number You Are Applying For	4. Date Completed

ADDITIONAL WORK EXPERIENCE BLOCKS IF NEEDED

C Name and address of employer's organization (include ZIP Code, if known)	Dates employed (give month and year)	Number of hours per week
Resolution Trust Corporation (RTC) 2910 North 44th Street Phoenix, AZ 85018	From: 2/90 To: 6/92	40

	Salary or earnings	Place of Employment
	Starting $ 53,112 per year Ending $ 64,073 per year	City Phoenix, State AZ

Exact title of your job COUNSEL / SECTION CHIEF	Your immediate supervisor Name XXXXXXX	Area Code 202	Telephone Number 000-0000	Number and job titles of any employees you supervised 41: legal / support staff

Kind of business or organization (marketing, accounting, social service, etc.) US. Government	If Federal Employment (civilian or military) list series grade rank and the date of your last promotion GG-905-14/3 5/92	Your reason for wanting to leave. Office was being closed; career advancement

Description of work: Describe your specific duties, responsibilities and accomplishments in this job. If you describe more than one type of work (for example, carpentry and painting or personnel and budget), write the appropriate percentage of time you spent doing each.

OVERVIEW   <u>MANAGERIAL:</u> **Section Chief, Legal Division**, Central Western Consolidated Office, Phoenix, Arizona (CWCO) for Lincoln Savings and Loan and Great American Bank. **Supervised and managed a 41-person staff,** including 7 attorneys and paralegals from the Coastal Consolidated Office (CCO) as part of a transition of the legal management of Great American Bank from CWCO to CCO.

<u>TECHNICAL:</u> **Reviewed a wide range of cases and made recommendations** regarding the wisdom and suitability of initiating, continuing, or settling cases involving complex litigation concerning issues of national interest. **Served as Acting Managing Senior Attorney** in the absence of the Managing Senior Attorney and the Deputy Managing Senior Attorney.

KEY ACTIVITIES   <u>MANAGERIAL</u>

Supervised and managed a staff of 34 professionals, including CWCO staff attorneys, financial institution in-house attorneys, and support personnel. In addition, as of April 1, 1992, I also supervised and managed another 7 attorneys and paralegals from the CCO as part of an assignment to complete the orderly transition of legal management of Great American Bank from CWCO to CCO.

Assigned, directed, and evaluated the work performance of all staff members. In addition, developed and coordinated plans for the accomplishment of work assigned to my Section. Directed and reviewed the work of the attorneys, paralegals and support staff assigned to my section.

Litigation Manager for the RTC Legal Division within CWCO. supervised legal and cost-effective aspects of more than 5,000 litigation cases.

Maintained extensive inter-organizational liaison, ensuring that high-level managers were kept informed of all significant developments. Conferred with and advised the Managing Senior Attorney, the Deputy Managing Senior Attorney, and all CWCO Section Chiefs regarding the application of the RTC's litigation policy to a broad spectrum of legal matters.

SEE NEXT PAGE   For Agency Use (skill codes, etc.

<u>XXXX XXXXXX</u>
SSN 000-00-0000

#24-C, continued – <u>KEY ACTIVITIES:</u>

<u>TECHNICAL</u>

Participated in and contributed to negotiations and settlements of complex asset dispositions and major litigation involving issues of national interest by providing legal advice and legal strategies to RTC legal and business executives. **Participated in the formulation strategy, trial preparation, and settlements** of the RTC's Civil Racketeering (RICO) Lawsuit against Charles Keating, Jr. and other Lincoln Savings and Loan directors, officers, accountants and lawyers, including various insurance carriers with policies affected thereby.

<u>RESULT:</u>
- Worked successfully with outside counsel, and with the RTC's Acting General Counsel and the Assistant General Counsel (PLS), in negotiating approximately $295 Million in pretrial settlements which included the largest (to date) pretrial settlements with a national law firm and a big six accounting firm by the RTC/FDIC.

- Successfully argued an entry of summary judgment against Keating for an amount in excess of $4.3 Billion.

- Successfully argued for Federal criminal convictions of Keating on 77 federal felony counts; and of his son, Charles H. Keating, on 64 felony counts for bank fraud, wire fraud, securities fraud, bankruptcy fraud, and racketeering.

Negotiated with representatives from the government of Kuwait regarding the sale of the Phoenician and Crescent Hotels which were part of the Keating/Lincoln S&L holdings.

<u>RESULT:</u>
- Developed the strategy which enhanced RTC's negotiating position by restructuring the ownership of the hotels, placing RTC in a position to repudiate the Shareholders' Agreement. This strategy resulted in the sale of the RTC's 55 % interest in the hotels for a sum which exceeded the Kuwait government's offer prior to the Gulf War by 159%.

Prepared with outside counsel what became known as the Drexel Task Force questionnaire, based upon our knowledge of Keating and Milken's junk bond transactions at Lincoln.

<u>RESULT:</u>
- The questionnaire was used to gather evidence to support the RTC's claims against Drexel, Milken, and others from thrifts within the RTC's control around the country.

Negotiated favorable settlements with 35 subcontractors and the general contractor in the McCarthy case which involved the foreclosure of a $18.5 Million mechanics lien against the Phoenician Hotel.

<u>RESULT:</u>
- Settlements with 35 subcontractors were negotiated for approximately 79% of their claimed lien amount, exclusive of attorneys' fees and interest. The settlement with the general contractor represented approximately 57 % of the amount it claimed under its lien, exclusive of other subcontractors' claims, attorneys' fees and interest.

SEE NEXT PAGE

XXXXX XXXXXXX
SSN 000-00-0000

#24-C, continued – KEY ACTIVITIES:

TECHNICAL

Developed a Litigation Claims Procedure Manual which was used by RTC in-house and outside counsel.

RESULT: • By using standard forms and pleadings for routine, recurring claims issues, our unit successfully eliminated the need for duplicative yet expensive legal research and pleading preparation associated with many FIRREA claims issues.

Compiled a standard forms pleading book.

RESULT: • By using standard pleadings and briefs for routine RTC matters, our unit reduced outside counsel expense substantially.

Supervised and managed the review of 1,087 contracts, issued legal opinions as to the advisability of repudiation, and prepared 260 repudiation cases for the client, as part of Great American Bank's liquidation.

Organized, supervised, and managed the RTC Legal Division Fraud Task Force's investigation of Western Savings & Loan Association.

RESULT: • This investigation led to the RTC's filing of a civil RICO complaint against Western's former officers, directors, accountants, attorneys, and accommodation parties.

• To date, the RTC and FDIC have recovered over $87 Million, at an approximate cost of $9.5 Million.

• In addition to the RTC's civil RICO action against Western's former insiders, professionals and accommodation parties, the Arizona and Los Angeles U.S. attorneys have indicted four of Western's former insiders or accommodation parties. One has plead guilty to, and three have been convicted of, various federal criminal bank fraud charges.

EVALUATION OF PERFORMANCE

"He balances competing goals and interests deftly. Energetic and resourceful. Notwithstanding the enormity of the workload, complexity of the issues, and rapidity of the pace, his staff is well-motivated and loyal, and morale is high. A highly effective manager.

"Possesses superb substantive legal skills. As one of our most experienced trial lawyers on staff, Mr. Xxxx serves as litigation coordinator for our office. His personal involvement in the day-to-day management of the highly successful Lincoln Savings/Charles Keating, Jr. racketeering litigation is but one example of Mr. Xxxx's consistently exceptional performance.

"Mr. Xxxx enjoys an excellent working relationship with members of the Legal Department staff and our client alike. He has earned the respect of others at all levels within the RTC, as well as outside the agency. An extremely valuable employee."

(Evaluation, 1992)

← **ATTACH ANY ADDITIONAL FORMS AND SHEETS HERE**

EDUCATION

25 Did you graduate from high school? If you have a GED high school equivalency or will graduate within the next nine months, answer "YES".

YES X   If "Yes", give month and year graduated or received GED equivalency: 6/71
If "NO", give the highest grade you

26 Write the name and location (*city and state*) of the last high school you attended or where you obtained your GED high school equivalency.

Westside H.S. - Omaha, NE

27 Have you ever attended college or graduate school   **YES** X ► If "YES", continue with **28**
NO ► If "NO", go to **31**.

28 NAME AND LOCATION (city, state and ZIP Code) OF COLLEGE OR UNIVERSITY. If you expect to graduate within nine months, give the *month* and *year* you expect to receive your degree:

Name	City	State	ZIP Code	MONTH AND YEAR ATTENDED From	To	NUMBER OF CREDIT HOURS COMPLETED Semester	Quarter	TYPE OF DEGREE (e.g. B.A., M.A.)	MONTH AND YEAR OF DEGREE
1) Creighton University School of Law	Omaha	NE	68012	9/75	5/78	75		J.D.	5/78
2) University of Nebraska	Lincoln	NE	68501	9/71	5/75	135		B.A.	5/75
3)									

29 CHIEF UNDERGRADUATE SUBJECTS
Show major on the first line

	NUMBER OF CREDIT HOURS COMPLETED Semester	Quarter
1) English	50	
2) History	15	
3) Philosophy	15	

30 CHIEF GRADUATE SUBJECTS
Show major on the first line

	NUMBER OF CREDIT HOURS COMPLETED Semester	Quarter
1) Law	75	
2)		
3)		

31 If you have completed any other courses or training related to the kind of jobs you are applying for *(trade, vocational, Armed Forces, business)* give information below

NAME AND LOCATION (city, state and ZIP Code) OF SCHOOL	MONTH AND YEAR ATTENDED From	To	CLASS-ROOM HOURS	SUBJECT(S)	TRAINING COMPLETED YES	NO
School Name 1) National Institute fore Trial Advocacy - NITA City Notre Dame State Indiana ZIP Code 46556	6/96	6/96	74	Trial Advocacy Building Trial Skills	X	
School Name 2) Hastings College of the Law City San Francisco State CA ZIP Code 94018	8/79	8/79	40	Civil and Criminal Trial Advocacy	X	

SPECIAL SKILLS, ACCOMPLISHMENTS AND AWARDS

32 Give the title and year of any honors, awards or fellowships you have received. List your special qualifications, skills or accomplishments that may help you get a job. Some examples are: skills with computers or other machines; most important publications (do not submit copies); public speaking and writing experience; membership in professional or scientific

PLEASE SEE ATTACHED SHEET

33 How many words per minute can you:

TYPE? TAKE DICTATION?
25   N/A
Agencies may test your skills before hiring you.

34 List job-related licenses or certificates that you have, such as: registered nurse; lawyer; radio operator; driver's; pilot's; etc.

LICENSE OR CERTIFICATE	DATE OF LATEST LICENSE OR CERTIFICATE	STATE OR OTHER LICENSING AGENCY
1) Attorney	1978-present	Nebraska
2) Attorney	1986-present	Iowa

35 So you speak or read a language other than English (include sign language)? Applicants for jobs that require a language other than English may be given an interview conducted solely in that language.

YES X   If "YES", list each language and place an "X" in each column that applies to you.
NO   If "NO", go to **36**.

LANGUAGE(S)	CAN PREPARE AND GIVE LECTURES Fluently	With Difficulty	CAN SPEAK AND UNDERSTAND Fluently	Passably	CAN TRANSLATE ARTICLES Into English	From English	CAN READ ARTICLES FOR OWN USE Easily	With Difficulty
1) French		X		X		X		X
2)								

REFERENCES

36 List three people who are not related to you and are not supervisors you listed under **24** who know your qualifications and fitness for the kind of job for which you are applying.

FULL NAME OF REFERENCE	TELEPHONE NUMBER(S) (include Area Code)	PRESENT BUSINESS OR HOME ADDRESS (Number, street and city)	STATE	ZIP CODE
1) XXXXXX	404-000-0000	285 XXXXXX Street Atlanta	GA	30303
2) XXXXXX	202-000-0000	1717 XXXX Street – Room 000 Washington	DC	20434
3) XXXXXX (US District Court Judge, retired)	619-000-0000	101 West XXXXXX– Suite 1700 San Diego	CA	92101

Page 3

XXXX, XXXXXX
SSN 568-76-5020

#31, continued: ADVANCED TRAINING

FBI / RTC Bank Failure School   December 7-10, 1993
    This was a highly intensive course focusing on the aspects of fraud involving financial institutions.
    Topics covered included:
        Fraud Detection and Investigation
        Forensic Accounting Approach
        Prosecution of Financial Institution Fraud Cases
        The Importance of CPAs to Bank Examiners and Criminal Investigations

Basic Examination School for Attorneys   January 1988
    This was a week-long concentrated course focusing on:
        Fundamentals of bank supervision
        Basic report analysis
        Bank accrual accounting
        Loan classifications
        Financial analysis

#32, continued: HONORS AND AWARDS

August 6, 1995: Special Act or Service Award
    Recognizing my efforts in developing, supervising, and implementing RTC's civil fraud program.

July 10, 1994: Performance Award & Special Act or Service Award
    Recognizing my leadership in RTC/DOJ joint civil forfeiture which recovered $13.6 Million in cash, and eliminated contractual obligations of at least $9.8 Million.

November 3, 1991: Special Act or Service Award
    Recognizing my role in developing successful "repudiation" of Shareholder Agreement strategy and employing it in negotiating favorable sale of RTC's interest in Phoenician Hotel.

LICENSES

Attorney:	1978-present	U.S. District Court, Nebraska
	1987-present	U.S. Court of Appeals, Eighth Circuit
	1988-present	U.S. District Court, Southern District, Iowa
	1988-present	U.S. District Court, Northern District, Iowa

BACKGROUND INFORMATION—*You must answer each question in this section before we can process your application.*

	YES	NO
37 Are you a citizen of the United States? *(In most cases you must be a U.S. citizen to be hired. You will be required to submit proof of identity and citizenship at the time you are hired.)* If "NO", give the country or countries you are a citizen of:		X

NOTE: It is important that you give complete and truthful answers to questions 38 through 44. If you answer "YES" to any of them, provide your explanation(s) in Item 45. Include convictions resulting from a plea of nolo contendere (no contest). **Omit:** 1) traffic fines of $100.00 or less: 2) any violation of law committed before your 16th birthday; 3) any violation of law committed before your 18th birthday, if finally decided in juvenile court or under a Youth Offender law; 4) any conviction set aside under the Federal Youth Corrections Act or similar State law; 5) any conviction whose record was expunged under Federal law. We will consider the date, facts, and circumstances of each event you list. In most cases you can still be considered for Federal jobs. However, **if you fail to tell the truth or fail to list all relevant** events or circumstances, this may be grounds for not hiring you, for firing you after you begin work, or for criminal prosecution (18 USC 1001).

	YES	NO
38 During the last **10 years**, were you **fired from any job** for any reason, did you **quit after being told that you would be fired,** or did you leave by mutual agreement because of specific problems?		X
39 Have you **ever** been convicted of, or forfeited collateral for **any felony violation?** *(Generally, a felony is defined as any violation of law punishable by imprisonment of longer than one year, except for violations called misdemeanors under State law which are punishable by imprisonment of two years or less.)*		X
40 Have you **ever** been convicted of, or forfeited collateral for **any firearms or explosives violation?**		X
41 Are you **now** under charges for **any** violation of law?		X
42 During the last 10 years have you forfeited collateral, been convicted, been imprisoned, been on probation, or been on parole? Do not include violations reported in 39, 40, or 41, above		X
43 Have you **ever** been convicted by a military **court-martial?** If no military service, answer "NO"		X
44 Are you **delinquent** on any **Federal debt?** *(Include delinquencies arising from Federal taxes, loans, overpayment of benefits, and other debts t the U.S. Government plus defaults on Federally guaranteed or insured loans such as student and home mortgage loans.)*		X

45 If "YES" in: 38 - Explain for each job the problem(s) and your reason(s) for leaving. Give the employer's name and address.
39 through 43 - Explain each violation. Give place of occurrence and name/address of police or court involved.
44 - Explain the type, length and amount of the delinquency or default, and steps you are taking to correct errors or repay the debt. Give any identification number associated with the debt and the address of the Federal agency involved.
NOTE: If you need more space, use a sheet of paper, and include the item number.

Item No.	Date (Mo./Yr.)	Explanation	Mailing Address
			Name of Employer, Police, Court or Federal Agency City State ZIP Code
			Name of Employer, Police, Court or Federal Agency City State ZIP Code

	YES	NO
46 Do you receive, or have you ever applied for retirement pay, pension, or other pay based on military, Federal civilian, or District of Columbia Government service?		X
47 Do any of your relatives work for the United States Government or the United States Armed Forces? Include: father; mother; husband; wife; son; daughter; brother; sister; uncle; aunt; first cousin; nephew; niece; father-in-law; son-in-law; daughter-in-law; brother-in-law; sister-in-law; stepmother; stepson; stepdaughter; stepbrother; stepsister; half brother; and half sister		X

Name	Relationship	Department, Agency or Branch of Armed Forces

SIGNATURE, CERTIFICATION, AND RELEASE OF INFORMATION

YOU MUST SIGN THIS APPLICATION. Read the following carefully before you sign.

- A false statement on any part of your application may be grounds for not hiring you, or for firing you after you begin work. Also, you may be punished by fine or imprisonment (U.S. Code, title 18, section 1001).
- If you are a male born after December 31, 1959 you must be registered with the Selective Service System or have a valid exemption in order to be eligible for Federal employment. You will be required to certify as to your status at the time of appointment.
- I understand that any information I give may be investigated as allowed by law or Presidential order.
- I consent to the release of information about my ability and fitness for Federal employment by *employers, schools, law enforcement agencies and other individuals and organizations,* to *investigators, personnel staffing specialists, and other authorized employees of the Federal Government.*
- I certify that, to the best of my knowledge and belief, **all** of my statements are true, correct, complete, and made in good faith.

48 SIGNATURE *(Sign each application in dark ink)*   **49** DATE SIGNED *(Month, day, year)*

*U.S. Government Printing Office: 1991 -281-782-20310

A COMPLETED OF-612

OPTIONAL APPLICATION FOR FEDERAL EMPLOYMENT - OF 612

You may apply for jobs with a resume, this form, or any other format. If your resume or application does not provide all the information requested on this form and in the job vacancy announcement, you may lose consideration for a job.

1 Job title in announcement		2 Grade(s) applying for	3 Announcement number
Computer Specialist, Supervisory		GS-0334-14/15	99-63-AP

4 Last name	First and Middle names	5 Social Security Number
XXXXXXX	XXXXXX	000-00-0000

6 Mailing address	7 Phone Numbers (include area code)
000 Stillwater Place	Daytime (703) 000-0000

City	State	ZIP Code	
XXXXXXX	MD	00000	Evening (301) 000-0000

WORK EXPERIENCE

8 Describe your paid and nonpaid work experience related to the job for which you are applying. Do **not** attach job descriptions.

1) Job title (if Federal, include series and grade)
COMPUTER SPECIALIST, GS-0334-13

From (MM/YY)	To (MM/YY)	Salary	per	Hours per week
8/96	present	$71,565	year	40

Employer's name and address	Supervisor's name and phone number
Defense Information System Agency (DISA)	John XXXXX
00000 XXXXXXX Square; XXXX, VA 00000	703-000-0000

Describe your duties and accomplishments

OVERVIEW
- **Computer Specialist** in the Defense Message System (DMS)Operations Branch on the staff of the DMS Global Service Manager. DMS is a computer-based (X.400/X.500) worldwide Department of Defense-wide Area Network messaging system that will replace the obsolete Automated Digital Network (AUTODIN) now in place. The mission of the Branch is to exercise day-to-day management control of, and provide staff level operational direction over, deployed elements of the DMS.

- **Personally responsible** for ensuring that reliable, efficient, effective, and economic DMS operations meet the customer's requirements.

KEY ACTIVITIES

Oversee and manage the global system of Regional Operations and Security Centers (ROSC).
- RESULT • Visited ROSC-C to assist in bring the center to full operational status prior to the start of IOT&E.
- • Coordinated the requirements and assessments of the three ROSC to prepare the final format of the Continuity of Operation Plan for the DMS portion of the ROSC's worldwide structure.

Develop policy and directives which provide a framework for processes and procedures in the execution of system implementation as well as operational tasks.
- RESULT • Developed, coordinated, and established the ALLDMSSTA general message in order to establish an electronic means of formally disseminating policy and procedure changes.
- • Drawing on program management and cryptologic background, assessed (in concert with D4) the requirements for instituting a viable maintenance management program.

SEE NEXT PAGE

XXXXXX XXXXX. — SSN: 000-00-00000

#1, continued, WORK EXPERIENCE

Monitor the implementation of all hardware and software changes/enhancements to the DMS components and infrastructure.
> RESULT • Formally approved all Field Engineering Notes for distribution and implementation during IOT&E using newly established software distribution procedures, a process that proved to be highly organized and successful.

Conduct operational performance evaluations and ensure overall compliance with technical criteria to maintain the DMS performance above management thresholds.

Maintain liaison with representatives of the Joint Staff, military departments, and other government agencies. Represent the Branch at meetings and conferences with higher echelons.

Obtain, direct, and coordinate necessary technical support when problem resolution requires expertise beyond that of on-site personnel.
> RESULT • Worked closely with the DISA PAC and DISA EUR Regional Service Management staff and the WESTHEM Columbus RCC to develop and implement an interim problem reporting mechanism pending arrival of the DMS Contractor products.

Function as the task monitor for cognizant portions of the DMS that are staffed under contract support and ensure contractor personnel and contract deliverables are in full compliance with requirements as detailed in the contract.

Provide operations input to the implementation design validation process.

EVALUATION OF PERFORMANCE:

"A self-starter who uses initiative to research exiting activities associated with system and network management tools and capabilities to ensure DMS will be able to readily migrate to a fully integrated system." (from Evaluation, 1996)

2) Job title (if Federal, include series and grade)
TELECOMMUNICATIONS SPECIALIST, GS-0391-13

From (MM/YY)	To (MM/YY)	Salary	per	Hours per week
5/95	8/96	$63,442	year	40

Employer's name and address
Space and Naval Warfare (SPAWAR) Systems Command
2451 Crystal Drive; Arlington, VA 22245-5200

Supervisor's name and phone number
CDR XXXXXX
703-000-0000

Describe your duties and accomplishments

OVERVIEW • **Project Manager** for computer/communication systems deployments of the Nova and MMS (Multi-level Mail Server), which were designated as Navy Defense Messaging System transitional components, and provided for the upgrade of automated messaging services while allowing the Naval Telecommunications System to transition from legacy platforms to the Defense Messaging System (DMS) target X.400 and X.500 architecture and components.

KEY ACTIVITIES

Managed and evaluated the execution of contractor performance for acquisition, installation, maintenance, and software support services. Directed and approved contractor efforts in the development of computer integrated logistic support planning (ILSP) and developed and coordinated site survey and system installation schedules.

RESULT • Mediated and resolved numerous difficulties, discrepancies, disagreements between and/or among installation support activities (engineering field activities, contractors, and others).

Provided technical information and direction relative to DMS transitional components which interfaced to host computers.

Reviewed and evaluated computer/communications systems architecture and wiring plans and diagrams. As part of the review process, also developed and submitted detail wiring schematics and diagrams which described errors and corrections.

RESULT • Used knowledge of Naval Telecommunication System architecture, interface techniques, and capabilities to provide input to the formulation of a system architecture and connectivity between Navy, Marine, Coast Guard, and other DoD and civil agency components where the object was to provide a seamless transition to the target X.400/X.500 DMS architecture.

Primary liaison with various organizational DMS coordinators in order to ensure timely update of requirements and fielding priorities. Represented the Division at internal or external committees, working groups, and meetings.

RESULT • Prepared and presented a variety of well-received point papers and briefings to provide information, recommendations, and defense of program positions or actions to be executed.

• Established working relationships across organizational boundaries which were essential to process improvement in the delivery of quality customer services.

SEE NEXT PAGE

XXXXXX XXXXX.— SSN: 000-00-00000

#2, continued, WORK EXPERIENCE

Provided administrative management for project implementation tracking and monitoring.

As a member of the Software Configuration Control Board, evaluated and recommended adoption or disapproval of software changes and proposals which were relevant to the Nova, MMS, and related systems.

RESULT • Made significant contributions to SPAWAR in the economy, efficiency, and service in the implementation of transitional system platforms (Nova, PCMT, GATEGUARD, and MMS).

EVALUATION OF PERFORMANCE:

"....a model employee who has proven during this period his value to the organization. He has taken the changes driven by organizational restructuring and realignment in stride and has actively promoted the goals and objectives of SPAWAR." (from Evaluation, 1996)

9 May we contact your current supervisor

YES [X]   NO [   ]   If we need to contact your current supervisor before making an offer, we will contact you first.

EDUCATION

10 Mark highest level completed   Some HS [   ]   HS/GED [   ]   Associate [   ]   Bachelor [   ]   Master [X]   Doctoral [   ]

11 Last high school (HS) or GED school. Give the school's name, City, State, ZIP Code (if known), and year diploma or GED received.

Eastern High School, Washington DC

12 Colleges and universities attended. Do **not** attach a copy with your transcript unless requested.

Name		Total Credits Earned		Major(s)	Degree - Year
		Semester	Quarter		(if any) Received
University of the District of Columbia				Electronic Technology	A.S., 1979
City Washington	State DC	ZIP Code			
Name National-Louis University				Managment	B.S., 1995
City McLean	State VA	ZIP Code 22102			
Name Eastern Michigan University				Information Security	M.S., 1997
City Ypsilanti	State MI	ZIP Code 48197			

OTHER QUALIFICATIONS

13 **Job-related** training courses (give title and year). Job-related skills (other languages, computer software/hardware, tools, machinery, typing speed, etc.). **Job-related** certificates and licenses (current only). **Job-related** honors, awards, and special accomplishments (publications, memberships in professional/honor societies, leadership activities, public speaking, and performance awards). Give dates, but do **not** send documents unless requested.

PLEASE SEE ATTACHED

GENERAL

14 Are you a U.S. citizen?   YES [X]   NO [   ]   Give the country of your citizenship
....

15 Do you claim veteran's preference?   NO [   ]   YES [X]   Mark your claim of 5 or 10 points below
5 points [X]   Attach your DD214 or other proof. 1   0 points [   ]   Attach an Application for 10-Point Veterans' Preference (SF-15) and proof required.

16 Were you ever a Federal civilian employee?

		Series	Grade	From (MM/YY)	To (mm/YY)
NO [ ] YES [X] For highest civilian grade give:		0391/0334	13	10/90	present

17 Are you eligible for reinstatement based on career or career-conditional Federal status?
NO [X]   YES [   ]   If requested, attach SF 50 proof.

18 I certify that, to the best of my knowledge and belief, all of the information on and attached to this application is true, correct, complete and made in good faith. **I understand** that false or fraudulent information on or attached to this application may be grounds for not hiring me or for firing me after I begin work, and may be punishable by fine or imprisonment. **I understand** that any information I give may be investigated.

SIGNATURE   DATE SIGNED

XXXXXX XXXXX. — SSN: 000-00-00000

#13 — OTHER QUALIFICATIONS

Successfully completed numerous courses on COMSEC and computer equipment and systems. Classes of COMSEC equipment and systems on which trained include general purpose data, voice, specialized tactical, bulk, and broadcast. Specific details will be provided on request.

1) George Washington University
       Fiber-Optic Technology for Communications, 2.16 CEUs   28 Jun 90
       Application of T-Carrier to Private Networking, 3.60 CEUs   27 Jul 90
       Data Communication Standards: Interfaces and Protocols for Open Systems
           Network Architectures, 2.16 CEUs   14 Sep 90

2) Data-Tech Institute
       Intensive Introduction to T1/T3 Networking, 1.50 CEUs   10 Aug 90

3) Naval Electronic Systems Security Engineering Center
       Contracting Officer's Technical Representative (COTR's) Course   23 Aug 89

4) Office of Personnel Management
       Instructor Training Workshop   14 May 82
       Project Management: Planning, Scheduling, and Control   14 Feb 92

5) Human Resources Office, NW NMCNCR
       Supervisory Development I   16 May 86
       Supervisory Development II   20 Aug 86

6) Management Concepts Incorporated
       Statement of Work / Specification Preparation   1 Jul 87

7) Human Resources Office, Washington NY
       Managing Conflict   19 Apr 90
       How To Negotiate   11 May 90
       Value Engineering   06 Aug 92

8) Naval Computer & Telecommunication Command
       Acquisition Streamlining   15 Mar 91
       Total Quality Leadership Awareness   15 Apr 92

9) Department of Navy Program Information Center
       Planning, Programming and Budgeting System (PEBS) Course   30 Sep 92

10) National Defense University, Information Resources Management College
       Information Engineering   28 May 93

SEE NEXT PAGE

XXXXXX, Alfred L. — SSN: XXXXXX

#13, continued — OTHER QUALIFICATIONS

11) Defense Information Systems Agency
    Defense Data Network Seminar   26 Aug 93

12) Naval Computer & Telecommunication Command
    X.400/X.500 DMS/MSP Training (J.G.Van Dyke)   10 Mar 95

13) National Security Agency
    Information Systems Security Engineering Course   12 May 95

AWARDS:

Graduated with honors, B.S. Management, 1995

Honors Student Award, MLS Information Security, 1997

Letter of Appreciation for Technical Professionalism from Commanding Officer NAS Memphis, 1980

Sustained Superior Performance Awards: 1982, 1983

Outstanding Performance Awards: 1992, 1993, 1994, 1995, 1996

A COMPLETED FEDERAL RESUME

XXXXX XXXXXXXX

000000 Alex Guerrero Circle
El Paso, Texas 79936

Home / Fax: (915) 000-0000
Email: xxxxxx@xxx.com
Office: xxxxxxxxxx
Email:xxxxx@xxx.org
U.S. citizen
Highest security clearance held: TOP SECRET (1985-90)
Highest Federal civilian grade: GG-1102-12
Date of last promotion : December, 1996

GOAL

Announcement Number:
Position title:

PROFILE

Current responsibility:
Contracting Officer
Border Environment Cooperation Commission
Assigned to facility in Juarez, Mexico

Proven experience managing budgets for contracts ranging in value up to $200 million. Experience supervising up to 5 employees.

Primary focal point for the award of several multi-million dollar construction, architectural and engineering, and management services contracts.

Strategic liaison responsibility. Frequently interact with high-ranking city, county, and state officials, as well as consultants and the general public to provide funding and construction of border projects in Mexico and the United States.

Served as Equal Employment Opportunity Counselor. Also served on Qualification Review Boards to rank applicants for Federal positions.

Designed and implemented operating policies and procedures. Automated library operations and recorded retrieval procedures. Participated in establishment of computerized accounting program for non-appropriated funds.

Accomplished communicator. Principal point-of-contact and lead negotiator during contract deliberations.

Strong written communication skills. Developed and wrote Agency-wide operating standards.

CURRENT TITLE: CONTRACTING OFFICER
Border Environment Cooperation Commission (BECC)   Juarez, Mexico 32470
GRADE: N/A   **SALARY:** $57,000   **HOURS:** 40/week
DATE: January 1998-present   **SUPERVISOR:** XXXXXX

Direct, monitor, and personally oversee the award of architectural and engineering and other management services contracts for the BECC, a quasi-government agency.

> RESULT   Responsible for the development of water/waste water and sanitation master plans, cost and price analysis, development of pre-negotiation memorandums and projects' negotiations, and assembling documentation required to certify projects for construction funds. Selected to fill in for the incumbent Technical Assistance Program Manager during her travel or absence.

Serve as lead negotiator and facilitator for the evaluation team. Responsible for coordinating all business development and contract administration activities for the organization. Direct proposal efforts, lead negotiation teams and chair status meetings with all disciplines involved in complex, high-dollar development projects.

> RESULT   Expertly guiding principals through the contracting process, successfully directed contracting efforts (cradle to grave) for multi-year, multi-million dollar projects.

Supervise and coordinate the work of subordinate staff of U.S. and Mexican nationals, managing planning efforts, devising organizational structures to support quality control, task management, technical operations and administrative functions.

> RESULT   Establish work schedules, assign tasks, advise subordinates on proper techniques and procedures and prepare annual performance reviews.

Review Mexico's contracting law and procedures and the United Nations Model Law on Procurement in order to develop Agency specific procurement standards. Because the BECC was created under a North American Free Trade Agreement (NAFTA) side-agreement and is a bi-national agency, funded by both the United States and Mexican governments and the U.S. Environmental Protection Agency (USEPA), the BECC is not required to conform to Federal Acquisition Regulations (FAR). As a result, no such procurement regulations were in place.

> RESULT   Developed procurement standards and procedures for this relatively new Agency.
>
> IMPACT   These procedures are written in a clear, concise and detailed manner and contain information that is vital to the efficient and effective administration of the procurement program. These procedures were instrumental in securing new contracts with the corporate community and launched the procurement program.

Prepare reviews for the agency's Legal Counsel on contract clauses and other legal issues. Review financial feasibility of projects. Examine environmental and sustainability aspects, as well as criteria required to qualify for construction funding. Where possible, work is coordinated with graduate studies in the MPA program at the University of Texas at El Paso (UTEP).

> RESULT   Successfully handled two protests for disqualification of proposals during the evaluation stage.
>
> IMPACT   This early resolution of the problem prevented a more serious challenge.

Point-of-Contact for management study and internal needs assessment.

> RESULT   Coordinate project tracking systems, electronic and hard copy record keeping, general operating procedures, manual writing, and accounting/budgeting processes.
>
> IMPACT   Until my intervention there were few standards or operational practices in place. Recipient, "Excellent" job performance rating.

TITLE: Contract Specialist (NOTE: hired as GS-1102-7 Intern; promoted to GS-9/11/12)
U.S. Section, International Boundary and Water Commission   El Paso, TX 79902-1441
GRADE: GG-1102-12   **SALARY:** $45,000   **HOURS:** 40/week
DATE: 12/90-1/98   **SUPERVISOR:** XXXXXX

Served as contracting officer and contract administrator for multi-million dollar supplies and services, construction, and architectural and engineering contracts. Possessed a contracting officer's warrant. Performed pre-award, award, and contract administration duties.

> RESULT   Prepared *Commerce Business Daily* synopses and advertisements, developed and reviewed technical specifications, and issued solicitations and Requests For Proposals (RFPs). Headed evaluation teams reviewing potential contractors' financial data. Prepared lease agreements for properties where contractors performed construction work.

Performed price and costs analyses, conducted contract negotiations, monitored expenditures, and developed legal interpretations. Presided over bid openings and site visits.

Set priorities and demonstrated effective leadership. Since contracting does not leave much room for variance, it was my responsibility to ensure that rules were strictly adhered to.

> RESULT   Established good working relationships with diverse groups of individuals in order to effectively solicit compliance with regulatory requirements.
>
> IMPACT   Anticipated questions and provided necessary information and guidance.

Instituted policy and procedures for Acquisition Division in areas of Ethics, Imprest Funds, and Memorandums of Understanding for grants and cooperative agreements with Federal agencies.

> RESULT   Developed technical expertise in all phases of the contracting cycle from per-award through negotiations and contract administration.
>
> IMPACT   Led staff members through the process of changing and updating old habits and implementing required procedures.

Coordinated with technical and engineering staff, end users, and senior executives within the client organizations and Federal contract managers to ensure timely compliance with all terms of the contracts and the Federal Acquisition Regulations (FAR).

> RESULT   Worked with diverse individuals to create cohesive plans and strategies, incorporating the often-divergent objectives of many disciplines. Oversaw several projects of national interest.
>
> IMPACT   In the operation and maintenance of the Nogales International Wastewater Treatment Plant, made the determination that it would be more cost effective to contract the work out to a private firm than to have the government continue its operation of the plant. As a result of contracting out, the government was able to realize a cost savings over a five year period.

Main point-of-contact, internally and externally, ensuring that client organizations were satisfied and that contractors delivered goods/services in accordance with Statements-of-Work documents.

Served as Equal Employment Opportunity (EEO) Counselor. Provided supervisors and managers with detailed explanations of applicable EEO laws and regulations prohibiting discrimination. Participated in EEO workshops.

> RESULT   Often called upon to provide assistance in matters involving disciplinary actions, grievances, EEO complaints and illegal separations.
>
> IMPACT   Used tact to provide practical advisory services in potentially volatile situations.

Facilitated affirmative action hiring, providing advice and support for manager involved. explaining Federal regulations to assist them in devising effective job search strategies.

> RESULT   Gained the support of management and employees throughout the organization.
>
> IMPACT   As a result, was able to resolve all issues presented to me at the local level without the need for expensive and disruptive litigation.
> Recipient of several "Excellent" job performance ratings during this period.

TITLE: Records Officer (Mail and File Assistant)
U.S. Section, International Boundary and Water Commission   El Paso, TX 79902-1441
GRADE: GG-307-07   **SALARY:** $25,000   **HOURS:** 40/week
DATE: 6/85-6/90   **SUPERVISOR:** XXXXXX

Chief, Headquarters Communications and Records Branch with TOP SECRET security clearance and purview over 12 field offices throughout the U.S. and Mexico border region.

> RESULT   Exercised primary responsibility for the Agency's records management, mail management, correspondence management, library (legal and technical) operations, Freedom of Information and Privacy Act programs, and public relations program.

Conducted assistance visits to field offices to conduct operational audits in records management. Wrote reports of my findings and made recommendations. Taught classes in records management, records disposition, correspondence management, mail management, micrographics management, directives management, copier use and ADP management.

> RESULT   Wrote the Agency's Freedom of Information Act regulations, and rewrote the records disposition and correspondence manuals.

Initiated a records control program for Privacy Act records.

> RESULT   Established a directives system, and initiated a micrographics program. Computerized the library's operations as well as its records retrieval procedures.
>
> IMPACT   My ideas were adopted, implemented, and maintained. When completed, these new or revised documents and procedures went a long way in reducing turnaround time, enabling our staff members to make renewed progress toward mission goals.

Supervised and directed the activities of subordinate staff.

> RESULT   Managed planning and designed organizational structures capable of supporting strong quality control, task management, technical and administrative functions.
>
> IMPACT   Established work schedules, assigned tasks, advised subordinates on proper techniques and procedures and prepared annual performance reviews.
> Recipient, several "Excellent" job performance ratings during this period.

TITLE: Administrative Clerk
Loan Servicing Department, Small Business Administration   El Paso, TX 79935
GRADE: GS-301-4   **SALARY:** $16,800   **HOURS:** 40/week
DATE: 5/84-6/85   **SUPERVISOR:** XXXXXXX

Planned, organized, and coordinated administrative activities of the office.

> RESULT   Completed special projects that involved contact with administrative and management staff at all levels within the Agency.
>
> IMPACT   Given greater responsibilities than the job called for while in this position.
> NOTE: *Accepted this position in order to return to Federal service.*

XXXX XXXXXXX
Announcement number:

TITLE: Homemaker
xxxxxx Alex Guerrero Circle   xxxxxx, Texas 00000
GRADE: N/A   **SALARY:** N/A   **HOURS:** N/A
DATE: 5/83-5/84   **SUPERVISOR:** N/A

Stayed home to care for newborn child. Responsible for child care, home operations, budgeting and family support.

TITLE: Administrative Officer
Administration Division, Department of the Army   WSMR, NM 88022
GRADE: GS-341-9   **SALARY:** $21,000   **HOURS:** 40/week
DATE: 9/81-5/83   **SUPERVISOR:** XXXXXX

Administrative management for Morale Support Activities Division's budget, procurement of supplies, publicity, personnel and manpower, and property and facilities management. **Monitored expenditures and developed annual budget forecasts.** Established five-year budget plans. Funding was provided through either non-appropriated (self earning) or appropriated means. Served as principal conduit for all information flow to the Director.

RESULT   Applied accounting techniques which determined if activities were profitable, identified ways of improving activities' income, and determined the need for supplemental funding through appropriated means.

IMPACT   Computerized accounting program for non-appropriated funds resulted in savings to the government.
         Recipient, Letter of Appreciation (1982).

Main point-of-contact for all budget issues for the Division, providing interpretation of accounting statements to supervisor, activity managers, and the Colonel. Worked with both appropriated and non-appropriated funds. Performed audits of private organizations at the Missile Range to assure their financial soundness and their compliance with regulatory requirements.

RESULT   Implemented mandated financial data format changes for private organizations.

IMPACT   Earned the trust and cooperation of all private organizations serviced and brought them into compliance with regulatory requirements.
         Recipient, Special Act Award for working with private organization (1982).

Supervised and directed the work of five staff members (3 civilians and 2 military). Managed planning efforts, devised organizational structures to support quality control, task management, technical operations and administrative functions.

RESULT   Established work schedules, assigned tasks, advised subordinates on proper techniques and procedures and prepared annual performance reviews.

TITLE: Management Assistant
Administration Division, Department of the Army   WSMR, NM 88002
GRADE: GS-344-7   **SALARY:** $16,000   **HOURS:** 40/week
DATE: 8/79-9/81   **SUPERVISOR:** XXXXXX

XXXX XXXXXXX
Announcement number:

Assisted in the analysis and assessment of management issues for the Administrative
Management Branch.

RESULT   Suggested solutions to administrative and management problems. Collected data,
reviewed and analyzed information. Interviewed managers and employees while
observing their operations, taking into account the nature of the organization, the
relationship it had with other organizations, its internal organization and culture.

IMPACT   Reported findings and recommendations to client organization, often in writing.
In addition, made oral recommendations. Assisted in implementation of
suggestions.

Taught classes in records management, records disposition, correspondence management, mail
management, micrographics and directives management, copier use and ADP management.

RESULT   Recipient, Letter of Appreciation for instructing military personnel in records
management (1980).

Conducted audits, and wrote reports of findings with recommendations. Allocated timeframes
to offices to correct deficiencies and did follow-up visits where appropriate. Held secret security
clearance. Acted in behalf of supervisor during her absence.

RESULT   Led individuals to change what they were doing incorrectly in order to conform to
regulatory requirements.

IMPACT   Facility was upgraded to exceed all records management requirements.

EDUCATION
Bachelor of Business Administration (B.B.A.)
University of Texas at El Paso, 1993

Masters of Public Administration candidate (M.P.A. degree due: May 1999)
University of Texas at El Paso

PROFESSIONAL ORGANIZATIONS
National Institute of Government Purchasing (NIGP)
National and Local Chapters

RELATED SKILLS
Computer literate in Windows, WordPerfect, MS Word and Works, Lotus (Quattro Pro), and
database management software, the Internet, intranets, and on-line services.

LANGUAGE SKILLS
Fluent in spoken and written Spanish

A COMPUTER-SCANNABLE RESUME OR RESUMIX™

XXXXXXXXX
SSN 000-00-0000

XXXXXX XXXXX
SSN 000-00-0000
0000 Spain Drive
Stafford, Virginia 00000
Home: (540) 000-0000
Work: (703) 000-0000
DSN: 000-0000
E-mail: xxxx@xxx.xxx

SUMMARY OF SKILLS
Military Satellite Communications
Manager, Defense Satellite Communications System (DSCS)
Proven Staff Leadership
Task Manager
Lead Evaluator
Contractor Supervision
Liaison and representation
Technical Troubleshooting
Spacecraft Reconfiguration
Data Integration
Operating Parameters
Control and Coordination
Operational Assessments
Contingency Planning
Specialized Engineering
Contingency Communications
Earth Terminals Optimization
System Reliability
Maintainability Standards
Control Concepts
System Capabilities
Interface Requirements
Requirements Analysis
Project Coordination
High-level Briefings
Frequency Modulation
Digital Baseband Equipment
Common-user Communications
Modeling and Simulation
Network Management
Information Security
Communications Link Configurations
System Optimization
Detection of Degradations

EXPERIENCE:
January 1991 to present. 40-50 hours/week.
Telecommunications Manager.
TOP SECRET / SCI security clearance
Defense Information Systems Agency (DISA)
Supervisor: XXXXXXX
Pay-grade: GS-391-14
Functional leader within DOD for the DSCS Operational Control System. Integrate complex data and conclusions from various functional areas to formulate policy and develop procedures for operating DSCS to serve DOD and other Federal agencies. Recruited by DSCS Operations Branch (DOT) at DCA/DISA. Promoted to GS-0391-14 as of 10-19-92 due
to "accretion of duties" and assigned as Deputy/Assistant to the Senior Satellite Communications System Manager; served as primary in his absence. Assumed all management duties effective October 1998 during his transition to retirement. Acting in that capacity to date. Supervise management of DSCS and technical direction of DSCS Operations Control Centers. Manage satellite communication payloads and network coordination. Establish parameters of satellite service. Exercise managerial authority regarding access to DSCS. Prepare and issue Telecommunications Service Requests (TSR). Develop implementation directives for the O&M commands. Coordinate execution of these directives. Develop objectives, policies and procedures for the Joint Staff concerning current and projected DSCS operations. Provide liaison and representation regarding operational requirements in the planning, development, programming, budgeting, acquisition and deployment of DSCS space and ground equipment and related operational control systems. Extensive use of DCAD 800-70-1 and 310-65-1 for TSR services, as governed by MOP 37. Evaluate all requests for DSCS access; prepare DISA's recommendations to the Joint Staff for its approval/disapproval and subsequent entry into the Integrated Consolidated SATCOM Data Base (ICDB). Serve as DNSO representative on ICDB-related matters. Extensive interaction with, and instruction of, DISA and other Defense and Intelligence Community managers, frequently including decision-makers with limited knowledge of satellite technology. Provide recommendations for communications link configurations that optimize the use of DSCS satellite resources. Plan satellite cut-overs and frequency plans to optimize loading of operational satellites.
RESULTS PRODUCED: Key player in ensuring highly efficient utilization of assets. Instrumental in developing and implementing a reconstitution effort during unexpected transponder failures. Planned and implemented error-free satellite Telecommunications Service Requests. Develop and maintain policies, procedures, concepts of operation, parameters and standards for DSCS, including ECCM and the use of partial satellites. Develop, produce, and publish operational and control concepts for DSCS in DISAC 800-70-1. Develop new and modified concepts and configurations in support of ongoing missions. Extensive troubleshooting in the following areas: limited bandwidth, restricted available power from satellite transponders, antenna patterns and earth terminal characteristics, shortage of specific filters or multiplexers, front-line coordination with field sites, creating cut-over plans. Provide inputs for updated edition of DCAC 800-70-1. Initiated change of ENR codes for all strategic satellite terminals in use worldwide.

1989 to 1991. 40-50 hours/week. **MilNet Manager.**
Defense Data Network, Operations
Supervisor: XXXXXXXX
Assigned to DDN Operations as DDN MilNetManger. Operational manager of the DOD global MilNet. Provided direction in network design and implementation from user level to nodal points, including fielding of NACs and CISCO routers.

1987 to 1989. 40 hours/week. **Integrated Test Facility Manager.**
Defense Data Network
Supervisor: LTC XXXX
Managed the Defense Data Network (DDN) Integrated Test Facility (ITF) in Reston, VA. Responsible for baseline development of BLACKER encryption device. Was detailed into position as Branch Chief upon transfer of LTC XXXX.

1985 to 1987. 50-60 hours/week. **Head, Communications Department.**
NAVELEXDETPAX, Patuxent River, MD.
Supervisor: XXXXXXX
Managed four (4) Telecommuncation Facilities (2 Strategic Genser, 1 Tactical, 1 SCIF) providing Air, Land and Sea Test & Evaluation Platforms. Conducted performance evaluations at all participating test facilities.

SECURITY CLEARANCE:
TOP SECRET / SCI

EDUCATION
Graduate, Southwest XXXX XXXXX Public High School, April 1961

ADVANCED PROFESSIONAL TRAINING
Customer Service Orientation (40 hour course), 1995
DSCS DOSS/DASA Course (80 hour course), 1991
DSCS Network Engineering Course (40 hour course), 1991
Orientation to Contracting (16 hour course), 1987
COTR Training (40 hour course), 1985
Leadership Management Education and Training, 1981
Satellite Controller Course (three month course), 1978
Radioman "B" School, (six month course),1971
Teletype Maintenance and Operation, 1966
Radioman "A" School (seven month course), 1962

AWARDS AND HONORS
Joint Service Commendation Medal
Vietnam Service Medal, with two Bronze Stars
Recipient of continuous "Outstanding" performance appraisals throughout my tenure at DISA.

KSAs OR RANKING FACTORS

XXXXXXX

xxxxx

EVALUATION FACTORS

1. **ABILITY TO SELECT, DEVELOP, AND SUPERVISE A SUBORDINATE STAFF, WHICH INCLUDED THE ABILITY TO ACTIVELY PURSUE MANAGEMENT GOALS AND SUPPORT THE EQUAL OPPORTUNITY PROGRAM.**

I believe my ability to lead and facilitate the work of others has been demonstrably evident throughout my career. For example, on numerous occasions I have interacted with staffs that I have led by (1) providing a clear sense of direction and (2) setting my expected performance levels at a level that is commensurate with these organizations' objectives, thereby (3) motivating my staff toward a higher level of goal accomplishments.

In addition, I have promoted quality performance through effective use of the agency's performance management system and I have established performance standards, appraised subordinate staffs' accomplishments, and acted to reward or counsel them, as their performance indicated was appropriate. I also have made it my practice to assess my employees' developmental needs and provide opportunities to help maximize their skills, capabilities, and ongoing professional development.

I welcome and value cultural diversity and I use these and other differences as one more tool to foster an environment where people can work together cooperatively, while achieving organizational goals. In all of my leadership roles, I have worked to promote commitment, pride, trust and group identity, and I have sought to prevent situations that could have resulted in unpleasant confrontations.

Examples of my ability in this area include:

Recruited, supervised and led the activities of subordinate staff in five (5) separate assignments.

RESULT
- Managed planning efforts, devised organizational structures to support quality control, task management, technical and administrative functions.
- Established work schedules, assigned tasks, advised subordinates on proper techniques and procedures; prepared annual performance reviews.

Conducted local Title 10 training sessions to familiarize personnel with Army MDAPs and associated reporting requirements and to equip them to recognize potential threshold breaches when they occur.

RESULT
- Sponsored an Army developmental assignment program whereby individuals within Army competed to participate at HQ, DA. Candidates were screened from applications received from HQ, DA and PEO/PM offices. Those participating gained hands-on experience with the various Title 10 reporting requirements associated with the Armyís Major Defense Acquisition Programs (MDAPs).

SEE NEXT PAGE

XXXXXXX

XXXXX

<u>EVALUATION FACTORS</u>

1.   **ABILITY TO SELECT, DEVELOP, AND SUPERVISE A
SUBORDINATE STAFF, WHICH INCLUDED THE ABILITY
TO ACTIVELY PURSUE MANAGEMENT GOALS AND SUPPORT
THE EQUAL OPPORTUNITY PROGRAM.** (continued)

Served as Team Leader during major financial management exercises, making
determinations regarding proper and effective procedures.

<u>RESULT</u>   • Designed studies, coordinated planning, developed strategy, and identified
potential sources for reliable and responsive information and assigned
tasks.   Teamwork included the compilation and review of budget data
reflecting existing operations and data from feasibility studies on proposed
programs.

Participated in the development and implementation of recruiting programs to meet
EEO requirements and Affirmative Action objectives.

<u>RESULT</u>   • Identified appropriate advertising vehicles for minority recruiting.

   • Provided assistance and input in matters involving career development,
training, disciplinary actions, grievances, EEO complaints and separations.

Actively recruited, interviewed, and selected individuals from or for the following
positions: Computer Programmers, Budget Analyst, Program Analysts, Budget Clerks,
Facilities Managers, and Engineering Technicians.

<u>RESULT</u>   • I have maintained a better than 50% ratio of women/minority positions
within the organizations affected.

   • Successfully achieved minority representation in key staff positions within
both the Program Management Resource Divison and in the Directorate
for Assessment and Evaluation.

   • All offices in which I have worked have met or exceeded workplace
diversity goals during my tenure. I believe that having diversity tools
available is crucial for managers to help ensure fair and equitable
treatment of employees. Also, I believe if done right, culturally diverse
offices can be rewarding and conducive to a high-performing, healthy
work environment.

Actively recruited and mentored individuals to fill developmental assignments within
the division.

<u>RESULT</u>   • Managed the developmental program in such a way that their parent
organizations continued to support our developmental program by staffing
vacancies. I keep in touch with many of our former developmental
employees and monitor their professional development and progress.

XXXXXXX

XXXXX

<u>EVALUATION FACTORS</u>

2.   **KNOWLEDGE OF MATERIEL LIFE CYCLE MANAGEMENT FUNCTIONS, PROGRAMS AND SYSTEMS USED TO PROVIDE LOGISTICAL SUPPORT.**

My current job includes a very substantial degree of life-cycle management responsibility.

For example, I currently run the policy operation of Acquisition Life Cycle management. In this capacity, the information related to guidance addressing Army's Acquisition Program Baselines (APBs) for Army Acquisition Category (ACAT) I, II and some representative III programs.

Examples of my strong working knowledge in this area include the following:

Analyze the content of the APBs and ensure that APBs adequately address program requirements.

<u>RESULT</u>   • I recently issued APB policy which now requires APBs to address "total life cycle costs" which by definition includes operating and support (O&S) costs.

Keep Army and OSD leadership informed regarding how the Army executes their cost, schedule and performance parameters within their respective APBs.

<u>RESULT</u>   • Maintain close ties and frequent contacts with officials at all levels in the Army and DoD as well as the respective PEOs and PMs and Command Groups.
  • Any known logistical support requirements would also be captured within the respective APBs.

I have gained substantial working knowledge and hands-on experience through interacting with officials in the Comptroller and Acquisition communities related to acquisition life cycle subject matter contained within APBs, SARs and DAES reports, as well as through managing these processes.

<u>RESULT</u>   • My effort to include O&S costs within APBs is unique. To this point, the other Military Services have not yet followed suit but will likely do so soon, since it is DoD policy to make Program Managers responsible for "total life cycle management".
  • If and when this happens, these Program Managers would have total "cradle-to-grave" program responsibility—as well as operational control of the budget dollars to make sure that this level of responsibility is discharged fully and effectively.

XXXXXXX
xxxxx

EVALUATION FACTORS

3.   **KNOWLEDGE OF ADVANCED LIFE CYCLE MANAGEMENT PLANNING PRINCIPLES AND PRACTICES.**

My strong background in the Comptrollership and Acquisition areas has given me an unusually broad set of qualifications in this area.

Examples of my knowledge in this area include the following:

Gained valuable understanding of military facilities planning while serving as Acting Chief of the Facilities Management office.

<u>RESULT</u>   • This experience exposed me to requirements associated with our proposed military construction, Army (MCA) projects and the MCA processor.

Currently responsible for issuing policy at HQ, DA level, pertaining to the total acquisition life cycle baseline parameters (cost, schedule and performance) for the Armyís major programs.

<u>RESULT</u>   • In 1996, the Army adopted the idea to include operating and support cost estimates within Acquisition Program Baselines (APBs). I began enforcing the policy in earnest several months later .

• Soon, the Army will have "total life cycle" cost data captured routinely in the APBs. This is one example of the "high-level" Army policy areas for which I am responsible (APBs, CARS, DAES, UCRs and SECDEF program certification) and in which I am intimately involved.

Strong working knowledge of PPBES, the DoD planning, programming, budgeting and execution system.

<u>RESULT</u>   • Oversee the submission of three budget cycle positions each year (POM, BES and PB) as they relate to the Armyís ACAT I programs.

• Prepared substantial portions of the internal operating budget (IOB) at the installation level.

Broad experience writing, revising, and implementing policy at HQ, DA level, as it relates to legal reporting requirements associated with Title 10, United States Code.

<u>RESULT</u>   • Review, update and issue revised policy and guidance pertaining to the required content of Major Defense Acquisition Programs (MDAPs - Section 2430), Selected Acquisition Reports (SARs - Section 2432), Nunn-McCurdy Unit Cost Reporting (UCRs - Section 2433) and Acquisition Program Baselines (APBs-Section 2435). Since Title 10 is generally DoD-wide in scope, it must not conflict with DoD policy and guidance. I work closely with the other services and DoD to ensure communication is clear.

XXXXXXX
xxxxx

EVALUATION FACTORS

4. ABILITY TO EFFECTIVELY COMMUNICATE BOTH ORALLY AND IN WRITING REGARDING THE DUTIES OF THIS POSITION.

I have had extensive experience communicating, both orally and in writing. For example, I have defended/advocated my organizations' programs to Congress, DoD, DA and industry. As a steward of government funds, I often have written to determine the disposition of un-liquidated obligations to ensure that the government's money was properly accounted for.

Examples of my ability in this critical skill area include the following:

Frequently prepare written correspondence for senior officials of the Army, DoD, and Congress.

RESULT • Represent the Army in writing—and in person—in a variety of areas. Much of the interaction is in the form of Integrated Product Teams (IPTs) which often includes aspects of Title 10, DoD 5000 and AR 70-1, which requires substantial subject matter expertise which must be communicated either by written policy or correspondence or both. Some of these areas include:
  • Major Defense Acquisition Programs (MDAPs)- 10, USC, Section 2430.
  • Selected Acquisition Reports (SARs) - 10, USC, Section 2432.
  • Nunn-McCurdy Unit Cost Reporting (UCRs) - 10, USC, Section 2433
  • Acquisition Program Baselines (APBs) - 10, USC, Section 2435
  • Defense Acquisition Executive Summary (DAES - DoD 5000)

Extensive personal liaison with senior Army and other DoD officials.

RESULT • Selected to brief the Secretary and Under Secretary of the Army regarding our Title 10, United States Code reporting requirements.

Issue written guidance and policy related to a broad area of responsibilities under my authority.

RESULT • Recently issued new Title 10 policy to the Program Executive Offices (PEOs) and their Project Managers (PMs).
  • Wrote Congressional Notification Letters to the House and Senate Leaders informing them of the NM unit cost breaches, for which we subsequently sent Congress reports.

Held managerial and staff leadership positions at installation and HQ, DA levels.

RESULT • At the installation level, was intimately involved with frequent manpower surveys and writing justifications to defend our TDA.

How to Give Yourself the Edge Filling Out a Federal Job Application

The key to filling out an eye-catching federal job application is attitude. Just keep reminding yourself how capable you are and that what you're being asked to do is no different from what many less-qualified people were able to do. Once you have yourself pumped up with as much enthusiasm as you can get, follow these tips:

- Be sure your application or resume includes all the mandatory information requested in the job vacancy announcement.
- Leave no lines blank. Fill in "N/A" or "not applicable" to show you're responding.
- Write up your application or resume. Then, go back and write it again, using the first as an outline to expand wherever possible.
- Quantify where possible. How much money did you save the company? How many people did you supervise? How many convictions did you get? How many programs did you institute?
- Remember to respond to the KSAs, ranking factors, or selection criteria separately. For grade levels at or above GS-7, respond with a full page to each KSA.
- Sign your application in colored ink, not black, and remember to mail the original, not the copy.

TWO

Representative Civil Service Jobs

CONTENTS

Glossary of Important Terms

The following list of terms applies to most of the positions discussed in Part II. It is a good idea, therefore, to read through this list before you embark upon this highly informative section of *Federal Civil Service Jobs*. Exceptions to and/or qualifications of any of these terms will be indicated and described at length for relevant positions.

ACADEMIC YEAR: Consists of approximately 36 weeks of full-time study, 30 semester hours, 45 quarter hours, or the equivalent. One academic year equals approximately nine months of experience.

CREDITING EDUCATION or TRAINING: Study completed in an institution above the high school level is evaluated as evidence of ability in terms of its relatedness to the knowledge, skills, and abilities required to assume the position of interest successfully. Study completed in a business or secretarial school or other comparable institution above the high school level is creditable provided subjects related to the position of interest were studied. Study completed in a junior college, college, or university is creditable provided such study included a minimum of six semester hours, or the equivalent, per year in subjects that equipped the candidate with the knowledge, skills, and abilities required at the level of the position of interest.

FULL-TIME STUDY: In the case of business and commercial schools, it is the equivalent of at least 20 classroom hours of instruction per week, plus necessary outside study. Part-time study is prorated on this basis also but is creditable only in amounts equivalent to one-half academic year or multiples thereof.

INTERVIEWS: The purpose of interviews is to observe and evaluate personal characteristics and qualifications that are essential to the successful performance of the duties of the position.

PHYSICAL REQUIREMENTS: Applicants must be physically and mentally able to efficiently perform the essential functions of the position without hazard to themselves or others. Depending on the essential duties of a specific position, usable vision, color vision, hearing, or speech may be required. However, in most cases, a specific physical condition or impairment of a specific function may be compensated for by the satisfactory use of a prosthesis or mechanical aid. Reasonable accommodation may also be considered in determining an applicant's ability to perform the duties of a position. Reasonable accommodation may include but is not limited to the use of assistive devices, job modification or restructuring, provision of readers and interpreters, or adjusted work schedules. Also, all positions involving federal motor vehicle operation carry the additional medical requirements.

QUALITY OF EXPERIENCE: For positions at any grade, the required amount of experience will not in itself be accepted as proof of qualifications. The candidate's record of experience and training must show that he/she has the ability to perform the duties of the position.

QUALITY RANKING FACTORS: A quality ranking factor is a knowledge, skill, or ability that could be expected to significantly enhance performance in a position, but could not reasonably be considered necessary for satisfactory performance. Quality-ranking factors may be used to distinguish the better-qualified candidates from those who meet all other requirements, including selective factors.

SELECTIVE FACTORS*: Selective factors must be job related, represent an extension of the basic knowledge and skills required of the position, and be essential to successful performance of the position. Selective factors are knowledge and skills of a kind and level that reasonably could not be acquired on the job without undue interruption of the organization's production. Selective factors for positions at higher grades typically will be more narrowly defined and/or set at a higher level than is necessary at lower grades. What may be appropriate as a quality-ranking factor at a lower grade may have to be a selective factor in a higher-graded position.

Alternative definition: a knowledge, skill, or ability that is essential for satisfactory performance in a position, and represents an addition to the basic minimum requirements in this standard.

Clerical Positions

CLERK (VARIOUS POSITIONS), GS-1/3

Description of Work

Clerical positions involve the orderly processing of papers and the performance of routine work supporting an office or organization. Within a framework of procedures, regulations, precedents, and instructions, clerks process and maintain the records and written materials that represent the transactions or business of the office or organization served. Basic duties that may be performed include the following:

- Maintaining records
- Receiving, screening, reviewing, and verifying documents
- Searching for and compiling information and data
- Providing a central source of information on the activities of the organization orally or by correspondence
- Preparing and/or verifying the validity of documents with which the organization is concerned

Requirements

A. General Background

In order to be considered for appointment, the applicant's overall background, work history, personal characteristics, work habits, and general behavior and reputation in his/her community, school, and previous employment must be of such nature as to provide positive evidence that he/she can and will perform clerical or office work in a successful and productive manner in an office environment.

B. Experience

GS-1—No written test, experience, training, or education is required.

GS-2—Six months of general experience; or graduation from a full four-year or senior high school or possession of a General Educational Development High School Equivalency Certificate (GED).

GS-3—One year of general experience; or one academic year of business or secretarial school, junior college, or college in addition to graduation from high school.

Written Tests

Applicants for positions at grades GS-2 and GS-3 are required to pass written tests.

For some positions, only applicants who receive suitably high scores on parts of the test specifically pertinent to the particular kind of work to be done will be considered.

Basis for Rating and Ranking Candidates

For GS-1: An evaluation of the applicant's willingness to do simple and repetitive clerical work, dependability, and the ability to perform work safely.

For GS-2 and GS-3: The score on the written test *and* an evaluation of the extent and quality of experience, education, and training.

Applicable Standards for Clerical Positions Also Requiring Skill in Typing or Stenography

Some positions requiring typing or stenographic skill as high as that required under the competitive standard for typing or stenographic work, are so constituted that other work skills or abilities, rather than typing or stenographic skills, form the main qualification requirements for the positions. An appropriate means should be used to ensure that applicants possess sufficient skill in typing or stenography to perform the duties of all such positions (for example, a performance test, certificate of proficiency, or some method of certification acceptable to the Office of Personnel Management).

Requirements for Clerical Positions Involving Public Contact

Some clerical positions (for example, information receptionists) that involve substantial contact with others require a clear speaking voice, tact, courtesy, and capacity for effective public contacts. In filling such positions competitively and non-competitively, appointing officers will assure themselves by reference checks, personal interviews, or other appropriate means that applicants possess these qualities to the degree necessary for satisfactory performance of the duties of such positions.

OFFICE MACHINE OPERATOR (VARIOUS POSITIONS), GS-1/3

Description of Work

Persons employed in these positions have as their primary responsibility the operation of the specific office machine described in the individual job title, although clerical work of varying degrees is also involved in many such positions.

Education and Experience Requirements

GS-1—No experience or education required; however, the appropriate tests must be passed.

GS-2—Must pass the appropriate written test and

Alternative 1. Pass appropriate performance test (if any);

or

Alternative 2. Have had six months of office clerical experience or office machine operation experience;

or

Alternative 3. Have completed a specialized course of instruction in the operation of the appropriate machine and either

a.   had three months of general or specialized experience

or

b.   have graduated from high school.

The specialized course of instruction on appropriate machines may have been completed as part of the high school curriculum. Evidence of successful completion of such courses will be required.

GS-3—Must pass the written test *and* the appropriate performance test (if any) and have had either

  a. one year of acceptable experience of which at least six months is specialized experience

          or

  b. one academic year of business or secretarial school or junior college

For occupations for which no performance test is available, education offered under B must have included training in the operation of appropriate office machines.

Written Test

All applicants are required to pass tests covering verbal abilities and clerical abilities (alphabetizing and arithmetic), and eye-hand coordination and perception of differences. All applicants for positions of operators of machines equipped with an alphabetic keyboard will be required to pass a performance test on a typewriter-style keyboard. Applicants for positions of EAM Operator must pass a test of abstract reasoning ability.

  Higher scores may be required for the higher grades.

Basis for Rating and Ranking Candidates

Applicants will be ranked on the basis of their score on the verbal abilities test, and the extent and quality of their experience and education. Other required tests must be passed but are not used to rank the eligibles.

General Note as to Applicable Standards for Positions Also Requiring Skill in Typing or Stenography

Some Office Machine Operator positions may require typing or stenographic skill at or above the level of proficiency required under the competitive standard for entry-level clerk-typist or clerk-stenographer positions, but may be so constituted that the machine operator skills, rather than the typing or stenographic skills, form the main qualification requirements for the positions. Positions so constituted are classified in the Office Machine Operator series appropriate for the main requirement and are identified by the parenthetical addition of the words "typing" or "stenography" to the titles otherwise prescribed for those series.

SECRETARY, ALL GRADES
SECRETARY (STENOGRAPHY), ALL GRADES
SECRETARY (TYPING), ALL GRADES

Description of Work

This series includes all positions whose duties are to assist one individual, and in some cases the subordinate staff of that individual, by performing general office work auxiliary to the work of the organization. To be included in this series, a position must be the principal clerical or administrative support position in the office, operating independently of any other such position in the office. The duties require knowledge of clerical and administrative procedures and requirements, various office skills, and the ability to apply such skills in a way that increases the effectiveness of others. The duties do not require a technical or professional knowledge of a specialized subject-matter area.

Experience Requirements

The requirements at all levels discussed below are purposely stated in terms of knowledge, skills, and abilities, rather than specific duties. A candidate may demonstrate possession of the knowledge, skills, and abilities through various means. For example, a candidate with extensive writing experience could perhaps demonstrate the ability to compose non-technical correspondence without ever having performed that specific duty. Volunteer work for organizations such as civic groups or church groups may be used to fulfill experience requirements to the degree that such work can be verified and evaluated when such work demonstrates possession of the knowledge, skills, and abilities applicable to secretarial work.

GS-3—A general background in the performance of routine clerical duties that demonstrates that a candidate has *all* of the following:

- Basic knowledge of office routines and functions sufficient to refer visitors and telephone calls and to route correspondence by name or functional area
- Knowledge of clerical practices and filing procedures
- Knowledge of spelling, punctuation, and syntax

Experience acquired through the performance of most kinds of clerical work in an office setting is normally considered qualifying.

GS-4—A background in the performance of a variety of clerical duties that demonstrates that a candidate has *all* of the following:

- Working knowledge of many different office procedures such as those needed to request a variety of office equipment, supplies, publication material, and maintenance services, when each of these requires a different procedure
- Ability to understand an organization and its functions sufficient to establish file systems for classifying, retrieving, and disposing of materials; refer telephone calls and visitors; distribute and control mail; maintain leave records; and provide general and non-technical information

GS-5—Experience in administrative or clerical work that demonstrates possession of the knowledge, skills, and abilities required to serve as a principal office assistant at these levels, including *all* of the following:

- Ability to organize effectively the flow of clerical processes in an office
- Ability to organize and design a filing system
- Ability to make arrangements for such things as travel, conferences, and meetings
- Ability to locate and assemble information for various reports, briefings, and conferences
- Ability to compose non-technical correspondence

Length of experience will not necessarily in itself be considered qualifying. The candidate's record must show the ability to perform the duties of the position to be filled.

GS-3—A candidate must have had six months of qualifying experience at GS-2 in the General Schedule or equivalent experience outside the General Schedule.

GS-4 and GS-5—A candidate must have had one year of qualifying experience at the next lower grade in the General Schedule or equivalent experience outside the General Schedule.

GS-6—A candidate must have had six months of qualifying experience at GS-5 in the General Schedule or equivalent experience outside the General Schedule.

GS-7–GS-11—A candidate must have had six months of qualifying experience at the next lower grade in the General Schedule or equivalent experience outside the General Schedule *or* one year of qualifying experience at the second lower grade in the General Schedule or equivalent experience outside the General Schedule.

GS-12 and above—A candidate must have had one year of qualifying experience at the next lower grade in the General Schedule or equivalent experience outside the General Schedule.

Substitution of Education and Training for Experience

Except for any requirement for passing performance tests to demonstrate skill in shorthand and/or typing (when required), the following will apply:

GS-3—All experience requirements for the GS-3 level may be met by completion of one academic year of full-time business school or one academic year of education above the high-school level.

GS-4—All experience requirements for the GS-4 level may be met by completion of two academic years of full-time business school or two academic years of education above the high-school level.

GS-5—All experience requirements for the GS-5 level may be met by completion of four academic years of education in an accredited college or university.

Note: Academic study alone is not creditable as qualifying experience for positions above the GS-5 level; that is, no more than four years of academic study is creditable toward meeting experience requirements.

Combination of education and experience may be used to meet the minimum qualification requirements.

Courses that are not measurable in terms of credit hours (for example, "certificate courses") should be treated as if they were work experience. However, no credit will be allowed for training obtained only or primarily in the basic skills of shorthand or typing or refresher courses.

Typing and Stenographic Skills

When secretarial positions require skill in typing or stenography at or above the level of proficiency required under the competitive standards for these skills, the qualification standard for the skill should be used in conjunction with this standard to ensure that candidates possess at least the minimum degree of skill required to perform the typing or stenographic duties of the position.

The level of stenographic proficiency required by positions classified as Secretary (Stenography) is based on the classification of the *stenography* duties and not necessarily on the grade level of the position. Therefore, before applying for positions of this type, first determine the skill level required by the stenographic duties.

Written Test

No written test is required at any grade level to establish basic qualifications of candidates, or to rank candidates. Performance tests may be required to demonstrate possession of stenographic or typing skill.

Basis for Rating and Ranking Candidates

Candidates who meet the minimum qualification requirements are rated on a scale of 70 to 100 based on an evaluation of the quality and extent of their experience, education, training, or other achievements pertinent to the duties of the positions to be filled.

Some kinds of training and experience that enhance the candidate's qualifications may be treated as factors to award extra credit for rating and ranking purposes. These include, but are not limited to, the following:

- Possession of a certificate as a "Certified Professional Secretary"
- Successful completion of in-service courses that offered training in areas related to the secretarial function, general management or administration, or the program area with which the supervisor is concerned
- Successful completion of work-related educational courses in excess of those used to meet minimum requirements
- Recognition for exceptional work performance

PERSONNEL CLERK
STAFFING CLERK
CLASSIFICATION CLERK
EMPLOYEE DEVELOPMENT CLERK
EMPLOYEE RELATIONS CLERK
GS-4/6
PERSONNEL ASSISTANT
STAFFING ASSISTANT
CLASSIFICATION ASSISTANT
EMPLOYEE DEVELOPMENT ASSISTANT
EMPLOYEE RELATIONS ASSISTANT
GS-6/10

Description of Work

Personnel Clerks perform a variety of clerical tasks in connection with processing paperwork, compiling and presenting data for reports, and providing basic information on personnel matters. Individual assignments may involve such duties as

- Processing personnel actions
- Maintaining registers and issuing certificates of eligibles
- Compiling data for and preparing periodic and special personnel reports
- Providing basic information about personnel regulations, procedures, programs, or benefits to employees, management officials, or the general public
- Providing clerical support in a personnel office or specialized unit within a personnel office where the work requires substantial knowledge of civilian personnel rules, regulations, procedures, and program requirements

Personnel Assistants perform a variety of technical support tasks that are usually related to one of the recognized personnel-management specialties. This work may take the form of assisting one or more fully qualified personnel specialists in a limited area of assignment. It also may involve independent performance of assignments in a prescribed segment of a personnel program where a fully qualified personnel specialist is not required.

Experience and Education

Except for the substitution of education or training provided for below, applicants must have had the kind and amount of experience shown in the following table, and as described in the statements immediately following:

Grade	Total (years)	General (years)	Specialized (years)
GS-4	2	1	1
GS-5	3	1	2
GS-6	4	1	3
GS-7 and above	5	1	4

Note: The work of clerical positions (as distinguished from assistant positions) at grades GS-5 and above requires the application of specialized knowledge gained through experience in civilian personnel operations. These positions are generally filled through non-competitive action.

These requirements for directly related experience will ordinarily apply. However, the requirement may be waived under certain circumstances where a lateral reassignment is involved, as provided elsewhere in this standard. In addition, the requirement for directly related experience may be waived for individuals under consideration for promotion in the relatively few instances where it can be clearly shown that the candidate's background gives positive evidence that he possesses to a superior degree the essential skills and abilities needed for the position.

Substitution of Education and Training for Experience

For a maximum of three years of the required experience (one year of general plus two years of specialized experience), study successfully completed in a resident school or institution may be substituted as follows.

For general experience only, the following substitutions apply:

- Study completed in a college, university, or junior college, above the high-school level may be substituted on the basis of one-half an academic year of study for six months of experience.
- Full-time study completed in a business or secretarial school or other comparable institution above the high-school level may be substituted on the basis of one-half an academic year of study for six months of experience provided such subjects as business English, office machines, filing and indexing, office practices, business mathematics, bookkeeping, or accounting were studied. No credit will be allowed for training that has been obtained only or primarily in the basic skills of shorthand or typing or refresher courses.

For specialized experience only, the following substitutions apply:

- For the first year of specialized experience, study successfully completed in a resident school above the high-school level may be substituted at the rate of one-half an academic year of study for six months of specialized experience provided the study included a minimum of six semester hours, or the equivalent, per year in subjects closely related to the personnel field. Such subjects include statistics;

psychology; sociology or other social sciences; courses where primary emphasis is on writing skill; public administration; personnel administration, industrial relations, or similar courses dealing directly with subjects in the personnel field; organization and management; and management analysis.

- For the second year of specialized experience, study of the type described in the preceding bullet may be substituted at the rate of one academic year of study for six months of specialized experience. Therefore, a full four-year course of this type of study may be substituted for a maximum of three years of the required experience and is fully qualifying for grade GS-5.

Computer Positions

COMPUTER CLERK, GS-2/4
COMPUTER ASSISTANT, GS-5/9

Description of Work

Computer Clerks and *Computer Assistants* perform a variety of tasks in support of specialists and computer operators engaged in the design and operation of computer systems. Employees in this occupation also support functional users of computer systems by accepting processing requirements, preparing them for execution, and in some cases performing or directing program execution through remote terminals, distributing the products and performing related control and processing support duties. These tasks are complementary to and support such specialized computer systems work as analysis, design, programming, installation, operations and system management.

Computer Clerks perform such tasks as

- Labeling, maintaining, and controlling tapes, disks, and other storage media and documentation in tape libraries
- Preparing processing schedules for jobs that are executed in simple sequence and have dependencies that are readily accommodated
- Maintaining a variety of computer program files, records, manuals, and related documents
- Tracing sources of procedural errors in documents, data, and control records

Computer Assistants perform limited phases of computer-specialist functions in addition to project control and scheduling work such as

- Translating program routines and detailed logic steps designed by others into instructions, codes, or languages that machines can accept
- Preparing charts showing the flow of documents and data in assigned subject areas
- Preparing daily or longer schedules for program processing sequences where multiple systems, multi-processing, dependencies, contentions, and similar conditions affect the scheduling processes
- Assembling, modifying controls, annotating instructions, and staging the materials and documentation required for machine processing
- Tracing and identifying the sources of processing failures, correcting those associated with system controls, introducing new or revised schedules of program processing, and providing control-stream modifications to take advantage of alternative operating system hardware configurations and processing techniques

Experience Requirements

Applicants must have the kind, quality, and amount of experience indicated in the following table and explanatory information.

Grade	General Experience (Years)	Specialized Experience (Years)	Total Experience (Years)
GS-1	None	None	None
GS-2	$1/2$	None	$1/2$
GS-3	1	None	1
GS-4	2	None	2
GS-5	2	1	3
GS-6	2	2	4
GS-7 and above	2	3	5

General Experience: Any experience that includes work associated with following written directions, procedures, or systematic work methods such as in classifying and maintaining records, or comparable clerical support work that gives evidence of the ability to perform this kind of work.

Specialized Experience: Any experience in computer clerical or other computer-related support work requiring knowledge of computer terminology, processing methods, controls, media, and data flow *or* experience requiring proficiency in translating actions into a computer programming language (COBOL, FORTRAN, ALGOL, and so on); preparing and interpreting program and system charts and instructions; or other work requiring comparable knowledge of computer-processing techniques.

Substitution of Education and Training for Experience

Education may be substituted for work experience according to the following criteria:

GS-2—Graduation from a four-year high school or GED equivalent.

GS-3—Successful completion of a two-year course, including instruction and practice in data processing in high school that provides knowledge of electronic computer systems, programming, media (tape, disks, and/or drum), input, and retrieval methods. Specific knowledge or ability as computer operators is not essential to this occupation and is not required when crediting high school ADP training

or

Successful completion of one year of education above the high-school level that includes at least six semester hours, or equivalent, in data processing courses

or

Successful completion of a full-time concentrated course of study of at least six months' duration that includes systems design and programming instruction and practice in a technical school above the high-school level.

GS-4—Successful completion of two years of study above the high-school level that includes at least 12 semester hours (or equivalent) in courses such as computer mathematics, basic and advanced programming, data processing, computer operations, or other ADP-related courses of study and practice.

GS-5—Successful completion of four years of study above the high-school level that includes at least 24 semester hours (or equivalent) in courses such as those described above for GS-4.

Quality of Experience

In evaluating combinations of experience, education, and training, one academic year of study may be substituted for one year of general experience or six months of specialized experience. Academic study may be substituted for a maximum of one year of specialized experience.

The applicant's record of experience and training must show the ability to perform the duties of the positions. In addition:

GS-5—For grade GS-5, except for those who qualify on the basis of education alone, the one year of required specialized experience must have been comparable in difficulty and responsibility to the GS-4 level in the same or closely related work.

GS-6—For grade GS-6 and above, at least one year of the required specialized experience must have been comparable in difficulty and responsibility to the next lower grade in the federal service or two years comparable to the second lower grade in the federal service.

Written Test

Applicants for competitive appointment to grades GS-2/4 must pass a written test. The written test is waived for applicants who qualify on the basis of specialized training or experience in the data-processing field.

Basis for Rating and Ranking Candidates

GS-2/4 applicants are rated on the basis of written test scores except for applicants for whom the written test is waived. For such applicants and for positions at grade GS-5 and above, applicants are rated on an evaluation of the quality and extent of their experience, education, or training.

FOR SUPERVISORY AND NON-SUPERVISORY POSITIONS
GS-2/13 IN THE COMPUTER OPERATION SERIES

Description of Work

Computer Operators are primarily responsible for the operation of the control console of a computer and all elements of the system that are directly connected with it. This involves readying the equipment for operation, starting it, monitoring its operation, and taking prompt action in response to machine commands or unscheduled halts.

Experience, Education, and Training Requirements

Applicants must have the kinds, quality, and amounts of experience indicated in the following table and explanatory information.

Grade	General Experience (Years)	Specialized Experience (Years)	Total Experience (Years)
GS-2	1/2	None	1/2
GS-3	1	None	1
GS-4	2	None	2
GS-5	2	1	3
GS-6	2	2	4
GS-7 and above	2	3	5

General Experience: General experience includes experience in the operation of electric accounting machines; or clerical experience; or experience in the operation of office business machines and other machines such as card punch, verifier, and the like.

Specialized Experience: Specialized experience includes experience in the operation of a computer system or peripheral device used in support of computer operations.

Specialized experience also may be experience in other computer-related occupations such as those involving programming, systems analysis, production control, scheduling, or others that are directly related.

Substitution of Education and Training for Experience: In crediting education above the high-school level, one year of study is equal to 30 semester hours or the equivalent. Education may be substituted for work experience according to the following criteria:

GS-2—Graduation from a four-year high school or GED equivalent

GS-3—Successful completion of one year of study in a school above the high-school level in any field of study

or

Successful completion of a full-time, or equivalent part-time, course of study in computer operations in an accredited vocational or technical school above the high-school level

GS-4—Successful completion of two years of study in a school above the high-school level

GS-5—Completion of four years of study above the high-school level, which includes at least 12 semester hours in any one or a combination of the following: mathematics, statistics, data processing, or other pertinent or related fields

In evaluating combinations of experience, education, and training, one academic year of study may be substituted for one year of general experience or six months of specialized experience. Academic study may be substituted for a maximum of one year of specialized experience.

Quality of Experience

For positions at any grade, the amount of experience will not in itself be accepted as proof of qualification. The applicant's record of experience and training must show that he/she has the ability to perform the duties of the position. In addition:

For grade GS-5, except for those who qualify on the basis of education alone, at least six months of the required specialized experience must have been comparable in difficulty and responsibility to the GS-4 level in the same or related work.

For grade GS-6 and above, in addition to education, training, and/or experience credited at lower levels, at least one year of the required specialized experience must have been comparable in difficulty and responsibility to the next lower grade in the federal service or two years comparable to the second lower grade in the federal service.

Written Test

Applicants for competitive appointment to grades GS-2/4 must pass a written test.

Basis for Rating and Ranking Candidates

For GS-2/4, applicants are rated on the basis of written test scores. For positions at grade GS-5 and above, applicants are rated on an evaluation of the quality and extent of their experience, education, or training.

Relating Qualifications of Candidates to Jobs Having Special Requirements

The numbers and kinds of computers, and the primary purposes they serve, differ among various work situations and may vary widely. Consequently, the particular demands of positions in these different work situations may vary widely. Referral of candidates for these positions may be limited to those whose records show evidence of the required capabilities.

COMPUTER SYSTEMS ANALYST, GS-5/15
COMPUTER PROGRAMMER, GS-5/15
COMPUTER PROGRAMMER ANALYST, GS-5/15
COMPUTER SYSTEMS PROGRAMMER, GS-5/15
COMPUTER EQUIPMENT ANALYST, GS-5/15
COMPUTER SPECIALIST, GS-5/15

Description of Work

Positions in this series advise on, supervise, or perform work necessary to design or implement systems for solving problems or accomplishing work processes by the use of digital computers. Except for entry-level positions, the primary requirement is knowledge of computer requirements and techniques.

Computer Systems Analysts are concerned with analysis of problems or processes and design of computerized systems for the accomplishment of work. Representative assignments include performance of feasibility studies for proposed computer applications in a subject matter area, development of an application's programming specifications, or analysis of existing applications' systems to correct problems.

Computer Programmers are concerned with translating system designs into the plans of instructions and logic by which computers can produce the desired actions or products. Knowledge of a particular programming language is an important consideration in recruitment for these positions.

Computer Programmer Analysts perform work that is a combination of Computer Systems Analyst and Computer Programmer duties.

Computer Systems Programmers are concerned with systems software. This typically involves maintenance and modification of assemblers, compilers, debugging routines, and similar internal computer programs necessary for the processing of other programs.

Computer Equipment Analysts are concerned with the selection or utilization of computer equipment. These positions do not involve design or repair of equipment; concern is with the relative merits of equipment items (for example, mainframe computers, disk memory devices, printers, terminals) and the arrangement of the items into equipment systems appropriate to an organization's needs.

Computer Specialists perform work of a kind or combination of duties that does not fall under one of the above specializations but does have as the main requirement knowledge of computer requirements and techniques.

Further information about the nature of the work performed by employees in the Computer Specialist series may be obtained from the position classification standard.

Knowledge, Skills, and Abilities

Knowledge and Skills

The requirements in this standard reflect the fact that proficiency in application of knowledge and skills at a given level indicates probability of success in similar work at the next higher level. The requirements are keyed to the progression of grade levels set forth in the classification standard. Successful accomplishment of assignments at the next lower grade in the normal line of promotion to the position being filled demonstrates capability to do work of the required level of difficulty and responsibility. Work in other fields that has provided the same kind and level of knowledge and skills similarly is qualifying. Education is substitutable for practical experience when the education has provided the knowledge and skills.

The GS-5 and GS-7 levels require basic analytic and communicative skills combined with broad general knowledge. The knowledge and skills required for GS-9 and above are more specialized. Persons typically gain and demonstrate the more specialized knowledge and skills through successful performance in lower grade level positions in this series, related work experience in other fields, or graduate study in fields such as data processing or computer science.

Selective Factors

Selective factors are knowledge and skills of a kind and level that reasonably could not be acquired on the job without undue interruption of the organization's production. Selective factors must be job related, represent an extension of the basic knowledge and skills required of the position, and be essential to successful performance of the position.

Owing to the diversity of work in the Computer Specialist series, the use of selective factors normally will be required in filling positions above the developmental level. Some factors, such as knowledge of a certain level of mathematics, may be appropriate for positions at any level. At the GS-9 and higher grades, knowledge and skills typically will be needed that relate to both the specialty of the position and the particular duties and responsibilities involved. For example, patterns of selective factors for a sample of full-performance positions might be as follows:

- For a Computer Programmer Analyst position—Proficiency in the use of a particular higher-level programming language (for example, COBOL), skill in the development and implementation of specifications for applications programs, and knowledge of techniques pertinent to the appropriate broad category of subject matter applications (for example, scientific applications or business applications).

- For a Computer Systems Programmer position—Proficiency in the use of a particular assembly level programming language (for example, ALC), knowledge of general techniques for analysis of system software requirements, and skill in the development and implementation of specifications for system software programs.

- For a Computer Equipment Analyst position—Knowledge of techniques for analysis of computer equipment requirements, knowledge of techniques for evaluation of computer equipment, skill in the development of specifications for the procurement of computer equipment, and knowledge of a broad category of equipment (for example, telecommunications-related computer equipment).

Positions at GS-12 and above commonly involve very demanding and responsible roles, often with little or no "back-up" expertise available in the organizational unit. Therefore, selective factors for positions at these grades typically will be more narrowly defined. What may be appropriate as a quality-ranking factor at a lower grade may have to be a selective factor in a higher-graded position. For example, knowledge of statistical methods and accounting techniques normally would be a quality-ranking factor in filling positions concerned with an automation project involving such methods and techniques. However, this knowledge normally would constitute a selective factor in filling the position of the project leader responsible for planning the overall approach and integrating segments of the system where these methods and techniques were of critical importance.

Minimum Qualification Requirements

GS-5

A. A background that includes one year of work at no lower than GS-4 or equivalent and demonstrates the following:
1. Skill in analyzing problems, to include identifying relevant factors, gathering pertinent information, and recognizing solutions
2. Skill in doing thorough, accurate work that requires planning a logical sequence of steps
3. Skill in communicating, both orally and in writing

Such skills typically are gained in administrative, technical, or investigative lines of work. It is also possible to acquire these skills through a variety of other means, such as volunteer work, vocational training, or substantive clerical work.

or

B. Completion of a four-year course in an accredited college leading to a bachelor's degree in any field
and (in the case of A or B)
C. Evidence of possession of any selective factors appropriate to the position to be filled.

GS-7

A. A background that includes one year of work at no lower than GS-5 or equivalent and demonstrates skills related to the computer field through performance of tasks such as the following:
1. Translating detailed logical steps developed by others into language codes that computers accept where this requires understanding of procedures and limitations appropriate to use of a programming language
2. Interviewing subject-matter personnel to get facts regarding work processes and synthesizing the resulting data into charts showing information flow
3. Operating computer consoles where this involves choice among various procedures in responding to machine commands or unscheduled halts
4. Scheduling the sequence of programs to be processed by computers where alternatives must be weighed with a view to production efficiency
5. Extracting and compiling information concerning an equipment feature where this involves selecting pertinent data from catalogs, manufacturers' literature, and previous studies
6. Preparing documentation on cost/benefit studies where this involves summarizing the materials and organizing them in logical fashion

Such skills typically are gained as a trainee in the Computer Specialist series, as a Computer Operator or Assistant, or through performance of work where the primary concern was the subject matter of the computer application (for example, supply, personnel, chemical process control) and one or more of the above types of computer-related efforts were required to facilitate the basic duties. Also, work in management analysis, program analysis, or a comparable field often provides such skills.

or

B. Superior academic achievement

or

C. Completion of one full academic year of graduate study in any field

and (in the case of A, B, or C)

D. Evidence of possession of any selective factors appropriate to the position to be filled

GS-9

A. A background that includes one year of work at no lower than GS-7 or equivalent and demonstrates knowledge of computer requirements and techniques in carrying out project assignments consisting of several related tasks. To qualify for the GS-9 level, the assignments must have shown completion of the following, or the equivalent:

   1. Analysis of the interrelationships of pertinent components of the system
   2. Planning the sequence of actions necessary to accomplish the assignment
   3. Personal responsibility for at least a segment of the overall project

Such knowledge and skills typically are gained in the Computer Specialist series or through performance of work where the primary concern was the subject matter of the computer application, and the above types of computer-related efforts were required to facilitate the basic duties. Also, work in management analysis, program analysis, or a comparable field often provides such knowledge and skills.

or

B. Completion of two full academic years of graduate study, or all requirements for a master's or equivalent degree, in a computer-related field such as computer science, data processing, or information-processing science

and (in the case of A or B)

C. Evidence of possession of any selective factors appropriate to the position to be filled

GS-11

A. A background that includes one year of work at no lower than GS-9 or equivalent and demonstrates accomplishment of computer project assignments that required a range of knowledge of computer requirements and techniques. For example, this level would be shown by assignments where, on the basis of general design criteria provided, the person developed modifications to parts of a system that required significant revisions in the logic or techniques used in the original development. In addition to the characteristics noted for the GS-9 level, qualifying accomplishments for the GS-11 level involve the following, or the equivalent:

   1. Knowledge of the customary approaches, techniques, and requirements appropriate to an assigned computer applications area or computer specialty area in an organization
   2. Planning the sequence of actions necessary to accomplish the assignment where this has entailed (a) coordination with others outside the organizational unit and (b) development of project controls
   3. Adaptation of guidelines or precedents to the needs of the assignment

Such knowledge and skills typically are gained in the Computer Specialist series or through performance of work where the primary concern was the subject matter of the computer application (for example, supply, personnel, chemical process control) and the above types of computer-related efforts were required to facilitate the basic duties. Also, work in management analysis, program analysis, or a comparable field occasionally provides such knowledge and skills.

or

B. Completion of three full academic years of graduate study, or all requirements for a doctoral degree (Ph.D. or equivalent), in a computer field such as computer science, data processing, or information processing science when (1) the position to be filled involves highly specialized work and (2) the graduate work is directly pertinent to the duties and responsibilities of the position

and (in the case of A or B)

C. Evidence of possession of any selective factors appropriate to the position to be filled

GS-12

A. A background that includes one year of work at no lower than the next lower grade or equivalent and demonstrates accomplishment of computer project assignments that required a wide range of knowledge of computer requirements and techniques pertinent to the position to be filled. This normally will have included knowledge of how the work is carried out in other organizations. In addition to the characteristics noted for the GS-9 and GS-11 levels, to qualify for GS-12 and above, the assignments will have involved performance of studies, such as feasibility studies, where alternatives were evaluated, reports prepared, and recommendations made. Such knowledge and skills typically are gained in the Computer Specialist series.

and

B. Evidence of possession of any selective factors appropriate to the position to be filled

Ranking Qualified Candidates

A suggested procedure is to analyze the requirements of the position and determine, in addition to selective factors essential to satisfactory performance, quality-ranking factors that would distinguish the better-qualified candidates among those who meet the minimum requirements. (Where appropriate, selective factors may also serve as quality-ranking factors.)

Positions at GS-5 and GS-7

Evaluation of candidates for positions at GS-5 and GS-7 should be based on evidence indicating probable success at higher level assignments. Other things being equal, candidates who can be expected to achieve full performance competence most quickly usually will be distinguished by the following:

- The quality of achievements that indicate ability in analyzing problems
- The caliber, job relatedness, and extent of education or experience that provided familiarity with data-processing concepts, terminology, and techniques
- For applications-oriented positions (for example, Computer Programmer), the degree of subject matter knowledge of the work process to be automated

Positions at GS-9 and Above

Evaluation of candidates for positions at GS-9 and above should be based on the following:

- Knowledge and skills specific to the position vacancy
- Evidence of the capacity to accept change and keep pace with the rapidly evolving computer technology

Examples of quality-ranking factors specific to a position, when supported by the position description, could be the degree of

- Skill in planning, developing, and conducting training
- Knowledge of a specific application
- Familiarity with a specific model of computer
- Knowledge of techniques for development of ADP standards
- Knowledge of database design
- Skill in simulation of new applications
- Familiarity with specific operating modes

Considerations in evaluating the capacity to accept change and keep pace with the technology could include the extent to which the candidate's background shows

- Success in a diversity of work in the computer field
- Development of systems or programs for which no precedents exist
- Accomplishments that involved the use of advanced design or programming techniques
- Evidence of continuing self development, such as pertinent course work or publication of papers in ADP society journals

Accounting, Budgeting, and Fiscal Management Positions

ACCOUNTING CLERICAL, SUPERVISORY, AND ADMINISTRATIVE POSITIONS, GS-7/15

Experience, Training, and Related Requirements

This standard is considered appropriate for filling such positions as Cash Accounting Assistant; Voucher Examiner; Time, Leave, and Payroll Supervisor; Benefit-Payment Roll Supervisor; and so on.

A. Length and Kind of Training and Experience Required

Except for the substitutions provided for below, applicants must have had as a minimum the length of experience specified in the following table.

Grade of Position	Length of Experience Required		
	Total (Years)	General (Years)	Specialized (Years)
GS-7	4	2	2
GS-8	$4\frac{1}{2}$	2	$2\frac{1}{2}$
GS-9	5	2	3
GS-10	$5\frac{1}{2}$	2	$3\frac{1}{2}$
GS-11 and above	6	2	4

General experience consists of work in

A. Accounting, auditing, or bookkeeping of a commercial type in such fields as cost accounting, financial accounting, and so on

or

B. Maintaining or examining fiscal records for the issuance, collection, safekeeping, or disbursing of money and securities by municipal, state, or federal government agencies, or commercial, industrial, or eleemosynary concerns and institutions

or

C. Supervising work described in A and B above with responsibility for the technical adequacy thereof, including supervision of machine accounting groups

Specialized experience is experience in the kind of work that is to be done in the position for which the examination is held and for which application is made. (Specialized experience in excess of the required length may be accepted as general experience.)

B. Provision for Substitution of Education for Experience

For a maximum of two years of the required general experience and one year of the specialized experience, applicants may substitute the following:

A. Study successfully completed in a resident school above high-school level with a major in the field of accounting or business administration on the basis of one academic year of study for nine months of experience

or

B. Teaching of any of the fields named in A above in a resident school above high-school level on the basis of one academic year of teaching for months of experience

or

C. Any time-equivalent combination of A and B above

or

D. The possession of a certificate as a Certified Public Accountant in a state, territory, or the District of Columbia, provided the certificate number, date, and place of issuance are clearly stated in the application

E. In addition, applicants who offer a bachelor's degree (or its equivalent) within 24 semester hours in any of the fields named in A above as a substitution for two years of the required general experience and one year of the specialized experience may substitute a master's degree in any of the fields named for one additional year of specialized experience. Under this provision, an applicant with a master's degree in the named fields of study may qualify at the GS-7 level.

C. Other Requirements

Quality of Experience. Applicants must have had progressively responsible experience of a scope and quality sufficient to demonstrate conclusively the ability to handle the duties of the position. The degree of fiscal responsibility involved must have been proportionately greater for each successively higher grade for which the applicant is being considered. The prescribed lengths and levels of experience must be met, but meeting them does not of itself entitle one to an eligible rating. The measure of total performance must be so full as to give promise of at least satisfactory performance at the grade or grades for which the applicant is being considered.

For grades GS-12 and above, at least one year of the required specialized experience must have been at a level of difficulty comparable at least to that of the next lower grade in the federal service. For grades GS-11 and below, at least six months of the required specialized experience must have been at a level of difficulty comparable to that of the next lower grade in the federal service, or one year must have been at a level comparable at least to that of the second lower grade.

BUDGET AND ACCOUNTING OFFICER, GS-11/15

Description of Work

Budget and Accounting Officers are typically responsible for the day-to-day supervision of the budget and the accounting operations, and may also be responsible for auxiliary areas such as credit and finance, internal audit, contractor accounts, and so on. As specialists, budget and accounting officers serve as technical experts for the organization's management staff on budget and accounting matters, provide specialized accounting and budget advice, interpret the results and needs of the budget and of the accounting programs, and coordinate these two separate functions (within the subordinate staff supervised) to the extent required for the effective conduct of each function.

To perform this work, the budget and accounting officer should have a high degree of knowledge of budget and/or accounting functions and operations, plus the ability to manage and direct the accounting, budgeting, and auxiliary staffs so as to provide the organization's management staff with the necessary specialized accounting and budget information and advice that that staff needs.

Experience

All applicants must have had a total of six years of progressively responsible administrative, technical, or specialist experience that provided a thorough knowledge of methods of supervision, administration, and management; and a demonstrated ability to deal with others. Of the six years, at least three years must have been *specialized* experience as defined below. The applicant's experience must include significant supervisory or administrative responsibilities, and also responsible technical or specialist experience in either the budget or accounting field, but *preferably in both*. If actual experience has been obtained in only one of these fields, the applicant must demonstrate possession of basic knowledge of the other area.

For some positions, the services of a professionally qualified accountant are desirable. For such positions, only those applicants will be considered who also meet the qualification requirements for the Accounting series—including, where required, passing a written test. (Some types of experience may satisfy the requirements of both the Accounting series and this standard and may be credited accordingly.)

Eligibility in any grade level will be based upon a clear showing that the applicant has had experience of a scope and quality sufficient to give him the ability to handle technical and/or supervisory problems commensurate with the duties of the grade for which he is being considered.

Specialized Experience

Specialized experience is progressively responsible experience in the fields of budget administration and/or accounting, or in any of the major kinds of work that are to be supervised and/or managed in the position for which the applicant is being considered. Experience in closely related fields is also acceptable, provided that the experience demonstrated competence in and knowledge of budget or accounting functions and also demonstrated the following:

- The ability to plan, direct, and coordinate a budget and accounting program, and to provide service thereon
- The ability to select, develop, and supervise a subordinate staff
- The ability to establish and maintain effective working relationships with all levels of key management officials and subordinate staff

The degree of technical ability involved must be proportionately greater for each successively higher grade for which the applicant is considered. Among the kinds of work that may be accepted as specialized experience are the following:

- The development, direction, evaluation, or revision of budgetary control systems
- Budget preparation and presentation, budget analysis, and/or program analysis
- Supervision or maintenance of commercial type accounts in such fields as cost accounting, financial accounting, and so on
- Supervision of the maintenance or examination of records for the issuance, collection, safekeeping, or disbursing of money and securities by municipal, state, or federal government agencies or private industry (including such records as cost, time, payroll, expenses, revenues, expenditures, appropriations, revolving funds, working capital, trust funds, or other fiscal records)
- Planning, directing, or supervising a program for collecting, classifying, compiling, or evaluating accounting data
- Planning, developing, or installing new accounting systems, or revising existing accounting systems
- Preparing financial or cost statements and reports used to evaluate performance or to determine status of activities or programs
- Auditing or examining accounting systems, records, or financial statements
- Examining or appraising organizational procedures, operations, or internal controls that involve financial systems or are accomplished primarily for budget or accounting purposes
- Preparing or reviewing reports of financial audits
- Experience as an office manager, owner, and so on, which has involved direct supervision of accountants, auditors, or Budget Analysts, provided that budget and accounting responsibilities comprised a major part of the position

Quality of Experience

For grade GS-11, at least six months of the required specialized experience must have been at a level of difficulty comparable to that of the next lower grade in the federal service, or one year must have been at a level comparable at least to that of the second lower grade. For grades GS-12 and above, at least one year of the required specialized experience must have been at a level of difficulty comparable at least to that of the next lower grade in the federal service.

Educational and Other Substitutions

Successfully completed study in a residence school above high-school level in any field may be substituted for a maximum of three years of general experience at the rate of one academic year of study for nine months of experience.

Full-time graduate education may be substituted for experience on the following basis. The education must have equipped the candidate with the knowledge and ability to perform fully the work of the position for which he is being considered.

A. *For one year of specialized experience*—One full academic year of graduate education in business administration, public administration, economics, industrial engineering or management, government, political science, or in other directly related fields
B. *For two years of specialized experience*—Completion of all requirements for a master's or an equivalent degree, or two full academic years of graduate education, which is in the fields described in paragraph A above.

The possession of a certificate as a Certified Public Accountant obtained through written examination in a state, territory, or the District of Columbia, provided the certificate number, date, and place of issuance are clearly stated in the application, may be substituted for three years of general experience.

ACCOUNTING SERIES, GS-5/15
AUDITING SERIES, GS-5/15

Description of Work

*Accountants** and *Auditors** perform professional work in any of several capacities depending upon the accounting system involved, the organizations and operating programs served, the financial data sought, and the needs of management. Accountants classify and evaluate financial data; record transactions in financial records; develop and install new accounting systems, and revise existing accounting systems; and prepare and analyze financial statements, records, and reports. Auditors examine accounts for the purpose of certifying or attesting that as of a certain date or for a stated period, various financial statements fairly present the financial position of the activity audited in terms of assets, liabilities, net worth, and income and expenses.

Auditors evaluate such matters as the degree of compliance with laws, regulations, and principles of sound financial management; the effectiveness, economy, and efficiency of resource utilization and management systems; and the extent to which desired results or benefits are being achieved. Audit emphasis includes evaluating internal controls to determine the reliability of reported results and ensuring that generally accepted accounting principles have been consistently applied by the activity audited.

Basic Requirements for All Grades

Candidates for all grades must meet the requirements of paragraph A, B, or C below. The basic requirements are fully qualifying for grade GS-5.

A. A full four-year course of study in an accredited college or university that meets all of that institution's requirements for a bachelor's degree with an accounting major.

B. A full four-year course of study in an accredited college or university that meets all requirements for a bachelor's degree and that included or was supplemented by at least 24 semester hours in accounting.

C. At least four years of experience in accounting, or an equivalent combination of accounting experience, college-level education, and training that provided professional accounting knowledge equivalent in type, scope, and thoroughness to that acquired through successful completion of a four-year college curriculum in accounting as in A above.

The background of candidates who meet the requirements of this paragraph must also include one of the following:

A. Twenty-four semester hours in accounting or auditing courses of appropriate type and quality. Note: Resident or home-study academic courses conducted by a federal agency or a non-accredited institution that are determined to be fully equivalent to accounting and auditing courses in an accredited college may be accepted.

B. A certificate as Certified Public Accountant or a Certified Internal Auditor, obtained through written examination

C. Recognized, well-established professional stature in accounting or auditing based on a combination

---

*Generally, for editorial convenience, the term "accounting" is used in lieu of "accounting and/or auditing." Similarly, "accountant" should be interpreted, generally, as "accountants and/or auditors."

of

1. Successful experience in a variety of highly responsible accounting functions in positions equivalent to GS-12 or higher

and

2. Significant documented contributions to the accounting or auditing profession through publications, leadership in professional organizations, development of new methods and techniques, or comparable achievements

D. Completion of the requirements for a bachelor's or higher degree with major study in accounting, auditing, or a related field that includes substantial course work in accounting or auditing (for example, 15 semester hours), but that does not fully satisfy the 24 semester hour requirement of paragraph A provided that

1. The candidate has successfully demonstrated the ability to perform work of the GS-12 or higher grade level in accounting, auditing, or a related field, such as valuation engineering or financial institution examining

2. A panel of at least two higher level professional accountants or auditors has determined that the candidate has demonstrated a good knowledge of accounting and of related and underlying fields that equals in breadth, depth, currency, and level of advancement that normally obtained with successful completion of the four-year course of study at an accredited college or university

and

3. Except for literal non-conformance to the requirement of 24 semester hours in accounting, the candidate's education, training, and experience fully meet the specified requirements

Additional Experience and Training Requirements

Candidates for grades GS-7 and above must have had either professional experience or graduate education, or an equivalent combination of both, in addition to meeting the basic requirements. This professional experience or graduate education must have been in or directly related to accounting or auditing or in a field closely related to the position to be filled.

1. Experience

In addition to the basic requirements, the following amounts of professional experience are required for grades GS-7 and above:

Grade	Total Experience (Years)
GS-7	1
GS-9	2
GS-11 and above	3

For grades GS-11 and below, at least six months of the required experience must have been at a level of difficulty comparable to that of the next lower grade or one year comparable to the second lower grade in the federal service. For grades GS-12 and above, at least one year of the required experience must have been at a level of difficulty comparable to that of the next lower grade in the federal service.

2. Education

In addition to the basic requirements, the following amounts and levels of education are qualifying for grades GS-7 and above. This education must have been either in accounting and auditing or in directly related fields:

GS-7—One full academic year of graduate education

GS-9—Completion of all requirements for a master's or equivalent degree *or* two full academic years of graduate education

Equivalent combinations of professional experience and graduate education of the type described above are acceptable at each grade.

3. Alternate Requirements

Superior academic achievement at the baccalaureate level or one year of student trainee experience in accounting or auditing is qualifying at grade GS-7. A combination of superior academic achievement at the baccalaureate level and one year of appropriate professional experience is qualifying at grade GS-9.

For Technician positions at GS-7 only, candidates who have completed the required 24 semester hours in accounting and who have experience—in addition to that needed to satisfy the basic requirement for all positions—as an accounting technician equivalent to grade GS-5 or higher may have that experience credited for GS-7 on a month-for-month basis up to a maximum of 12 months.

Selective and Quality-Ranking Factors

In general, candidates who meet the basic requirements for all grades are qualified for positions at the entrance and lower levels in any specialized branch of accounting such as cost, systems, staff, and auditing. Specific knowledge, skills, and/or abilities are used as quality-ranking factors under justification that shows:

- How the quality-ranking factor is directly related to the duties and responsibilities of the position
- Why possession of the desired knowledge, skill, and/or ability would predict superior performance

For other specialized positions, only candidates who possess specific job-related knowledge, skills, and/or abilities may be qualified. Justification for selective placement factors must show the following:

- How the selective factor is directly related to the duties and responsibilities of the position
- Why possession of the knowledge, skills, and/or abilities identified as selective factors are necessary for successful performance in the position

The Office of Personnel Management Position—Classification Standard for the Accounting Series and the Auditing Series includes a great deal of valuable information on the various specialized branches of accounting.

Written Test

No written test is required.

Basis for Rating and Ranking Candidates

Candidates will be rated on a scale of 100 on the extent and quality of their experience and training. Ratings are based on candidates' statements in their applications and on any additional information that may be secured by the Office of Personnel Management.

Professional knowledge of accounting is defined as

- A thorough knowledge of the concepts, theories, principles, and practices of general and cost accounting; public industrial and/or governmental accounting; auditing, taxation, budgeting, and analysis of financial statements; and trends and current developments in the accounting profession in government, industry, and public accounting firms
- An understanding of the legal principles that govern financial transactions and relationships in government or industry
- A basic foundation in related fields such as banking, mathematical analysis, statistics, automatic data processing systems and techniques, business organization, and the principles and processes of management

Professional ability to apply accounting knowledge is defined as the ability to

- Apply fundamental and diversified professional accounting concepts, theories, and practices to achieve financial management objectives with versatility, judgment, and perception
- Adapt and apply methods and techniques of related disciplines such as economics and statistical analysis
- Organize, analyze, interpret, and evaluate financial data in the solution of management and accounting problems

Positive and continuing development of professional knowledge and ability is defined as an action program involving activities such as the following as appropriate to the circumstances:

- Developing new approaches, methods, or techniques for the solution of problems in accounting or auditing
- Formal or informal training and guidance on the job by specialists or more mature professionals
- College-level academic study
- Participation in seminars, conferences, and technical committees of professional societies and other organizations
- Review and study of the professional literature of accounting and related fields
- Publication of professional papers

Professional work in accounting, like that of other professions, is marked by continuing personal effort to keep abreast of the advancing and changing discipline. Continuing education in accounting and related fields is an important element of full professional competence as an accountant that should be considered in evaluating the qualifications of candidates for professional accountant positions. Accounting technicians who desire to make the upward transition to professional accountant must not only satisfy the essential requirement of 24 semester hours in accounting, but should plan on continued academic course work.

Education in Accounting

Undergraduate Education

Most accounting majors consist of 24 semester hours of accounting courses that have easily recognizable titles such as "Elementary Accounting," "Intermediate Accounting," "Advanced Accounting," "Auditing," "Federal Tax Accounting," "Cost Accounting," "CPA Problems," "Accounting Systems," "Internal Auditing," "Government Accounting," "Accounting Theory," "Accounting Seminar," and the like. However, not all professional accounting courses have the words "accounting" or "auditing" in their titles. Courses entitled, for example, "Analysis of Financial Statements," "Business Budgeting," "Cost

Analysis and Control," "Investment Analysis," and "Statement and Report Presentation and Analysis" are considered professional accounting courses when they

- Have as a prerequisite one or more clearly identifiable professional accounting courses such as principles of accounting
- Are primarily concerned with the development, analysis, and presentation of financial data and/or the interpretation and evaluation of financial information and its application to management problems

Graduate Education

Graduate education may have been either in accounting or in directly related fields such as business administration, finance, comptrollership, and management. Normally, such study includes one or more courses in accounting.

Acceptance of Technician Experience

At grade GS-7, for competitive appointment and for in-service placement, accounting technician experience at the grade GS-5 level and above may be accepted toward meeting the professional experience requirements as described on page 91, provided the candidate meets the basic requirements for all grades on page 88.

ACCOUNTING TECHNICIAN GS-4/9

Description of Duties

Accounting Technicians perform non-professional work necessary to insure the effective operation of established accounting systems. They apply a basic understanding of accounting concepts and procedures in performing such functions as classifying accounting transactions; maintaining, balancing, and reconciling accounting records; examining accounting records to verify accuracy; determining appropriate adjustments and special entries; preparing and verifying accounting statements and reports; and performing prescribed analyses of accounting data and reports. These functions may involve a narrow range of accounts or may encompass the entire accounting system of the activity, depending on the nature and level of assignments.

Experience Requirements

Except for the substitutions provided for below, candidates must have had the kind and amount of experience shown in the table and described in the statements immediately following.

Grade	General Experience (Years)	Specialized Experience (Years)	Total Experience (Years)
GS-4	2	None	2
GS-5	2	1	3
GS-6	2	2	4
GS-7	2	3	5
GS-8 and above	2	4	6

General Experience

This is clerical work that has demonstrated arithmetic aptitude and ability, accuracy and attention to detail, and the ability to apply established procedures for recording and compiling data. Such work may have involved

- Maintaining various types of records requiring accuracy in selecting, posting, and consolidating pertinent data
- Coding, compiling, or verifying statistical data
- Making arithmetic computations, applying formulas or conversion tables, and so on
- Screening various types of documents to verify the accuracy of codes, amounts, or similar data in numeric form against related documents or guides
- Operating various calculating or posting machines, provided this work included responsibility for verifying accuracy
- Similar work that demonstrated the relevant abilities

Specialized Experience

This is work that required the candidate to acquire and apply a knowledge of established accounting procedures and techniques in the performance of such functions as

- Analyzing and classifying or recording transactions
- Balancing, reconciling, adjusting, or examining accounts
- Developing or verifying accounting data for reports, statements, and schedules
- Performing prescribed analyses of accounting data

Directly related specialized experience is defined as experience gained in the same specialized area of accounting technician work as the position for which application is made.

Quality of Experience

Candidates for any grade must have at least one year of experience at a level of difficulty comparable to the next lower grade or two years of experience at the level of difficulty comparable to the second lower grade in the federal service.

Substitution Allowed

A. Study successfully completed in a resident college, university, or junior college may be substituted for *general* experience on the basis of one-half academic year of study for six months of experience, provided it included at least three semester hours per year in the fields of bookkeeping or accounting.
B. Study successfully completed in a resident business or commercial school or other comparable institution above the high-school level may be substituted for *general* experience on the basis of one-half academic year of study for six months of experience, provided such study included accounting or bookkeeping as well as other subjects such as business English, office machines, filing and indexing, office practices, or business mathematics. No credit will be allowed for training that has been obtained only or primarily in the basic skills of shorthand or typing or refresher courses.
C. Study of the nature described in A and B above may be substituted for the first year of specialized experience on the basis of one academic year of study for six months of specialized experience.

Under these provisions, a two-year course of study of the above nature meets the experience requirements for grade GS-4, and a full four-year course of study meets the experience requirements for grade GS-5.

Written Test

A written test of abilities necessary to learn and perform the duties of these positions is required for positions at grade GS-4.

Basis for Rating and Ranking Candidates

Competitors for all positions will be rated on a scale of 100. Rankings are made as follows:

- **For competitive appointments at GS-4:** On the basis of the written test
- **For competitive appointments above GS-4 and for in-service placement actions at all grades:** On the basis of the extent and quality of experience and training relevant to the duties of the position

In-Service Placement Provisions

Substitution for Specialized Experience

Responsible work in closely related occupations that has demonstrated potential for advancement and aptitude for accounting technician work may be substituted for a maximum of one year of specialized experience. Experience in related work may be credited, provided it involved the following:

- Demonstrated analytical ability in interpreting and applying a body of regulations and procedures under varying conditions
- Substantial responsibilities for verifying the accuracy and completeness of data in source and supporting documents or reports and for tracing and correcting discrepancies

and

- Reconciling records maintained with related accounting data or performing prescribed analyses of the records maintained

Work in related areas that does not fully meet the above conditions is creditable as *general* experience only.

Waiver of Directly Related Experience Requirement

The requirement for directly related experience may be waived under the following conditions:

- For lateral reassignments when:
   A. The candidate has had experience that provided a general familiarity with the work of the position for which he is being considered

   and

   B. A review of the candidate's experience and performance discloses possession of the necessary skills and abilities, and evidences potential for successful performance of the work

- For promotion actions, where it is clearly shown that:
   A. Despite the lack of directly related experience, the candidate's background gives positive evidence that he possessed to a superior degree the essential skills and abilities needed for the position

   and

   B. The candidate has had experience that has provided a general familiarity with the work of the position for which he is being considered

   and

C. The overall evaluation of the candidate's background provides strong evidence that he can successfully perform the higher grade work without prolonged training

Suggestions for Evaluating Employers for In-Service Placement

In evaluating candidates for in-service placement to Accounting Technician jobs, it is suggested that inquiries be made of former supervisors of the candidate to elicit detailed information concerning demonstrated abilities, type of work experience, and past responsibilities.

Inquiries should develop information on

A. The kind and extent of knowledge of double-entry accounting processes or of closely related recordkeeping techniques. (Note: The accounting and finance unit is not the only place where such pertinent experience can be gained)

B. The degree of responsibility for interpreting guidelines and procedures, and the relative degree of supervision

and

C. Such personal characteristics and interests as
- Interest and aptitude in working with figures
- Ability to maintain a high level of accuracy in work requiring close attention to detail
- Interest in the purpose and effect of prescribed procedures

or

- Initiative in questioning unusual actions or in obtaining information to support or verify questionable actions

In ranking individuals, other things being equal, the greatest credit should be given to those with the greatest amount of directly related experience, and to those who have had the greatest responsibility and freedom from supervision. Extra credit may be given for a broader range of experience (in addition to any required directly related experience) when the broader experience will be of benefit in the position and if it gives evidence of greater potential for development. Extra credit may also be given for completion of correspondence courses or part-time study, not credited under educational substitution provisions, in accounting or bookkeeping.

BUDGET ANALYST, GS-5/15
BUDGET OFFICER, GS-11/15
BUDGET EXAMINER, GS-5/15 (OMB ONLY)

Description of Work

Positions in this series perform, advise on, or supervise work in the phases or systems of budget administration currently in use in the federal service. Such work primarily requires knowledge and skill in the application of related laws, regulations, policies, precedents, methods, and techniques of budgeting.

Budget Analysts perform a segment, but less than the full range of, the budget administration work done in the employing component or installation. The work requires knowledge of the particular phase(s) of budgeting; analytical method; processes; and procedures used in budgeting for assigned organizations, programs, or activities. Budget Analysts analyze the relative costs and benefits of alternate courses of budget and program action, check the propriety of obligations and expenditures, establish standard rates and charges to customers of industrially-funded activities, or develop budgetary policy and regulatory guidance.

Budget Officers are responsible for the full complement of budgetary operations that support the programs and personnel of the employing organizational component and level. At a minimum, a Budget Officer's responsibilities include formulation and execution of the annual operating budget for the employing component. However, most Budget Officers also provide expert staff advice and assistance to managers by developing budget plans and estimates; interpreting budget laws, policies, and regulations; analyzing the cost effectiveness of program operation; and recommending alternate sources of program funding.

Budget Examiners are budgetary experts in the Office of Management and Budget (OMB) actively engaged in the review, analysis, and control of the budgetary operations of federal agencies and departments. Budget Examiners approve, disapprove, or adjust agency requests for funds in proposed and approved annual budgets and provide budgetary guidance to federal agencies. These positions are established only in OMB.

For a more complete description of the work performed by Budget Analysts, Budget Officers, and Budget Examiners, refer to the position classification standard for the Budget Analysis series.

Experience Requirements

Applicants must show that they have met the general and specialized experience requirements summarized in the following chart:

Grade	Specialized (Years)	General (Years)	Total (Years)
GS-5	None	3	3
GS-7	1	3	4
GS-9	2	3	5
GS-11 and above	3	3	6

General Experience

This is experience from which the applicant gained a general knowledge of financial and management principles and practices applicable to organizations. Experience in specialized fields that are closely related to budget analysis or excess specialized experience is acceptable as general experience.

Specialized Experience

This is experience that provided specific knowledge and skill in the application of budgetary principles, practices, methods, and procedures directly related to the work of the position to be filled. Such experience must have included substantially full-time work or its part-time equivalent in one or more of the following budgetary functions:

- Budget preparation, justification, and presentation
- Budget execution (for example, monitoring and control of obligations and expenditures)
- Development of budgetary policies, procedures, and guides
- Development, evaluation, or revision of budgetary control systems
- Planning and budgeting for the operations of a working capital fund

Quality of Experience

Applicants must demonstrate progressively responsible experience of a scope, quality, and degree such as to have equipped them with the capability to perform duties at the grade level of the position for which application is made. Typically, this is demonstrated by accomplishment of assignments of the difficulty and responsibility described in the position classification standard used to evaluate positions at the next lower grade in the normal line of promotion to the position being filled.

Specialized experience that involved less than the majority of the candidate's time is to be prorated and credited on a month-to-month basis. In crediting experience gained in the federal service, the grade of specialized experience may or may not be equivalent to the grade level of the position in which it was gained. Whenever possible, determination of the grade level of specialized experience should be based on the classification evaluation of the budget work performed.

Substitution of Education and Training for Experience

Education may be substituted for the required experience as follows:

- Undergraduate education
    - Successful completion of a four-year course of study in an accredited college or university leading to a bachelor's degree or the equivalent is acceptable as meeting all requirements for the GS-5 level.
    - Part-time undergraduate education of the type described above may be substituted at the rate of one year of education for nine months of general experience.

- Graduate education
    - Successful completion of one full academic year of relevant graduate education in business, administration, economics, accounting, governmental budgeting, public administration, industrial engineering, political science, or an equally relevant field with comparable course work meets all requirements for grade GS-7.
    - Successful completion of all requirements for a master's or equivalent degree, or two full years of graduate education that is in one of the fields described in the preceding bullet meets all requirements for grade GS-9.
    - For some positions, notably those that also require intensive knowledge of the Congressional budget process, economics, or statistics, completion of all requirements for a doctoral degree in a field directly related to the work of the position to be filled is accepted as qualifying for grade GS-11.
    - Part-time graduate education of the type described above may be substituted at the rate of 30 semester hours for one year of specialized experience, or 15 semester hours for six months of specialized experience.

Education may not be substituted for the required experience above the GS-11 level.

Special Provisions for In-Service Placement

Positions covered by this standard may be filled at the GS-5 and GS-7 levels without regard to the experience or educational requirements listed previously by in-service lateral reassignment of employees from positions in the Budget Clerical and Assistance series, the Accounting Technician series, the General Accounting Clerical and Administrative series, or other series that provided comparable financial skills. Unless otherwise qualified under experience and educational requirements described in other parts of this standard, employees reassigned under this provision must serve at least one year in the position at the grade level at which reassigned before promotion within this series.

This provision is not to be used to promote an employee from a clerical, assistant, or technician occupation directly into a position in this series.

Basis for Rating and Ranking Candidates

Candidates for competitive appointment to all positions will be rated on the basis of their experience and/or education as it relates to the work or the position to be filled.

Guide for Evaluating Candidates

Positions at all grade levels in this series require the following:

- The ability to effectively express ideas and recommendations orally and in writing
- The ability to reason in quantitative terms (for example, in numerical concepts)
- Analytical ability, which includes the ability to conceptualize, generalize, and draw meaningful inferences and conclusions from financial and narrative data
- The ability to work effectively under pressure of tight time frames and rigid deadlines
- Some positions in this series require skill in presenting and gaining the acceptance of budgetary requests, recommendations, and decisions during formal negotiations with fund-granting and fund-reviewing authorities

For positions at the entry level (GS-5 and GS-7), credit should be given for experience and education that has demonstrated the candidate's ability to communicate effectively, both orally and in writing.

Analytical ability of the type required in this series is often demonstrated through the completion of college-level courses in logic, philosophy, economics, mathematics (for example, probability and statistics), computer science, chemistry, and physics. In ranking candidates, courses that included analytical methods and techniques commonly used in budget analysis may also be considered. While courses in business mathematics, financial management, statistics, economics, and accounting are highly desirable, they have not been specified as minimum educational requirements because to do so could possibly exclude some candidates who would otherwise be well-qualified to do the work.

Selective Placement Factors

In filling positions at grades above the entry levels, selective factors may be appropriate for screening candidates. If selective factors are used, the requirements must be job related, and need for them must be reflected in the official position description or other official communication. These will vary considerably, depending upon the nature of the position to be filled.

Quality-Ranking Factors

Candidates who meet or exceed the basic requirements, including any selective factors, may be ranked according to their degree of proficiency on quality-ranking factors that have been identified for use. Examples of quality-ranking factors could include

- Knowledge of the programs and work processes of organizations for which budgetary services are provided
- Skill in developing and presenting briefings on budgetary matters

Volunteer service (for example, in charitable, religious, or service organizations) is to be counted toward meeting experience requirements of this standard.

SAVINGS AND LOAN EXAMINER, GS-5/15
FARM CREDIT EXAMINER, GS-5/15
INVESTMENT COMPANY EXAMINER, GS-5/15
SAVINGS AND LOAN EXAMINING OFFICER, GS-12/15
FARM CREDIT EXAMINING OFFICER, GS-12/15
INVESTMENT COMPANY EXAMINING OFFICER, GS-12/15

Description of Work

Examiners in positions of these kinds make examinations and audits of savings and loan associations, farm credit associations, cooperative banks, investment institutions, national banks, or other financial institutions to determine financial condition, soundness of operations, compliance with regulatory laws and provisions, integrity of accounts, and other pertinent matters.

Examining Officers in positions of these kinds plan, manage, and direct the work of examiners of financial institutions.

Experience Requirements

Except for the substitutions provided for below, applicants must have had experience of the kinds and amounts specified below:

Grade	Specialized (Years)	General (Years)	Total (Years)
GS-5	3	3	None
GS-7	4	3	1
GS-9	5	3	2
GS-11 and above	6	3	3

General Experience

This consists of any of the following:

A. Experience in positions requiring a thorough knowledge and the application of commercial accounting or auditing principles and practices (but less than full professional accounting knowledge)—for example, experience that has provided an understanding of debits and credits, the principles of journalizing, balance sheets, and operating statements

or

B. Experience with a savings and loan association, savings or commercial bank, or other financial institution requiring knowledge of accounting or auditing principles as applied to such institutions

or

C. Any time-equivalent combination of A and B above

Specialized Experience, Type A (Usual Requirement)

This consists of any of the following:

A. Progressively responsible experience requiring a thorough knowledge and the application of accounting or auditing principles and practices (but less than full professional accounting knowledge) with a financial institution engaged in mortgage-lending operations; with the mortgage loan department of an insurance company; or with a federal agency making, insuring, guaranteeing, or supervising mortgage lending

B. Progressively responsible experience in the examining or auditing of such financial institutions as savings and loan associations, savings or commercial banking institutions or trust companies, Federal Reserve banks, farm credit associations, or federal or state credit unions

C. For up to a maximum of two years of experience, professional accounting or auditing work that provided a broad knowledge of the application of accounting or auditing principles and practices

D. Any time-equivalent combination of A, B, and C above

Specialized Experience, Type B (Optional Requirement)

This is experience that has provided a thorough knowledge of federal and state laws applicable to the type of financial institution involved and of the operations and practices of such institutions.

Specialized experience, type B may be required for some positions, but when required, this will not increase the total length of required experience. The specialized experience, type B may be required, therefore, in lieu of part of the above stated requirement for either general experience or specialized experience, or both. For grade GS-7, specialized experience, type B may be the sole specialized experience that is required.

Specialized experience, type A in excess of that required may be substituted for general experience.

Substitution of Education and Training for Experience

Study successfully completed in a resident institution above the high-school level may be substituted for general experience at the rate of one academic year of study for nine months of experience, provided that such study included an average of six semester hours (or the equivalent) in either one or two of the following, or directly related fields: accounting, banking, business administration, commercial or banking law, economics, or finance. For some positions, 12 semester hours of this study must have been in accounting. A total of four academic years of study as described in this paragraph is qualifying for grade GS-5.

Full-time graduate education may be substituted for experience on the following basis:

A. For one year of specialized experience: One full academic year of graduate education in one of the following: accounting, banking, business administration, economics, finance, or other directly related fields. (This amount and kind of education meets all the requirements for grade GS-7.)

B. For two years of specialized experience: Completion of all requirements for a master's or an equivalent degree, or two full academic years of graduate education, which is in the fields described in paragraph A above. (This amount and kind of education meets all the requirements for grade GS-9.)

Applicants may substitute the possession of a certificate as a Certified Public Accountant in a state, territory, or the District of Columbia for all of the three years of general experience, provided the certificate number and date of issuance are clearly shown.

Quality of Experience

The prescribed lengths and levels of experience must be met, but meeting them does not of itself entitle one to an eligible rating unless the quality of the applicant's total background gives promise of satisfactory performance at the grade level for which the applicant is being considered.

For grades GS-11 and below, at least six months of the required specialized experience must have been at a level of difficulty comparable to that of the next lower grade in the federal service, or one year must have been at a level of difficulty comparable at least to that of the second lower grade. For grades GS-12 and above, at least one year of the required specialized experience must have been at a level of difficulty comparable to that of the next lower grade in the federal service.

Additional Requirements

All applicants must demonstrate the ability to meet and deal successfully and effectively with the public.

Written Test

Applicants for grade GS-5 and GS-7 positions must pass an appropriate written test. Applicants for all positions at grades GS-9 and above will not be required to take a written test.

Basis for Rating and Ranking Candidates

Applicants for GS-5 and GS-7 positions will be rated on the basis of their test scores and an evaluation of their education and experience.

Applicants for all positions at GS-9 and above will be rated on the basis of the quality, diversity, and extent of their experience and its relevance to the duties of the position to be filled. Such ratings will be based on the competitors' statements in their applications and on any additional evidence that is obtained.

Law Enforcement Positions

INVESTIGATOR
SUPERVISORY INVESTIGATOR
CRIMINAL INVESTIGATOR
SUPERVISORY CRIMINAL INVESTIGATOR, GS-5/15

Coverage

These standards are intended to be used primarily in filling investigator and criminal investigator positions that involve the performance of fact-finding and reporting duties and related responsibilities described below, and other positions in these series for which actual investigative experience is essential. All parts of these standards apply to positions in both the General Investigating series and the Criminal Investigating series; where variations exist involving differences in investigating duties, specialized experience, physical standards, and minimum age requirements, these are so indicated.

Description of Work

Investigators

Investigators plan and conduct investigations relating to the administration of, or compliance with, federal laws and regulations. The duties performed typically include

- Collecting facts and obtaining information by observing conditions, examining records, and interviewing individuals
- Writing and securing affidavits
- Administering oaths
- Preparing investigative reports to be used as a basis for court or administrative action
- Testifying before administrative bodies, courts, or grand juries, or serving as a witness for the government

The work occasionally may involve criminal investigations. Performance of these duties may require work at irregular hours and considerable travel. Investigators may also be required to operate motor vehicles.

Criminal Investigators

Criminal Investigators plan and conduct investigations relating to alleged or suspected violations of federal laws. The duties typically performed include

- Obtaining physical and documentary evidence
- Interviewing witnesses
- Applying for and serving warrants for arrests, searches, and seizures
- Seizing contraband, equipment, and vehicles
- Examining files and records
- Maintaining surveillance
- Performing undercover assignments
- Preparing investigative reports
- Testifying in hearings and trials
- Assisting U.S. Attorneys in the prosecution of court cases

Most Criminal Investigators are required to carry firearms and to be proficient in their use. The work may occasionally involve noncriminal investigations.

Performance of these duties frequently requires irregular unscheduled hours, personal risks, exposure to all kinds of weather, considerable travel, and arduous exertion, under adverse environmental conditions. Criminal Investigators may also be required to operate motor vehicles.

Types of Positions

The kind of investigative work performed varies in respect to the investigative jurisdiction and functions of the employing agencies. The grade levels of the positions vary with the scope, complexity, and importance of investigations and the degree of individual responsibility required. At the higher grade levels, investigators may also serve as team leaders, group supervisors, case reviewers, unit coordinators, or in similar capacities, with responsibility for supervising the work of other investigators; or they may be responsible for the management or direction of an investigative program or program segment.

The duties of some positions require experience or equivalent educational backgrounds that have been obtained in or are closely related to particular industries, business operations, commercial enterprises, professions, or other occupational areas; or that have been obtained in both the investigative and the criminal investigative areas.

Experience Requirements

Except for the substitutions provided for below, applicants must have had experience of the length shown in the table and of the nature described in the paragraphs following:

Grade	General Experience (Years)	Specialized Experience (Years)	Total Experience (Years)
GS-5	3	None	3
GS-7	3	1	4
GS-9	3	2	5
GS-11 and above	3	3	6

General Experience

This must have been progressively responsible experience that has required

- The ability to work or deal effectively with individuals or groups of persons
- Skill in collecting and assembling pertinent facts
- The ability to prepare clear and concise reports

    and

- The ability and willingness to accept responsibility

Acceptable general experience may have been gained in types of work such as the following:

- Adjustment or investigation of claims arising under law, contract, or governmental order
- Analysis of reports or data or the preparation of surveys, studies, or reports requiring the development, organization, evaluation, and interpretation of substantive program, technical, or similar information
- Examining, administrative, or professional experience with government regulatory bodies requiring review of regulatory material or reports on compliance with regulations
- Experience requiring the ability to determine applicability of laws, rules, and regulations, and to explain legal requirements
- Responsible auditing and accounting work that included analyzing books and records, and preparation of statements and reports in accordance with recognized accounting standards, procedures, and principles
- Adjudication or examination of claims that required the collection and analysis of pertinent data and the preparation of written reports and recommendations on such claims
- Performance of preliminary record inspection, verification and procurement of documents required to establish prima facie cases from courts and law-enforcement agencies, and securing of related information from records of such courts and agencies
- Experience as a teacher of accounting or law in a resident college or university
- Experience described below under "Specialized Experience" for either Investigator or Criminal Investigator
- Any time-equivalent combination of any of the above or comparable types of experience

Specialized Experience

This must have been progressively responsible investigative experience that demonstrated

- Initiative, ingenuity, resourcefulness, and judgment required to collect, assemble, and develop facts and other pertinent data
- The ability to think logically and objectively; to analyze and evaluate facts, evidence, and related information; and to arrive at sound conclusions
- Skill in written and oral reports and presentation of investigative findings in a clear and concise manner

and

- Tact, discretion, and capacity for obtaining the cooperation and confidence of others

For Investigator positions, this may be either investigative or criminal-investigative experience, or comparable experience. For Criminal Investigator positions, this must have been criminal-investigative experience, or comparable experience.

Investigator Positions

Acceptable investigative experience may have been obtained in types of work such as the following:

- Investigations of difficult casualty or insurance claims
- Investigations conducted for a private detective agency that involved responsible fact-finding and reporting on substantial issues
- Newspaper reporting where the major responsibility involved personal investigations of facts pertaining to violations of law
- Investigations in connection with the prosecution or defense of civil or criminal cases
- Investigations for a federal, state, county, or municipal agency
- Investigations of important cases for practicing attorneys; or practice of law involving a substantial amount of investigative work or analysis of issues of fact and law
- Legal experience involving such activities as personal participation in court cases and interviewing of suspects or witnesses
- Investigations concerning compliance with, or violations of, governmental law, rules, and regulations
- Investigations of individuals for character, conduct, suitability, and fitness for employment
- Any of the types of specialized experience described below for Criminal Investigators
- Any time-equivalent combination of the above types or similar types of experience

Criminal-Investigator Positions

Acceptable criminal-investigative experience may have been gained in types of work such as the following:

- Investigative experience as a member of a military-intelligence or criminal-investigative component in any of the branches of the Armed Forces or in any of the various intelligence or investigative branches of the public service, in which the principal duties consisted of the supervision of or the independent conduct of investigations of security, intelligence, or criminal cases; the preparation of comprehensive documented reports; and responsibility for testifying in court
- Investigation of complex casualty or insurance claims that included a substantial number of cases involving suspected crimes or alleged fraud
- Investigation of criminal cases for practicing attorneys requiring the use of recognized investigative methods and techniques

- Experience in the general practice of criminal law that required appearing in court and interviewing suspects and witnesses, or that required a substantial amount of complex criminal investigative work
- Experience as a uniformed law officer where the principal duties (at least 50 percent of the time) were criminal investigations requiring the use of a variety of investigative methods and techniques such as surveillance, assuming an undercover role, and so on. (Investigative experience of this nature that has been acquired on less than a full-time basis will be prorated for credit.)
- Any time-equivalent combination of the above types or similar types of experience

Non-Qualifying Experience

Some types of experience are related to investigative work but are not acceptable as either general or specialized experience for either the position of Investigator or Criminal Investigator. Applicants who offer only these kinds of experience will be disqualified. Experience is not acceptable if:

- It has not afforded training in, or required the application of the knowledge, abilities, and skills described above

or

- It has been acquired in essentially clerical tasks or assignments

Examples of the kinds of experience that are not qualifying are

- Experience in performing the normal duties of policeman, guard, watchman, or private detective assigned principally to the protection of life or property, or similar experience in other kinds of positions
- Experience as a probation or parole officer that did not require pre-sentence investigations, investigations of parolees, objective development of facts, preparation of reports, or appearance in court to defend investigative findings
- The investigation of minor insurance damage claims or of the financial standing of individuals or firms for credit associations or for collection agencies
- Clerical work performed incidental to the adjudication of claims
- Experience generally acquired in such positions as payroll clerk or reviewer, or voucher clerk or reviewer; cash accounting clerk; cashier; teller; time and leave clerk; disbursing clerk; fiscal clerk; administrative clerk; and similar positions
- Experience as an inspector whose principal duties were to examine materials, plant facilities, or equipment to determine whether they conformed to prescribed specifications or standards

Quality of Experience

Length of experience is of less importance than demonstrated success in positions of a responsible nature, and of less importance than the breadth and scope of the pertinent knowledge, skills, and abilities possessed by the applicant and applied by him in the performance of the duties of such positions. Although no additional amount of experience beyond that required for grade GS-11 is required for grades GS-12 through GS-15, applicants for these higher grade levels must have had a progressively higher quality of experience.

For all grades through GS-11, at least six months of the required specialized experience must have been at a level of difficulty and responsibility comparable to that of the next lower grade, or at least one year of the specialized experience must have been at a level of difficulty and responsibility comparable to that of the second lower grade in the federal service. For the GS-12 level and above, at least one year of the specialized experience must have been at a level of difficulty and responsibility comparable to that of the next lower grade in the federal service.

Substitution of Education and Training for Experience

The following may be substituted for a maximum of three years of general experience (for both Investigator positions and Criminal Investigator positions):

- Study successfully completed in an accredited college or university may be substituted at the rate of one year of study for nine months of experience. (Four years of study in a college or university or completion of all requirements for a bachelor's degree qualifies for positions at grade GS-5.)
- Possession of a certificate as a Certified Public Accountant in a state, territory, or the District of Columbia.

Full-time graduate education may be substituted for experience on the following basis:

- One full academic year of graduate education may be substituted for one year of specialized experience for the positions of Investigator and Criminal Investigator. (This amount and kind of education meets all the requirements for both types of positions at grade GS-7.)
- Completion of all requirements for a master's or an equivalent degree, or two full academic years of graduate education in public administration, industrial relations, political science, government, business administration, law enforcement, police administration, criminology, or directly related fields can be substituted for two years of specialized experience for Investigator positions. (This amount and kind of education meets all the requirements for these positions at grade GS-9.)
- Completion of all requirements for a master's or an equivalent degree, or two full academic years of graduate education in law enforcement, police administration, criminology, or directly related fields can be substituted for two years of specialized experience for Criminal Investigator positions. (This amount and kind of education meets all the requirements for these positions at grade GS-9.)

Completion of a total of at least six years of legal and pre-legal education that meets all the requirements for an LL.B. or J.D. degree will provide eligibility in full at grade GS-9 for the positions of Investigator and Criminal Investigator.

Personal Qualities

In addition to meeting all other requirements, applicants for these positions must possess certain personal qualities essential for investigative work. Among these qualities are

- Ability in oral expression
- Poise and self-confidence
- Good personal appearance
- Tact
- Initiative and drive
- Capacity for effective public relations
- Practical intelligence

Written Test

Competitors for positions at the GS-5 and GS-7 levels must pass an appropriate written test. No written test is required for positions at GS-9 and above.

Basis for Rating and Ranking Candidates

Competitors for GS-5 and GS-7 are rated on the basis of the written test and an evaluation of their experience and education.

Competitors for GS-9 and above are rated on the basis of an evaluation of their experience, education, and investigative skills.

Interview

Competitors who pass the written test, as required, and who meet the experience and training requirements may be requested to appear for an interview at the time of consideration for appointment.

Special Physical Requirements

Investigator Positions

Applicants must be physically able to perform efficiently the duties of the position for which application is made. Good distant vision in one eye and the ability to read without strain printed material the size of typewritten characters are required, glasses permitted. Ability to hear the conversational voice, with or without a hearing aid, is required. In most instances, an amputation of arm, hand, leg, or foot will not disqualify an applicant for appointment, although it may be necessary that this condition be compensated by use of satisfactory prosthesis. Applicants must possess emotional and mental stability. Any physical condition that would cause the applicant to be a hazard to himself or to others will disqualify him for appointment.

Criminal Investigator Positions

The duties of the positions require moderate to arduous physical exertion involving walking and standing, the use of firearms, and exposure to inclement weather. Manual dexterity with comparatively free motion of finger, wrist, elbow, shoulder, hip, and knee joints is required. Arms, hands, legs, and feet must be sufficiently intact and functioning in order that applicants may perform the duties satisfactorily. Applicants must possess sufficiently good vision, with or without glasses, in each eye, in order that they may perform the duties satisfactorily. Near vision, glasses permitted, must be acute for the reading of printed material the size of typewritten characters. The ability of applicants to hear the conversational voice and whispered speech without the use of a hearing aid is required. Since the duties of the position are exacting and responsible, and involve activities under trying conditions, applicants must possess emotional and mental stability. Any physical condition that would cause the applicant to be a hazard to himself or to others will disqualify for appointment.

Motor Vehicle Operator Qualifications

For some positions, applicants must possess a valid automobile license at the time of appointment, and must also qualify after appointment for authorization to operate motor vehicles in accordance with applicable civil service regulations and with related requirements of the employing agency.

Age

Investigator Positions

Minimum of 18.

Criminal Investigator Positions

Minimum of 21; not waived for any applicants including those persons entitled to veterans' preference. Maximum entry age under 37; waived only for those already in a federal civilian law-enforcement position.

Evaluation of Experience and Education for Competitive and In-Service Placement Purposes

Education that has been acquired in fields directly or closely related to the positions to be filled should be rated at a higher level than that which has been acquired in less closely or unrelated fields.

Quality levels for rating investigator and criminal investigator experience should be established in accordance with the following guides:

- Experience that has concerned matters involving substantial ramifications or elements of investigative complexity should be rated at a higher quality level than experience that did not involve such ramifications or elements. Ordinarily, investigative complexity can be gauged by such indicators as
  - The size, diversity, and interrelationships of operations and activities investigated
  - The numbers of investigative matters growing out of the original case assignment
  - The numbers, size, and complexity of structure and subsidiary activities of the organizations involved
  - The geographic dispersion of the operations investigated
  - The degree of involvement of other principals
  - The degree of controversy surrounding the case
  - The potential deterrent value in successfully bringing the case to a conclusion
  - The delicacy of the legal issues involved
  - The absence of precedents, and so on
- Experience that has required individual responsibility on the part of the investigator for complete investigations should be rated at a higher quality level than experience that has involved responsibility for a segment or phase of an investigation, or that has involved limited responsibility for a complete investigation.
- Experience that has required the exercise of sound independent decision making and judgment while working under general technical and administrative supervision and direction should be rated at a higher quality level than experience that has been acquired while working under closer supervision.
- Experience that has required the exercise of a high degree of ingenuity, resourcefulness, and creative thinking should be rated at a higher quality level than experience that called for these qualities to a lesser degree.

Rating Procedure

Evaluation of the scope and level of the applicants' knowledge, skills, and abilities is of greater importance than evaluation of length of experience in individual types of positions.

POLICE OFFICER, GS-2/5
DETECTIVE, GS-6/7
SUPERVISORY POLICE OFFICER, GS-5/9
SUPERVISORY DETECTIVE, GS-7/8

Description of Work

Police perform or supervise performance of law-enforcement work involved in the protection of life, property, and the rights of individual citizens. They enforce federal, state, county, and municipal statutes, laws, and ordinances, and agency rules and regulations. They preserve the peace; prevent, detect, and investigate accidents and crimes; arrest violators; and aid citizens in emergency situations.

Experience, Training, and Related Requirements

Candidates for positions at GS-3 and above are required to show experience of the length and nature described below:

Minimum Experience and Training

Grade	Total Experience (Years)
GS-2	None
GS-3	1
GS-4	2
GS-5	3
GS-6	4
GS-7 and above	5

Acceptable Experience

For positions at GS-3, acceptable experience is that which clearly demonstrates that the candidate possesses knowledge of general law-enforcement methods and techniques that could be applied in performing police functions. This experience must have included protecting property, equipment, or materials; and person-to-person relationships in enforcing various rules and regulations.

For positions at GS-4 and above, acceptable experience is that which has given the candidate a broad knowledge of police operations, practices, and techniques. The experience must have included making arrests, protecting life and property, maintaining law and order, investigating accidents, preventing crime, and preserving the peace. Experience of this type normally may be acquired through regular, active service as a member of a federal, state, county, municipal, or local police force or similar organization; or through service as a military police officer in the Armed Forces or Coast Guard.

Quality and Level of Experience

For non-supervisory positions, at least six months of the required experience must have been at a level of difficulty and responsibility comparable to that of the next lower grade, or at least one year of required experience must have been at a level of difficulty and responsibility comparable to that of the second lower grade in the federal service.

Non-Qualifying Experience

Experience as a prison or jail guard, night watchman, or other position that did not provide knowledge and skills in general law-enforcement methods and techniques that could be applied in the performance of police functions will not be considered as acceptable experience.

Substitution of Education and Training for Experience

Successful completion of police recruit training in a large civilian police force, a police academy, or police school may be substituted for the experience requirements at GS-3.

Successful completion of a reserve police training course that included a minimum of 36 hours of actual lecture or training in police-department procedures and methods, and local laws and regulations, and that led to the award of a certificate of proficiency or issuance of a badge, may be substituted for a maximum of six months of the experience required for GS-3.

Successful completion of one year of study in a resident school above high-school level may be substituted in full for the GS-3 requirements, provided each semester of study included three semester hours, or the equivalent, in one or more of the following subjects:

- Police administration
- Police law and evidence
- Police investigation
- Criminology
- Law enforcement
- General law
- Similar subjects pertinent to police work

Successful completion of two years of study in a resident school above high-school level may be substituted in full for the GS-4 requirements, provided each semester of study included three semester hours, or the equivalent, in one or more of the following subjects:

- Police administration
- Police law and evidence
- Police investigation
- Criminology
- Law enforcement
- General law
- Similar subjects pertinent to police work

Successful completion of a full four-year course of study required for a B.S. degree in police science from a resident school above high-school level may be substituted in full for the GS-5 requirements.

Written Test

All candidates for positions in grade GS-2 must take a written test to demonstrate their abilities to understand the written word and to follow oral directions.

Motor Vehicle Operator Qualifications

For positions requiring the operation of a government-owned motor vehicle, candidates must

- Pass a practical road test, driving the appropriate type vehicle supplied by the agency to which the candidate is provisionally certified

- Possess a valid state or territory motor vehicle operator's license or obtain one within 30 days after entry on duty
- Have a satisfactory safe driving record

Basis for Rating and Ranking Candidates

Competitors for all positions are rated on a scale of 100. The basis of rating is as follows:

GS-2—Competitors are rated only on the basis of the written test. They are rated on a scale of 100. A rating of at least 70 must be obtained on the test as a whole.

GS-3 and above—An evaluation of experience and training is performed. Candidates must present evidence of ability to discharge the duties of the position.

Personal Qualities

Candidates, in addition to other qualifications, must demonstrate that they possess traits and characteristics that are important to success in police work. Among these are

- Alertness
- Ability to work in stressful situations
- Ability in oral expression
- Tact
- Integrity
- The capacity for effective public relations
- Practical intelligence
- Good judgment

Age Limits

Persons appointed to police positions must be at least 21 years of age. This requirement may be waived only for veterans. Persons between the ages of 20 and 21 may file applications for examinations. Such persons will be examined, but only veterans may enter on duty before attaining the age of 21 years.

Physical Requirements

Applicants must be physically able to perform efficiently the duties of the position, which are described elsewhere in this standard. For most positions, applicants must have binocular vision correctable to 20/20 (Snellen). Uncorrected vision must test at least 20/70 (Snellen) in each eye. Near vision corrected or uncorrected must be sufficient to read Yaeger Type 2 at 14 inches. However, there may be some positions suitable for persons with good vision in one eye only.

The ability to distinguish basic colors is essential. Ability to hear the conversational voice, without the use of a hearing aid, is required. Persons with an amputation of arm, hand, leg, or foot should not apply. Applicants must possess emotional and mental stability. Any physical condition that would cause the applicant to be a hazard to himself or to others will disqualify for appointment.

CORRECTIONAL OFFICER, GS-6/13

Description of Work

Correctional Officers supervise and perform work concerned with the correctional treatment, supervision, and custody of criminal offenders in correctional institutions or community-based treatment or rehabilitation centers. They have primary responsibility for guiding inmate conduct, supervising work details, carrying out plans for the correctional treatment and modification of attitudes of inmates, instructing and counseling inmates on institutional and personal problems, and generally ensuring the custody, safety, and well-being of inmates. On occasion, Correctional Officers are required to carry firearms.

Experience and Training

Except for the substitution of education provided below, applicants must have had the following kinds and length of experience:

Grade	General Experience (Years)	Specialized Experience (Years)	Total Experience (Years)
GS-6	$3^1/_2$	None	$3^1/_2$
GS-7	$3^1/_2$	1	$4^1/_2$
GS-8	$3^1/_2$	2	$5^1/_2$
GS-9/13	$3^1/_2$	3	$6^1/_2$

Note: When positions are to be filled at grades below the normal GS-6 level, the qualification requirements should be determined by a downward extension of the criteria in this standard—for example, three years of general experience is qualifying for grade GS-5.

General Experience

This is experience, paid or voluntary, full or part time, that demonstrates the applicant's aptitude for acquiring the skills and knowledge needed for correctional work, and in addition, demonstrates the possession of personal attributes important to the effectiveness of correctional officers, such as:

- The ability to meet and deal with people of differing backgrounds and behavioral patterns
- The ability to be persuasive in selling or influencing ideas
- The ability to lead, supervise, and instruct
- A sympathetic attitude toward the welfare of others
- The capacity to adapt to new ideas and changing conditions
- The ability to reason soundly and to think out practical solutions to problems
- The ability to pay attention to detail
- The ability to make decisions and act quickly, particularly under stress
- Poise and self-confidence
- The ability to remain calm during emergency situations

The following types of experience are illustrative of acceptable general experience, providing they meet the above criteria (this list is not intended to be all-inclusive):

- Social casework in a welfare agency
- Classroom teaching or instructing

- Responsible rehabilitation work—for example, in an alcoholic rehabilitation program
- Supervision of planned recreational activities
- Active participation in community action programs
- Employment with a counseling service in interviewing and counseling people
- Management of, or supervising work in, a business or other organization that included personnel-management responsibilities in addition to directing work performance
- Sales work (other than taking and filling orders as in over-the-counter sales)
- Active participation, as an officer or member, in extracurricular activities in college, such as student government, service organizations, college magazines or newspapers, fraternal organizations, and so on

Specialized Experience

This is experience in the correctional custody and supervision, in accordance with modern penological concepts, of inmates of a penal or correctional institution or community-based correctional-treatment facility. This experience must satisfy all of the following requirements:

- Must have included satisfactory completion of a federally operated in-service training course for correctional officers, or completion of a comparable training course covering modern correctional concepts and techniques
- Must have demonstrated the ability to supervise and control inmates in groups of 20 or more, and to make sound decisions in critical circumstances
- Must have shown the capacity to relate successfully to inmates with respect to matters such as close and continuous counseling, singly and in groups
- Must have shown the ability to work independently and to assume responsibility for the correctional custody and supervision of inmate activities; to direct, observe, and correct inmate behavior; and to take precautionary measures to ensure control in situations relatively critical to the security of the institution

In addition:

- For grade GS-8, the applicant must have demonstrated the ability and knowledge necessary to perform difficult post assignments that require the judgment, maturity, and knowledge of inmate behavior developed through experience gained in performing a variety of correctional assignments; to use and to make reports and recommendations based on the use of techniques such as informal counseling, guidance, interview, and observation; and to deal adequately with special problems of correctional custody made difficult by unusual conditions of supervision and control.
- For grade GS-9 nonsupervisory positions, the applicant must have demonstrated the knowledge of, and ability to apply technical treatment and/or counseling skills and techniques acquired through formal classroom and supervised practical training. These skills may have been utilized in a variety of assignments, typically as part of structured treatment or rehabilitation programs under the guidance of professionals in the behavioral sciences or social work.

Quality of Experience

The applicant's record of experience and training must show that he has the ability to perform the duties of the position. In addition:

- For grade GS-6, the applicant must have had at least six months of general experience comparable in difficulty and responsibility to that of the next lower grade, or one year comparable to the second lower grade in the federal service.
- For grades GS-7 through GS-11, at least one year of the specialized experience must have been comparable in difficulty and responsibility to the next lower grade, or two years comparable to the second lower grade in the federal service.
- For grades GS-12 and above, at least one year of the specialized experience must have been comparable in difficulty and responsibility to the next lower grade in the federal service.

Substitution of Education and Training for Experience

To be acceptable as substitution for general or specialized experience, the level and quality of the education and/or training (or of the combined experience and education and/or training) must have equipped the candidate to perform correctional duties at the grade level of the position to be filled.

General Experience

- Two years of study successfully completed in a resident school above high-school level may be substituted for two years of general experience.
- Successful completion of a full four-year course of college study may be substituted for three years of general experience.
- One full semester of graduate study successfully completed in an accredited college or university may be substituted for six months of general experience and is fully qualifying for grade GS-6.

At any grade, post–high school education may be partially substituted for required experience at the rates of substitution indicated above.

Specialized Experience

- One full semester of graduate study in correctional administration, criminology, penology, sociology, or social work successfully completed in an accredited college or university may be substituted for six months of specialized experience, up to a total of 18 months.

Credit for appropriate education and training other than that outlined above (such as manpower development programs, "New Careers" programs, rehabilitated offender programs, or in-service training programs) will be granted depending on the nature, extent, and applicability of the training in relation to the position to be filled.

Selective Placement

Additional knowledge and abilities may be required for some positions because of the concentration of inmates in distinct age, ethnic, cultural, or other specific groups in certain institutions. It is desirable for these institutions to have sufficient numbers of correctional officers who can successfully relate to the members of these groups. Selective placement consideration may be given to applicants having a thorough knowledge and understanding of the customs, language patterns, and problems of specific groups of inmates.

Basis for Rating and Ranking Candidates

Applicants for all grades will be rated on the basis of an evaluation and appraisal of experience, education, and training.

Employment Interview

The personal qualities and characteristics of the applicant are the most critical of all the requirements for Correctional Officer positions. He must be willing to perform arduous and prolonged duties on any of the three shifts. He must possess certain personal qualities in order to effectively relate to inmates in a correctional setting. These qualities include the following:

- Empathy
- Objectivity
- Perceptiveness
- Resourcefulness
- Adaptability and flexibility
- Stability
- Maturity

Before appointment, candidates may be required to appear before a panel of specialists in correctional administration for an employment interview. The interview will also serve to acquaint the applicant with further details of, and the environment surrounding, the position. A determination by the panel that a person who is otherwise qualified does not possess such personal characteristics to the required degree may result in removal of his application from further consideration. Notice will be given in advance of the date and place of the interview.

Physical Requirements

The duties of these positions involve unusual mental and nervous pressure and require arduous physical exertion involving prolonged walking and standing, restraining prisoners in emergencies, and participating in escape hunts. Applicants must be physically capable of performing efficiently the duties of the position, be free from such defects or diseases as may constitute employment hazards to themselves or others, and have no deformities, disfigurements, or abnormalities that tend to be conspicuous. Persons having remediable defects or curable diseases, and who are otherwise qualified, will be admitted to the examination but must submit proof, during the time the list of eligible competitors exists, that the defects or diseases have been remedied or cured before they may be considered for appointment.

No height or weight limits are specified, but weight must be in proportion to height. Male applicants under 66 inches and female applicants under 63 inches in height will be especially evaluated for stamina and vigor.

Vision

Uncorrected vision must be no less than 20/100 (Snellen) in each eye, capable of full correction to 20/30 (Snellen) in each eye, provided that defective vision is not due to active or progressive organic disease.

Hearing

Hearing in each ear must be normal, that is, 15/15 in each ear by the whispered voice test. Hearing aids are not acceptable.

General

The following conditions will disqualify an applicant from appointment:

- Hernia (with or without truss)
- Organic heart disease (whether or not compensated)
- Severe varicose veins
- Serious deformities or disabilities of extremities (including weak feet)
- Chronic constitutional disease
- Marked abnormality of speech
- Facial disfigurement
              or
- Other serious physical defect or disease

Disease of the nervous system or history or presence of mental disease or emotional instability may disqualify an applicant for appointment. Before entrance on duty, appointees will be given, without expense to themselves, a physical examination by a federal medical officer and will be rejected if they do not meet the standards specified above. Persons who are offered appointment must pay their own expenses in reporting for duty. Any person reporting for duty at the place of assignment and found ineligible because of physical defects cannot be appointed, and no part of his expense for reporting and returning home can be borne by the government.

Age

At time of appointment, applicants must not have reached their 37th birthday unless they have previously served in a federal civilian law-enforcement position.

Professional Positions

PARALEGAL SPECIALIST, GS-5 AND ABOVE

Description of Work

Paralegal Specialist positions involve such activities as

- Legal research; analyzing legal decisions, opinions, rulings, memoranda, and other legal material; selecting principles of law; and preparing digests of the points of law involved
- Selecting, assembling, summarizing, and compiling substantive information on statutes, treaties, contracts, other legal instruments, and specific legal subjects
- Case preparation for civil litigation, criminal law proceedings, or agency hearings, including the collection, analysis, and evaluation of evidence—for example, as to fraud and fraudulent and other irregular activities or violations of laws
- Analyzing facts and legal questions presented by personnel administering specific federal laws; answering the questions where they have been settled by interpretations of applicable legal provisions, regulations, precedents, and agency policy; and in some instances preparing informative and instructional material for general use
- Adjudicating applications or cases on the basis of pertinent laws, regulations, policies, and precedent decisions

or

- Performing other paralegal duties requiring discretion and independent judgment in the application of specialized knowledge of particular laws, regulations, precedents, or agency practices based thereon.

These duties may or may not be performed under the direction of a lawyer.

Experience and Training Requirements

Except for the substitution of education provided for below, candidates must have had both general and specialized experience as follows:

Grade	General Experience (Years)	Specialized Experience (Years)	Total Experience (Years)
GS-5	3	None	3
GS-7	3	1	4
GS-9	3	2	5
GS-11 and above	3	3	6

General Experience

This is progressively responsible experience that demonstrated the ability to explain, apply, or interpret rules, regulations, procedures, policies, precedents, or other kinds of criteria. Such experience may have been gained in administrative, professional, investigative, technical, high-level clerical, or other responsible work.

Specialized Experience

This is legal, quasi-legal, paralegal, legal technician, or related work that demonstrated:

- The ability to evaluate pertinent facts and evidence
- The ability to interpret and apply laws, rules, regulations, and precedents
- Skill and judgment in the analysis of cases
- The ability to communicate effectively orally and in writing
- As required, the ability to deal effectively with individuals and groups
- As required, knowledge of the pertinent subject area

Qualifying specialized experience may have been acquired in positions that involved, for example:

- Preparation, development, examination, review, or authorization of action on claims in accordance with applicable laws, rules, regulations, precedents, policies, office practices, and established procedures
- Examination and/or preparation of contracts, legal instruments, or other documents to ensure completeness of information and conformance to pertinent laws, rules, regulations, precedents, and office requirements that has required the application of a specialized knowledge of particular laws, or of regulations, precedents, or practices based thereon
- Analysis of legal decisions, opinions, rulings, memoranda, and other legal material and preparation of digests of the points of law involved for the internal use of the agency
- Interpretation and application of laws and related regulations in determining individual or agency responsibility

- Selection, compilation, and summarization of substantive information on statutes, treaties, and specific legal subjects for the use of others
- Conduct of hearings or adjudication of appeals arising under statute or regulations of a government agency
- Investigation and analysis of evidence of alleged or suspected violations of laws or regulations

Quality of Experience

The candidate's record of experience and training must show the ability to perform the duties of the position. For positions at grades GS-11 and below, at least six months of the required specialized experience must have been at a level of difficulty and responsibility equivalent to that of the next lower grade, or one year of such experience at a level equivalent to the second lower grade in the federal service. For positions at grades GS-12 and above, at least one year of the required specialized experience must have been at a level equivalent to the next lower grade in the federal service.

Substitution of Education for Experience

Successful completion of a full four-year course in an accredited college or university leading to a bachelor's degree may be substituted for three years of general experience. Such education successfully completed in a residence school above high-school level may be substituted at the rate of one academic year of study for nine months of experience, up to a maximum of four years of study for three years of general experience.

Completion of all requirements for an LL.B., J.D., or higher degree from a recognized law school, including at least six full years of resident college work, will meet the requirements for grade GS-9.

Successful completion of one full academic year of study in a paralegal or legal curriculum may be substituted for one year of specialized experience required for grades GS-7 and above; less than one full year of study will be credited on a pro-rata basis.

Written Test

Candidates for competitive appointment to grades GS-5 and GS-7 must pass an appropriate written test. In addition, the test may *not* be used in evaluating or ranking eligible employees unless the test is approved for this purpose by the Office of Personnel Management.

Basis for Rating and Ranking Candidates

Competitors for all positions are rated on a scale of 100. Rankings are made:

For competitive appointment at grades 5 and 7—On the basis of the written test

For competitive appointments above GS-7—On the basis of the extent and quality of experience and training relevant to the duties of the position

Special Physical Requirements

The ability to read without strain printed material the size of typewritten characters is required, corrective lenses permitted. The ability to speak without impediment may be required for some positions. The ability to hear the conversational voice, with or without a hearing aid, is required for most positions; however, some positions may be suitable for the deaf.

STATISTICIAN, GS-5
STATISTICIAN (APPROPRIATE SUBJECT-MATTER SPECIALIZATION), GS-7/15
SURVEY STATISTICIAN, GS-7/15

Description of Work

Statisticians do professional work or provide professional consultation requiring the application of statistical theory and technique in the collection, compilation, analysis, and interpretation of quantitative information in a variety of subject-matter fields, including the biological, social, and physical sciences; engineering; agriculture; and administration.

Statisticians (appropriate subject-matter specialization) are primarily concerned with the use of statistical theory, techniques, and methods to determine meaningful relationships or to measure the significance of quantified information in a particular subject-matter field—for example, biology, demography, engineering, economics, and so on.

Survey Statisticians are concerned with the application of statistical theory and technique to the planning, organization, and operation of programs for collecting, verifying, adjusting, processing, summarizing, and presenting information expressed numerically.

Basic Requirements for All Grades

Applicants for all grades must have successfully completed one of the following, A or B:

A. A full four-year course leading to a bachelor's degree in an accredited college or university that has included 15 semester hours in statistics (or in mathematics and statistics, provided at least six semester hours are in statistics) and nine additional hours in one of the following:
   - The physical or biological sciences
   - Medicine
   - Education or engineering
   - The social sciences, including demography, history, economics, social welfare, geography, international relations, social or cultural anthropology, health sociology, political science, public administration, psychology, and so on

   Credit toward meeting statistical course requirements should be given for courses in which 50 percent of the course content appears to be statistical method.

B. Courses given in A above, plus additional appropriate experience or education that, when combined with these courses, totals four years of education and experience and gives the applicant a technical knowledge comparable to that which would have been acquired through successful completion of a full four-year course.

   The experience offered in combination with specified educational courses to meet the requirements specified in paragraph B above should include evidence of professional statistical work such as the following:

- Sampling
- Collecting, computing, and analyzing statistical data

- Applying known statistical techniques to data such as measurement of central tendency, dispersion, skewness, sampling error, simple and multiple correlation, analysis of variance, and tests of significance

Without other indication of professional statistical experience, work in the processing of numerical or quantified information by other than statistical methods is not considered appropriate qualifying experience.

For positions involving highly technical research, development, or similar complex scientific functions, selection may be restricted to eligibles who show the successful completion of a full college course in the appropriate field as designated above.

The basic requirements that apply to all grades are fully qualifying for grade GS-5.

Additional Experience and Training Requirements

Candidates for grades GS-7 and above must have had either professional experience or graduate education (or an equivalent combination of both) in addition to meeting the basic requirements. Such professional experience or graduate education must have been in, or directly related to, statistics or an appropriate subject-matter field. For statistician positions at GS-9 and above in one of the specializations listed below, the experience or education must have provided specialized knowledge of the subject-matter field:

- Agriculture
- Biology
- Health
- Medicine
- Engineering
- Social science
- Operations and administration, including logistics
- Economics
- Demography
- Education
- Physical science

Experience

In addition to the basic requirements, the following amounts of professional experience in the appropriate subject-matter fields are required for grades GS-7 and above:

Grade	Minimum Amount of Professional Experience in Appropriate Subject-Matter Fields (Years)
GS-7	1
GS-9	2
GS-11 and above	3

For grades GS-11 and below, at least six months of the required experience must have been at the level of difficulty comparable to that of the next lower grade, or one year comparable to the second lower grade, in the federal service. For grades GS-12 and above, at least one year of the required experience must have been at a level of difficulty comparable to that of the next lower grade in the federal service.

Education

In addition to the basic requirements, the following amounts or levels of education in the appropriate subject-matter fields are qualifying for grades GS-7 and above, as shown:

GS-7—One full academic year of graduate education.

GS-9—Completion of all requirements for a master's or equivalent degree, or two full academic years of graduate education

GS-11— Completion of all requirements for a doctoral degree (Ph.D. or equivalent) or three full academic years of graduate education

GS-11 (analytical positions)—Completion of all requirements for a master's or an equivalent degree for which at least two years of graduate study is required when

- The position involves primarily analytical work of a creative or advanced scientific nature
- The knowledge required for the work is *typically and preferably* acquired through graduate study
- The work is of such character that the academic preparation will equip the candidate to perform fully the professional work at the GS-11 level after a short orientation period

To be acceptable, the graduate education must have included a course in statistical or related theory for which knowledge of calculus is required.

Combinations of Professional Experience and Graduate Education

Equivalent combinations of professional experience and graduate education of the types described above are acceptable at each grade.

Alternate Requirements

Superior academic achievement at the baccalaureate level or one year of student trainee experience is qualifying at grade GS-7. A combination of superior academic achievement at the baccalaureate level and one year of appropriate professional experience is qualifying at grade GS-9.

Basis for Rating and Ranking Candidates

No written test is required. Applicants' qualifications will be rated on a scale of 100 and will be evaluated on the basis of their education, training, and experience as shown in the application, and on corroborative evidence obtained by the Office of Personnel Management.

LIBRARIAN
ADMINISTRATIVE LIBRARIAN
SUPERVISORY LIBRARIAN
LIBRARY DIRECTOR (WITH SPECIALIZATIONS AS APPROPRIATE), GRADES GS-7/15
LIBRARIAN TRAINEE (SPECIAL PROVISION AT GS-5)

Description of Work

Positions involve work that primarily requires a full professional knowledge of the theories, principles, and techniques of librarianship. An inherent requirement of these positions is knowledge of literature resources. Such work is concerned with the collection, organization, preservation, and retrieval of recorded knowledge in printed, written, audio-visual, film, wax, near-print methods, magnetic tape, or other media. Typical library functions include one or more of the following:

- Selection
- Acquisition
- Cataloging and classification of materials
- Bibliographic and readers' advisory services
- Reference and literature searching services
- Library management and systems planning
- The development and strengthening of library services

Some positions may involve work in connection with the development of information-retrieval systems.

Specializations

Since many libraries are highly specialized, the work often lies chiefly in one subject-matter field, or closely related subject areas. To serve subject specialists who are the principal users of these libraries, some librarians require knowledge of a specialized subject or field of endeavor. Such subject-matter knowledge typically covers a broad field, rather than a deep subject knowledge and competence related to a specific discipline or a full knowledge of the state of the art. Because materials in libraries are often in foreign languages, some librarians also must have a proficient knowledge of one or more foreign languages.

To provide qualified personnel for librarian positions requiring knowledge of a subject-matter field and/or proficient knowledge of several foreign languages, the following specializations are authorized:

Subject-Matter Specializations

- Biological sciences
- Medical sciences
- Physical sciences
- Social sciences
- Business and industry
- Engineering

- Education
- Fine arts
- Humanities
- Law
- Music

Foreign-Language Specializations

- Germanic
- Oriental
- Romance
- Slavic
- Arabic

Experience and Education Requirements

All Librarians must meet the requirements for professional education in library science or possess equivalent experience as shown in IA, IB, IC or IIA, below. The usual way of entering the profession is to qualify at grade GS-9 on the basis of a master's degree in library science. However, it is possible to qualify for entrance at the GS-7 level on other bases as indicated.

For Librarian (appropriate specialization) positions, all candidates must also meet requirements that are directly related to the subject matter or language of the specialization. These requirements are in addition to the basic professional library science requirements that apply to all positions. However, these requirements may be included within, or may be supplemental to, those specified for all positions at GS-7 and GS-9.

I. Requirements for Librarian Positions, GS-7

To qualify for all Librarian GS-7 positions, the applicant must meet the requirements specified in paragraphs A, B, or C below. (Note: Applicants who qualify under provisions of paragraphs A or B will not be required to take a subject-matter test in library science.)

A. Completion of one full academic year of graduate study in library science in an accredited college or university, in addition to completion of all work required for a bachelor's degree

or

B. Completion of all requirements for a "5th-year" bachelor's degree in library science. In addition, the applicant must have had at least one year of library experience that included the performance of duties in one or more functional areas of librarianship at the GS-5 or higher grade level

or

C. A total, in some combination, of not less than five years of college-level education, training, and/or experience. To qualify on this basis, the applicant must establish conclusively that the education, training, and/or experience has provided a knowledge and understanding of the theories, principles, and techniques of professional librarianship; a knowledge of literature resources; and the knowledge and abilities essential for providing effective library services. Under this provision:

   1. Applicants must pass a subject-matter test in library science.
   2. If the applicant qualifies on the basis of a college-level education, he must have had at least one year of library experience comparable in difficulty and responsibility to that of a GS-5 (or higher level) library technician, technical information specialist, or subject-matter specialist performing library services.

3. If the applicant qualifies on the basis of experience alone, with no college-level education or training, he must have had at least two years of library experience comparable in difficulty and responsibility to that of a GS-5 (or higher level) library technician.

4. The applicant may qualify under any time and quality equivalent combinations of the requirements shown in paragraphs 2 and 3.

5. Specialized training—for example, training at a school for library technicians or through "in-house" courses—will be allowed appropriate credit depending upon its applicability and extent.

To qualify for Librarian (Appropriate Specialization) positions GS-7, the applicant must also possess specialized knowledge of a subject-matter field and/or proficiency in one or more foreign languages that are directly related to the positions being filled. When such knowledge is required by the position, the applicant's education or experience must have included or been supplemented by the requirements specified in one of the paragraphs below:

A. A full four-year course of study in an accredited college or university that meets all academic requirements for a bachelor's degree, and also

1. Has included at least 24 semester hour credits in the specialized field for which the applicant is being considered

or

2. Has included any combination of subjects with at least 15 semester hour credits in a major subject that is especially applicable to the position for which the applicant is being considered

or

B. Completion of at least 24 semester hours of legal study in an accredited law school for positions primarily concerned with providing library services in law or legislative reference.

or

C. Four years of successful and pertinent experience of such nature and level to provide a knowledge of the basic principles, theories, practices, techniques, terminology, and expressions of the appropriate discipline or subject-matter field; an understanding of the standard methods, procedures, and techniques of research and analysis in the subject-matter field; the ability to acquire additional information about the field and related fields; and some knowledge of literature resources in the field.

D. Any time-equivalent combination of experience as described in item C, with education as described in item 1 or 2 above.

E. Demonstrated ability as shown by education or experience to read or translate information from one or more foreign languages into English.

II. Requirements for Librarian Positions, GS-9

To qualify for all Librarian GS-9 positions, the applicant must meet the requirements specified below

A. Completion of all requirements for a master's degree or two full academic years of graduate study in library science, in an accredited college or university, meets all requirements for Librarian positions, GS-9.

B. In addition to meeting one of the requirements for GS-7 (A, B, or C), candidates must have had professional *or* advanced experience *or* graduate study as follows:

1. One year of professional experience in librarianship that included the performance, supervision, or administration of one or more major functional areas of librarianship. Some positions are highly specialized in one functional area, and may require that the advanced experience be in the appropriate function to qualify at these higher grade levels.

2. One year of professional or advanced experience in the subject matter or language that has provided the applicant with the professional, technical, linguistic, or other specialized knowledge and abilities required by the particular position for which he is being considered.

3. Graduate education in a subject-matter field that is especially applicable to the position, and provides the knowledge required to perform the duties of the position, as follows:

- Completion of all requirements for a master's degree

or

- Two full academic years of graduate education.

III. Requirements for Librarian Positions, GS-11 and Above

To qualify for all Librarian GS-11 (and above) positions, the applicant must meet the requirements specified below:

A. In addition to meeting the requirements for GS-9 (either A or B), candidates must have had either:

1. One year of professional experience in librarianship

or

2. One year of professional or advanced experience in a subject-matter or language area appropriate to the position

B. Completion of all the requirements for a doctoral degree (or equivalent) or three full academic years of graduate education in library science

C. In addition to possessing professional education in library science (or equivalent experience) as required for entrance at grades GS-7 or GS-9, candidates must have completed graduate study in a subject matter or language area appropriate to the position as follows:

1. All requirements for a doctoral degree (Ph.D. or equivalent)

or

2. Three full academic years of graduate education

IV. Combinations of Professional Experience and Graduate Education

Equivalent combinations of professional experience and graduate education of the types described above are acceptable at each grade.

Quality of Experience

For grades GS-11 and below, at least six months of the required experience must have been at the level of difficulty comparable to that of the next lower grade, or one year comparable to the second lower grade, in the federal service. For grades GS-12 and above, at least one year of the required experience must have been at a level of difficulty comparable to that of the next lower grade in the federal service.

Supervisory and Administrative Positions

For positions concerned with administration, management, or direction of library programs, candidates must meet all other requirements for the particular grade and also show that they possess the required administrative and/or managerial ability to perform successfully the duties of such positions. Education, training, or experience of the candidate should demonstrate, for example

- The ability to manage or direct a library, group of libraries, or library system
- The ability to plan, organize, and direct the development and execution of library programs, policies, and procedures
- The ability to plan or conduct management studies, public relations, and educational activities
- The ability to plan, develop, and carry out administrative activities of the library or library system concerned with budget and finance, personnel, plant and equipment, and so on

Basis for Rating and Ranking Candidates

All competitors who meet the education and experience requirements for GS-7 and above, and who pass the written test in library science when required, will be rated based upon an evaluation of their experience and training in library work. The library science written test, when required, will be used for qualification purposes only.

Evaluating Experience and Training

In evaluating experience and training, consideration will be given to the type, level, and scope of experience relating directly to the particular position or positions under consideration, as indicated in the application, and to any additional pertinent information obtained from references, employees, associates, and colleagues.

Non-Qualifying Experience and Training

No credit will be given toward meeting the experience requirements for positions in this series for work in the following situations:

- Work with collections of fiction, recreational, or other reading material where no formal cataloging or classification of material is performed
- Experience in wholesale or retail bookstores, circulating fiction and club libraries, or hospital record departments
- Experience as a library page, library attendant, or clerical worker, even though the duties included such work as charging and discharging books or typing catalog cards or orders for books and materials
- Non-professional work in a library on a part-time or volunteer basis
- Training in the particular use of library facilities such as is given in orientation courses to college freshmen

Written Test

Applicants for all grades who have a master's degree or the required education in library science, or have a 5th-year bachelor's degree in library science, will *not* be required to take a written test.

Applicants for all grades who qualify on the basis of experience alone or a combination of experience and education must pass a subject-matter test in library science. This written test is designed to measure the candidate's knowledge of the fundamentals underlying professional library science and his understanding of its methods and techniques and their applications to effective library science. Questions will be asked on facts, principles, applications, tools, practices, and theory of professional librarianship as found in a variety of libraries.

Special Provisions for All Librarian Positions

At GS-9 and above, Librarian positions concerned with acquisition, cataloging, or reference work are sometimes highly specialized. In filling such positions, consideration may be limited to those eligibles who have had experience in the appropriate specialization at a qualifying level of difficulty.

Special Provision for Filling Positions of Librarian (Trainee), GS-5

This is a special provision that may be used when there is a shortage of candidates who are fully qualified for GS-7 level Librarian or Librarian (appropriate specialization) positions. This provision is included because of the reported dearth of fully qualified librarians. It is intended for use in those situations where the Librarian (trainee) can be expected to complete his/her education or training in library science within a reasonable period of time, and thus meet requirements for librarian positions at the GS-7 level.

Under this provision, applicants for positions of Librarian (trainee), GS-5 must meet the following requirements:

- Completion of a full four-year course of study in an accredited college or university that meets all academic requirements for a bachelor's degree

or

- Equivalent experience

Qualification of candidates under this provision is demonstrated by eligibility on a civil service register, or an appropriate subject-matter register. Appointing officers may request certification of eligible candidates with major study in a subject-matter field that is considered appropriate for the position being filled.

Individuals hired as Librarian (trainee), GS-5, may not be employed or promoted to a position of Librarian GS-7 until they fully meet the requirement specified for GS-7 Librarian positions.

SOCIAL WORKER GS-7/15
SOCIAL, WORK PROGRAM SPECIALIST, GS-9/15

Description of Work

Social Workers perform professional social work involved in carrying out agency programs of service to people with whom they are concerned, such as patients in agency-operated hospitals and clinics, wards of child welfare agencies and their families, inmates of correctional institutions, and so on.

Most positions involve direct professional services to individuals. Some positions also include working with clients in groups when appropriate, and/or working with and advising members of the community in the development of local resources to prevent or alleviate social problems. Some positions are primarily concerned with supervision of social work staff and/or students, with directing programs of social work, or with researching to improve social-work practice.

Social Work Program Specialists advise on, develop, evaluate, and promote social-welfare programs and services administered by state agencies and other public and non-profit organizations and institutions. More specifically, they develop and issue material on new knowledge; set minimum standards for the administration and operation of programs; evaluate the soundness and effectiveness of program administration and operation; and work with state, community, and professional leaders who are interested in strengthening service programs, and so on.

Minimum Education Requirement

Applicants must have successfully completed a course of study in an accredited school of social work that has fulfilled all of the requirements for the master's degree in social work. The recognized accrediting association in the field is the Council on Social Work Education.

Additional Training and Experience Requirements

GS-7—No additional training or experience needed.

GS-9—In addition to meeting the requirements for grade GS-7, applicants must have successfully completed one of the following:

- Related practice training in professional social work during field placement as part of the graduate study
- At least one year of professional social-work experience under professional supervision

GS-11—In addition to meeting the requirements for grade GS-9, applicants must have had a minimum of one year of professional social-work experience under professional supervision. Experience must have demonstrated the ability to perform advanced assignments independently.

GS-12–15—In addition to meeting the requirements for GS-11, applicants must have had a minimum of one additional year of professional social-work experience that has demonstrated broad knowledge of the field of social work and superior skill and judgment in professional practice.

For program specialist positions—The experience must have included one or, in some cases, a combination of two or more functions, such as program planning, program development, program evaluation, consultation, and cooperative community relationships in an agency providing social work service to families, children, or adults

or

Supervisory, administrative, or consultative work in a public or voluntary welfare or health agency with an organized social-work program. For positions with staff-development responsibilities, the required experience must have included experience in planning or conducting a social work education or staff development program in a health or welfare agency, or teaching in an accredited school of social work.

Quality of Experience and Training

The number of years of experience required for any grade level represents the minimum amount of time necessary to qualify for the appropriate position, but length of time is not of itself qualifying. The applicant's work experience must also have been of a quality and scope sufficient to enable him to perform satisfactorily assignments typical of the grade level for which he is being considered. The evaluation of the applicant's performance and potentialities will be based upon information acquired through confidential inquiry of his supervisors and others familiar with the nature and quality of his work.

For positions at grade GS-9, at least one year of experience must have been at a level comparable in scope and difficulty to that of grade GS-7 in the federal service. For grade GS-11, at least one year of the required experience must have been comparable in scope and difficulty to that of GS-9. For GS-12 and above, at least one year must have been comparable in scope and difficulty to that of the next lower grade.

Non-Qualifying Experience

Except for the substitution of supervised field training completed as part of an educational curriculum (see above), experience acquired prior to completion of all requirements for the master's degree is not considered as qualifying.

An applicant who has been out of social work practice for 10 or more years may be asked to provide additional evidence that his qualifications fully meet the requirements of competence to practice in terms of current professional knowledge and standards of practice.

Qualification Inquiries

For all grades of these positions, confidential inquiries, including contacts with the applicant's supervisors and associates or with other persons familiar with his qualifications, may be made to obtain further information about qualifications, character, and suitability for these positions.

Selective Placement

Some positions will require the background and approach of a particular method of practice. For such positions, consideration may be restricted to eligibles who possess the pertinent experience and knowledge required to perform the duties of the positions covered in this occupation. At grade GS-11 and above, there are some positions that require experience specifically related to such fields of practice as programs of service to medical and psychiatric patients in hospitals and clinics, programs of rehabilitation for inmates of correctional institutions, or programs for the protection of children.

For some program specialist positions, some of the qualifying experience must have provided a knowledge of specific aspects of an agency program such as foster care, work with the aging, services to unmarried mothers, community planning, volunteer services, and so on.

Other positions may require experience that has provided a knowledge of one or more specific areas of child welfare, such as adoptions, foster family care, group care, day care, services to children in their own homes, homemaker service, services for mentally retarded and emotionally disturbed children, and so on.

Some positions in medical programs require experience that has provided knowledge of health and medical-care social services for mothers and children.

Agencies requesting selective referrals must show the connection between the kind of training or experience on which they wish to base selective consideration and the duties of the position to be filled.

Driver's License

For certain positions, applicants may be required to have a driver's license.

Written Test

No written test is required. Applicants are rated on a scale of 100 on the basis of education, experience, training, and personal qualifications in relation to the requirements of the specific position for which they are being considered. Ratings will be based upon competitors' statements in their applications and upon any additional evidence that may be secured through qualification inquiries or similar means.

Special Physical Requirements

There may be a few positions in larger offices where the casework load would permit the employment of a blind person in a restricted area of activity.

Health-Care Positions

PHYSICIAN'S ASSISTANT, GS-7/11

Description of Work

Physician's Assistants help physicians by providing diagnostic and therapeutic medical care and services under the physician's supervision. The work requires knowledge of specific observation and examination procedures, and the ability to perform designated diagnostic and therapeutic tasks. The work does not include the full scope of interpretation of medical findings requiring the professional background of the licensed physician.

In clinics or during hospital rounds, Physician's Assistants assist in the observation and evaluation of patients by performing such duties as taking case histories, conducting physical examinations, and ordering laboratory studies. As directed by a physician, Physician's Assistants carry out special procedures such as applying and removing casts, performing lumbar punctures, or suturing minor lacerations.

Experience, Training, and Related Requirements

Requirements for GS-7

Candidates for positions at GS-7 must meet the following requirements:

A. A broad background of knowledge of the medical environment, practices, and procedures such as would be acquired by a bachelor's degree in a health care occupation such as nursing, medical technology, or physical therapy or by three years of responsible and progressive health care experience such as medical corpsman, nursing assistant, or medical technician

and

B. Successful completion of a course of study of at least 12 months, including clinical training or preceptorship, specifically designed for professional-caliber physician's assistants.

The course of study or training must be approved by a nationally recognized professional medical body such as the American Medical Association or the Association of American Medical Colleges, or by a panel of physicians established by a federal agency for this purpose.

Requirements for GS-9 and GS-11

In addition to the requirements for GS-7, the following amounts of pertinent professional-caliber experience comparable to the work of a physician's assistant are required for grades GS-9 and GS-11:

Grade	Minimum Amount of Experience (Years)
GS-9	1
GS-11	2

The required education, training, and experience must have demonstrated the ability to perform professional-caliber medical work as a physician's assistant with minimal supervision, including the exercise of a degree of judgment in integrating and interpreting diagnostic findings and in determining the need for referral to a physician.

For all grades, at least six months of the required experience must have been at the level of difficulty comparable to that of the next lower grade, or one year comparable to the second lower grade, in the federal service.

Acceptance of Professional Medical Education

Candidates who have completed three full years of a curriculum in an accredited medical school leading to the doctor of medicine or doctor of osteopathy degree may be rated eligible at GS-9.

Candidates who have completed the requirements for the degree of doctor of medicine or osteopathy but who lack licensure to practice medicine in the United States may be rated eligible at GS-11.

Selective Placement Factors

Some positions demand specific competence in a particular specialty. For such positions, consideration may be limited to those candidates whose records show evidence of the required knowledge, abilities, skills, and personal characteristics.

Basis for Rating and Ranking Candidates

Ratings are based upon candidates' statements in their applications and all available evidence concerning the quality and scope of their knowledge and ability including the candidate's education, experience, training, avocations, and personal characteristics.

Required Knowledge and Abilities

Candidates are rated on the degree to which they possess the knowledge and abilities of the kinds listed below, as appropriate to the grade level:

- The ability to identify a medical problem and determine appropriate action to meet the problem, including referral to a physician
- Knowledge and understanding of the environment, principles, ethics, and special human relationships in the field of medicine
- Knowledge of the medical, biological, and physical sciences related to the applicable area of medicine
- Knowledge of and the ability to perform specified diagnostic and therapeutic practices and procedures
- The ability to work responsibly with physicians and other members of the medical team, and to deal effectively with patients
- The ability to communicate effectively, both orally and in writing

NON-SUPERVISORY NON-PROFESSIONAL
NURSING CARE POSITIONS, GS-1/6
NURSING AIDE
NURSING ASSISTANT
OPERATING ROOM NURSING ASSISTANT
PSYCHIATRIC NURSING ASSISTANT

Description of Work

Nursing Aides, under close supervision, perform simple and repetitive personal- and nursing-care procedures. Nursing Aide positions are normally established for training purposes.

Nursing Assistants receive on-the-job training in nursing care that requires some knowledge of human body functions and behavior for the purpose of providing personal nursing care, support duties for diagnostic procedures, technical treatment procedures, patient charting, and patient teaching.

Operating Room Nursing Assistants assist registered nurses and surgeons in a variety of operating- and delivery-room activities. They position and drape patients, ensure proper lighting, pass instruments and materials, maintain sterile conditions, assist in sponge and needle counts, and dispose of contaminated materials.

Psychiatric Nursing Assistants give general nursing care, observe and report changes in behavior, and provide reassurance and technical support to mentally ill patients.

Experience, Training, and Related Requirements

Except for the substitutions provided for in subsequent sections, candidates must have had qualifying experience in the amounts shown in the following table:

MINIMUM AMOUNTS OF EXPERIENCE

Grade	General Experience (Years)	Specialized Experience (Years)	Total Experience (Years)
GS-1	none	none	none*
GS-2	1/2	none	1/2
GS-3	1	none	1
GS-4	1 1/2	1/2	2
GS-5	2	1	3
GS-6	2	2	4

*It should be noted that for grade GS-1, no experience, training, or education is required. No written test is required. Candidates must be willing to do personal- and nursing-care work and show evidence of likelihood of success in assignments.

General Experience

This is experience that has demonstrated the ability:

- To learn and perform nursing care duties
- To deal successfully with people
        and
- To be adaptable to the work situation

Specialized Experience

This is experience in non-professional nursing-care work in a hospital, outpatient clinic, nursing home, or other supervised medical, nursing, or patient-care facility. Illustrative examples of nursing-care work follow:

- Caring for mentally ill patients, including observing, recording, and reporting changes in their behavior
- Providing reassurance and encouragement to mentally ill patients
- Assisting surgeons and registered nurses in operating-room activities, including passing instruments, maintaining sterile conditions, and draping and positioning patients
- Providing pre- and post-operative care
- Setting up and operating special medical equipment and apparatus

Candidates are not required to be proficient in all tasks listed above. However, their experience, education, and training must clearly show that they possess the skills and knowledge required to perform the work of the job at the grade level for which application is made. As a minimum, the candidate must show

A. A practical knowledge of
   1. Human body structure
   2. Sterile techniques and procedures
                    and
   3. How to meet, deal, and work with medical, surgical, and psychiatric patients
                    and
B. Knowledge of, and skill in, the performance of personal- and nursing-care procedures and techniques pertinent to the specialized area and grade for which application is made

Quality and Level of Experience

Applicants must demonstrate progressively responsible experience of a scope, quality, and degree such as to have equipped them with the ability to perform duties at the grade level of the position for which application is made. Typically, this is demonstrated by accomplishment of assignments of the difficulty and responsibility described in the position classification standard used to evaluate positions at the next lower grade in the normal line of promotion to the position being filled.

Substitution of Education and Training for Experience

Successfully completed education and training of acceptable type and quality may be substituted for experience requirements as specified below:

- Graduation from a high school or its equivalent may be substituted in full for the experience requirements at the GS-2 level. (High-school education or its equivalent may not be substituted for any part of the experience requirements for GS-3 and above.)
- Successful completion of a two-year associate-degree program in an accredited community college, junior college, or college or university in a field of study appropriate to the specialization of the position being filled, psychiatric technician, or operating-room technician may be substituted for the two years of experience required for GS-4.
- Partial completion of professional or practical nurse training in a school approved by the state-approving body may be substituted on a month-for-month basis up to one year of specialized experience when the following provisions are met:

- The candidate must have been in good standing when the training was interrupted.
- In order to substitute the training for specialized experience, the applicant must have satisfactorily completed courses that involved clinical practice in medical and surgical nursing and infant and child care. Candidates lacking clinical practice in infant and child care may substitute clinical practice in psychiatric or another specialized field of nursing.

Any excess specialized training may be credited as general experience.

- Education and training other than that outlined above will be allowed appropriate credit for either general or specialized experience, depending upon its applicability and extent.

The maximum amount of experience for which education or training of any kind may be substituted is three years (two years of general and one year of specialized experience).

Written Test

Candidates for positions at GS-2 and GS-3 must pass a written test of abilities necessary to learn and perform the duties of these positions. The written test should be waived for candidates who qualify on the basis of successful completion of specialized education or training that is substitutable for specialized experience.

Basis for Rating and Ranking Candidates

Applicants who meet the minimum qualification requirements, including a passing score on the written test, when required, will be rated on a scale of 70 to 100 based on the following:

GS-1—An evaluation of the applicant's willingness to do simple and repetitive work of the occupation, his dependability, and his ability to work safely

GS-2/3—The applicant's score on the written test, or for those competitors not required to pass the written test (see the "Written Test" section above), an evaluation of education, training, and/or experience

GS-4 and above—An evaluation of the quality and extent of the applicant's experience, education, training, or other achievements pertinent to the duties of the position to be filled

FOR POSITIONS IN THE PUBLIC HEALTH NURSE OCCUPATION, GRADES GS-5/15
PUBLIC HEALTH NURSE
CONSULTING PUBLIC HEALTH NURSE
PUBLIC HEALTH NURSE (TRAINING)
RESEARCH PUBLIC HEALTH NURSE

Description of Work

Public Health Nurses supervise or give public health nursing care, health teaching, and guidance to individuals and families in homes and schools. Such positions typically are found in public health nursing services that emphasize comprehensive care for mothers and children, and services to patients having communicable diseases and chronic illnesses.

A few Public Health Nurse positions primarily involve advice and consultation on public health nursing programs, teaching or training in public health nursing programs, teaching or training in public health nursing, or research in public health nursing.

Education, Experience, and Other Requirements

Basic Educational Requirements

Candidates for all positions must meet one of the following requirements:

- Graduation from a baccalaureate or higher degree program in nursing approved by the legally designated state approving body. To be acceptable, the program must have been accredited by the nationally recognized accrediting agency (or else must have included course content and field practice in public health nursing equivalent to that of programs that are accredited).
- Graduation from either a diploma or associate-degree program in professional nursing approved by the legally designated state approving body and at least one academic year in a university public health nursing program accredited by the nationally recognized accrediting agency.

or

- Graduation from a foreign school of professional nursing, provided that the nursing education and the nursing knowledge acquired therefrom are substantially comparable and equivalent to that of graduates of nursing schools as described in the first bullet. Such equivalence must have been evaluated by a school of nursing accredited by the nationally recognized accrediting agency as equivalent to that of its program.

Candidates for positions that involve highly technical research or development or comparable highly technical and scientific functional areas of nursing work must meet the requirements described in the first bullet above.

Registration Requirements

Applicants for all positions must have active, current registration as a professional nurse in a state, District of Columbia, the Commonwealth of Puerto Rico, or a territory of the United States.

An applicant who has, within the past 12 months, graduated from a baccalaureate or higher degree program in nursing approved by the legally designated state approving body, with qualifying preparation in public health nursing, may be appointed at the entrance grade level for which qualified, pending attaining state registration as a professional nurse within six months after appointment. No person appointed pending registration may be retained beyond six months or promoted if registration has not been attained.

The basic requirements that apply to all grades are fully qualifying for grade GS-5.

Additional Experience and Training Requirements

Candidates for grades GS-7 and above must have had either professional experience or graduate education (or an equivalent combination of both) in addition to meeting the basic educational requirements. Such professional experience must have been in public health nursing, general nursing, or another specialty area of nursing that is directly applicable to the position to be filled. For GS-9 at least one year, and for GS-11 and above at least two years of the required professional nursing experience must have been in the public health nursing field.

Such graduate education must have been in nursing in a field that is directly applicable to the position to be filled. An exception to this requirement is that one year of the graduate education may have been in directly related fields. Graduate education in the "directly related field" is qualifying for grade GS-7 only.

Experience

In addition to the basic educational requirements, the following amounts of professional experience in the appropriate subject-matter field are required for grades GS-7 and above:

Grade	Minimum Amount of Professional Experience in Appropriate Subject-Matter Fields (Years)
GS-7	1
GS-9	2
GS-11 and above	3

For grades GS-11 and below, at least six months of the required experience must have been at the level of difficulty comparable to that of the next lower grade, or one year comparable to the second lower grade, in the federal service. For grades GS-12 and above, at least one year of the required experience must have been at a level of difficulty comparable to that of the next lower grade in the federal service.

Education

In addition to the basic educational requirements, the following amounts and levels of education in the appropriate subject-matter field are qualifying for grades GS-7 and above, as shown:

Grade	Minimum Amount or Level of Education in Appropriate Subject-Matter Fields (Years)
GS-7	One full academic year of graduate education
GS-9	Completion of all requirements for a master's or equivalent degree or two full academic years of graduate education
GS-11	Completion of all requirements for a doctoral degree (Ph.D. or equivalent) or three full academic years of graduate education

Combinations of Professional Experience and Graduate Education

Equivalent combinations of professional experience and graduate education of the types described above are acceptable at each grade.

Alternate Requirements

Superior academic achievement at the baccalaureate level or one year of student trainee experience is qualifying at grade GS-7. A combination of superior academic achievement at the baccalaureate level and one year of appropriate professional experience is qualifying at grade GS-9.

Selective Placement Factors

Some Public Health Nurse positions demand specific competence in a particular specialty and/or in special functional areas such as giving advice and consultation, teaching, and research. For such positions, consideration may be limited to those candidates whose records show evidence of the required knowledge, abilities, skills, and personal characteristics.

Personal Characteristics Required

Public Health Nurse positions require the ability to work harmoniously and effectively with others in the organization and to establish and maintain satisfactory working relationships with others in hospitals, clinics, the school, social agencies, and so on. Public Health Nurses must have the ability to inspire confidence and motivate patients and their families to follow the treatment program and to use the available health facilities.

Many Public Health Nurses perform their work in homes and schools in which direction and supervision may not be immediately available. In these situations, the work requires an extra measure of personal traits such as maturity, objectivity, resourcefulness, and sound judgment.

Some Public Health Nurses require the knowledge, abilities, and skills to give advice and leadership to states and/or localities on the nursing aspects of health services in a specialty area such as maternal and child health, psychiatry, tuberculosis, and so on.

These factors should be considered in evaluating candidates in relationship to the requirements of the specific position to be filled.

Written Test

No written test is required.

Interview

Applicants who meet the education, experience, and other requirements may be requested to appear for an employment interview.

Qualification Inquiries

Reference inquiries, including contacts with a candidate's teachers, supervisors, or other persons familiar with the candidate's qualifications, may be made to obtain further information about the candidate's professional and personal qualifications for these positions.

Basis for Rating and Ranking Candidates

Applicants will be rated on the extent and quality of their education and experience.

NURSE, GS-4/15

Occupational Coverage: Nurse, Clinical Nurse, Community Health Nurse, Occupational Health Nurse, Operating Room Nurse, Psychiatric Nurse, Nurse Anesthetist, Nurse Consultant, Nurse Educator, Nurse Midwife, Nurse Practitioner, Nurse Specialist, Research Nurse.

Description of Work

Nurses apply a professional knowledge of nursing to advise on, administer, supervise, or perform direct or indirect care of patients in hospitals, clinics, health units, homes, schools, and communities. They administer anesthetic agents and supportive treatments to patients undergoing surgery or other medical procedures; promote better health practices; teach; perform research; act as nurse midwives; or consult with and advise nurses who provide direct care to patients.

Professional nursing includes a wide variety of categories of work, many of which are highly specialized.

Clinical Nurses provide direct nursing service in the assessment, planning, implementation, and evaluation of patient care in hospitals, clinics, or other patient-care facilities. They frequently work in a specialized clinical area—for example, a surgical ward, an ambulance, or an emergency room.

Community Health Nurses provide therapeutic services and coordinate patient and family health information and services to, between, or in homes, hospitals, clinics, schools, and communities. They function as client advocates and promote the health maintenance activities of early detection and prevention.

Occupational Health Nurses provide nursing and health services to employees in relation to their occupations and working environments. This entails both the nursing care and treatment of injuries and illnesses of employees; and participation in preventive health programs, health education, and counseling aimed at prevention of disease and health maintenance; and environmental surveys.

Operating Room Nurses provide specialized nursing care to meet the needs of patients undergoing surgical procedures, providing for patient counseling and continuity of care. This involves responsibility for and supervision of the preparation of the operating room and necessary equipment, and for the scheduling of facilities and personnel.

Psychiatric Nurses provide direct nursing service to patients in psychiatric hospitals, psychiatric units in general medical and surgical hospitals, or mental health clinics. This work requires advanced knowledge, skills, and experience in counseling and guidance, and communicative skills that contribute to the redirection of behavior of patients or their families.

Nurse Anesthetists administer anesthetic agents and provide supportive treatment to patients undergoing surgery or other medical procedures.

Nurse Consultants provide consultative and advisory service with respect to one or more facets of the nursing field. They work independently, and the services cover a broad range of activities involving assessing, planning, implementing, coordinating, and evaluating nursing programs both within and outside the employing agency.

Nurse Educators develop, provide, and administer educational programs and activities for nurses. They teach courses, develop technical phases of educational programs, plan curriculum content and methods of teaching, and advise on the application of approved educational methods for individual schools and communities.

Nurse Midwives provide care for mothers and babies throughout an essentially normal maternity cycle within the framework of a medically directed health service, and are responsible for management, counseling, and teaching.

Nurse Practitioners, through advanced competence in primary health care, provide direct, comprehensive nursing, preventive, and therapeutic health services to individuals, families, or groups. This includes assessing the health status of individuals; managing the care of selected patients; and providing treatment, health teaching, counseling, guidance, and instructions to individuals/families so that they participate in a plan of care.

Nurse Specialists have an advanced level of competence in the special field for which applying, with experience in clinical practice that demonstrates the ability to develop innovative techniques, practices, and approaches for patient care.

Research Nurses perform, participate in, and/or direct research activities toward development of new or expanded knowledge of the field of nursing or health systems that improve patient care and enhance the clinical practice of nursing.

Basic Registration Requirements for All Nurse Positions

Applicants for nurse positions must have active, current registration as a professional nurse in a state, District of Columbia, the Commonwealth of Puerto Rico, or a territory of the United States.

An applicant who has within the past 12 months graduated from a school of professional nursing approved by a legally designated state approving agency at the time of graduation may be appointed at the entrance grade level for which qualified, pending attaining state registration as a professional nurse within six months after appointment. No person appointed pending registration may be retained beyond six months or promoted if registration has not been attained.

Basic Educational Requirements for All Nurse Positions

Candidates for positions at all grades must meet one of the following requirements:

A. Graduation with a bachelor's or higher degree in nursing from a school of professional nursing, approved by the legally designated state accrediting agency at the time the program was completed by the candidate

B. Graduation from a three-year (at least 30 months) diploma program of professional nursing approved by the legally designated state accrediting agency at the time the program was completed by the candidate

C. Graduation from an associate-degree program or other program of at least two years, in a school of professional nursing approved by the legally designated state accrediting agency at the time the program was completed by the candidate

D. Graduation from a school of professional nursing (including foreign schools), of at least two years in length other than one covered by A, B, or C above, provided that the professional nurse training and the nursing knowledge acquired therefrom are substantially comparable and equivalent to that of graduates of an approved school as described above. Comparability should be evaluated by a State Board of Nursing. Registration as defined above meets this requirement

Note: Successfully completed college-level course work in nursing; the behavioral, physical, or biological sciences related to nursing; nutrition; public health; and maternal and child health in excess of the minimum basic education requirement may be substituted for professional nursing experience at the rate of one academic year of appropriate education for nine months of professional nursing experience in establishing eligibility for the GS-5 level. Tutorial or remedial work cannot be substituted.

Basic Educational Requirements for Certain Specialized Positions

In addition to meeting the basic requirements for all nurse positions, candidates for the following positions must meet the criteria listed below.

Community Health Nurse: Candidates for these positions at GS-5 and above must have graduated from a baccalaureate or higher degree program in nursing approved by the legally designated state approving body.

Nurse Anesthetist: Candidates for Nurse Anesthetist positions at GS-9 and above must have graduated from at least an 18-month course in a school of anesthesia for nurses accredited by the American Association of Nurse Anesthetists for the year of the applicant's graduation.

Nurse Midwife: Candidates for Nurse Midwife positions must have completed an organized program of study and clinical experience recognized by the American College of Nurse Midwives.

Entry-Level Credit for Military Experience

Nurse experience gained while in the military as a military corpsman will be accepted for initial appointment at grade GS-4 to the extent that it is accepted by a state licensing body.

Education and Experience Above the Entry Levels

Candidates for grades GS-7 and above must have had either professional experience or graduate education (or an equivalent combination of both) in addition to meeting the basic educational requirements for all nurse positions. Such professional experience must have been in nursing. Such graduate education must have been in nursing with a concentration in a field of nursing or closely related non-nursing fields directly applicable to the requirements for the position to be filled.

Experience

The required amounts of professional experience are

Grade	Associate Degree Program or Diploma Program of Less Than 30 Months (Years)	Diploma Program of 30 Months or More (Years)	Baccalaureate Degree Program (Years)
GS-4	None	None	None
GS-5	1	None	None
GS-7	2	1	1
GS-9	3	2	2
GS-11 and above	4	3	3

For positions at GS-5, graduates of an associate degree or diploma nursing program of less than 30 months' duration may have experience as a Practical Nurse or Nursing Assistant (either voluntary or paid) credited for grade GS-5 on a month-for-month basis to a maximum of 12 months. The practical nurse or nursing experience must have been:

- Gained under the supervision of a professional nurse
- Equivalent to GS-4 or higher

     and

- Relevant to the position to be filled

For grades GS-7–11, at least six months of the professional nursing experience must have been at the level of difficulty comparable to that of the next lower grade in the federal service, or one year comparable to the second lower grade.

For specialized positions at GS-9 and above, one year of professional nursing experience must be sufficiently related to the specialty in both subject matter and grade level, to demonstrate the candidate's ability to perform the major duties of the position being filled.

Candidates for positions at GS-12 and above must have at least one year of experience at the next lower grade. Candidates must demonstrate a record of accomplishment, professional competence, leadership, and recognition in the profession as in the planning, organizing, directing, and coordinating of nursing projects, or in well-established service as an expert and consultant.

Education

In addition to the basic requirements, the following amounts and levels of education in the appropriate subject-matter field are qualifying for grades GS-7 and above:

Grade	Minimum Amount or Level of Education in Appropriate Subject-Matter Fields
GS-7	One full academic year of graduate education
GS-9	Completion of all requirements for a master's or equivalent degree, or two full academic years of graduate education
GS-11	Completion of all requirements for a doctoral degree (Ph.D. or equivalent) or three full academic years of graduate education

Currency of Knowledge and Skills: At all grade levels, greater credit may be given to applicants who have knowledge of and skills in current nursing practices.

Alternate Requirements: Superior academic achievement at the baccalaureate level is qualifying at grade GS-7. A combination of superior academic achievement at the baccalaureate level and one year of appropriate professional experience is qualifying at grade GS-9.

Combinations of Professional Experience and Graduate Education

Equivalent combinations of professional experience and graduate education of the types described above are acceptable at each grade. Specialized areas of nursing (see the section titled "Description of Work") may require particular specialized education and experience.

Possible Selective Factors

Many nursing positions GS-9 and above demand competence in a particular area, gained through specialized experience and/or training. Selective factors for these positions should be reflected in the knowledge, skills, and abilities described in the position description.

Written Test

No written test is required.

Interview

Applicants who meet the education, experience, and other requirements may be required to appear for an employment interview.

Qualification Inquiries

Reference inquiries, including contacts with the candidate's teachers, supervisors, or other persons familiar with the candidate's qualifications, may be made to obtain further information about the candidate's professional and personal qualifications for these positions.

Basis for Rating and Ranking Candidates

Applicants are rated on the extent and quality of their education and experience. Such ratings are based upon the applicant's statements in the application and upon any additional information that may be secured, including that secured by inquiries made to supervisors, schools, and other references.

DIETITIAN, GS-5/15

NUTRITIONIST, GS-5/15

PUBLIC HEALTH NUTRITIONIST, GS-9/15

Description of Work

Dietitians and Nutritionists advise on, administer, supervise, or perform work that requires the application of a professional knowledge of the science of nutrition. Dietitians and Nutritionists are concerned with human nutrition needs and are responsible for the development of diet plans or programs for individuals or groups, for instructing others in nutrition matters, and for applying knowledge of socioeconomic conditions that affect the eating habits of individuals and groups. Dietitians usually perform work that is associated with institutional health care, such as hospitals, domiciliaries, or privately operated group-care facilities in the community, and that involves responsibility for individual diet plans and for the management of the food-service system. Public Health Nutritionists perform work associated with public health services and programs designed to meet the health needs of target groups within the population, such as maternal and child health, geriatrics, and American Indians. Nutritionists perform in non-treatment food-assistance programs designed to help target groups within the population, or in research. Major specialties and subspecialties are summarized as follows.

Dietitians are responsible for nutritional care in managing individual or group feeding, in imparting knowledge concerning food and nutrition, and in applying knowledge to developing and implementing plans for health maintenance and/or improvement.

Administrative Dietitians are members of the management team, responsible for planning and evaluating the food-service system, directing and managing food-service personnel, planning budgets and managing resources, establishing standards of safety and sanitation, developing specifications for the procurement of equipment and supplies, and developing menu patterns and evaluating client acceptance.

Clinical Dietitians are members of the health-care team concerned with continuously providing for the nutritional needs of individuals and groups in acute, intermediate, long-term care and hospital-based community-care facilities generally involving a specialized program. They are primarily concerned with assessing nutritional needs, developing therapeutic diets, recording progress in the medical records, providing nutritional education to the patient and family, and recommending changes to the physician. A dietitian may be responsible for one or more wards in a hospital involving patients with general or specialized problems, or for a nutrition or an outpatient clinic that provides similar care for ambulatory or outpatients.

Community Dietitians serve as members of the community health team, responsible for assessing the nutritional needs of individuals and groups located in nursing homes, private homes, or other group-care facilities, and for evaluating and advising on the nutritional services provided by the institution to the individual.

Research Dietitians assist physicians or research scientists by planning the diet for the proposed study, by developing precise and complete data on patient nutrient intake and output, and by stimulating participation by patients or volunteer subjects.

Consultant Dietitians provide advice or services in nutritional care that affect the management of resources, such as the evaluating of food-service systems, developing budgets and records systems, developing educational materials, recommending layout designs and equipment needs, or counseling clients and consulting with health-care teams.

Teaching Dietitians plan, schedule, or conduct educational programs for professional staff development, in-service training of non-professional staff, and may include training for medical interns, nurses, volunteers, patients, or dietetic interns or students.

Nutritionists are specialists in human nutrition concerned with nutritional or food-assistance services provided by social, agricultural, or educational agencies to target populations. They perform such duties as assessing the nutritional needs of groups, evaluating the nutrition component of programs, interpreting nutrition research or legislation, providing consultation and training, or participating in research.

Public Health Nutritionists serve as members of the health team and are responsible for planning and administering the community nutrition program for a geographical area or specialty area. This involves such duties as assessing the nutritive quality of food eaten by people in the community; providing consultation and training to administrators, health professionals, and food-service personnel in a variety of programs with a food service, nutrition education, and/or health component; conducting dietary studies and providing patient education to groups or individuals in normal and therapeutic nutrition; and consulting on the development and improvement of standards or services provided.

Nutritionists in Specialized Areas: Current major specializations include maternal and child health, school nutrition and health, group feeding, gerontology, chronic disease, rehabilitation, clinical dietetics, group food service, research, education, and training. The Nutritionist plans, develops, implements, evaluates, and promotes the nutrition component of the specialty area to serve the needs of the target population.

Community Nutritionists function as members of the community health team, assessing nutrition needs of individuals and groups in the community and providing education and information through individual and group counseling, and through displays, newspapers, radios, and other informational devices.

Nutritionists in Administration plan policy and action related to changing health, service, or program needs as influenced by nutrition practices and socioeconomic forces; determine program priorities through the projection of anticipated benefits and expected costs; and evaluate the effectiveness of program services provided.

Experience and Training Requirements

Basic Requirements for All Grades

Successful completion of a full four-year course of study in an accredited college or university creditable toward a baccalaureate or higher degree in dietetics, food, nutrition, food-service management, institution management, or a closely related science.

Dietitian: For positions of Dietitian, the curriculum must have been in accordance with the qualifying requirements established by The American Dietetic Association (ADA) in effect at the time of graduation. Professional registration as a Registered Dietitian (R.D.) is evidence of meeting ADA requirements.

For dietitians and nutritionists, completion of the basic requirement is qualifying for GS-5.

Public Health Nutritionist: Positions of Public Health Nutritionist require the successful completion of a master's degree in public health nutrition, community nutrition, or in nutrition supplemented by public health courses from an accredited college or university.

For Public Health Nutritionists, completion of the basic requirement is qualifying for GS-9.

Additional Experience and Training Requirements

Candidates for grades GS-7 and above must have had either professional experience or graduate education, or an equivalent combination of both, in addition to meeting the basic requirements. This professional experience or graduate education must have been in or directly related to dietetics or nutrition, or in a field closely related to the position to be filled.

In addition to the basic requirements, the following amounts of professional experience are required for grades GS-7 and above:

Grade	Total Experience (Years)
GS-7	1
GS-9	2
GS-11 and above	3

Completion of a coordinated undergraduate program, internship, or other clinical component approved by the American Dietetic Association, which was conducted as part of the undergraduate program, or after completion of the basic requirements for a baccalaureate degree, is qualifying at grade GS-7 for Dietitians or Nutritionists.

Candidates possessing professional registration as a Registered Dietitian meet the full requirements for eligibility at GS-7.

For grades GS-11 and below, at least six months of the required experience must have been at a level of difficulty comparable to that of the next lower grade, or one year comparable to the second lower grade in the federal service. For grades GS-12 and above, at least one year of the required experience must have been at a level of difficulty comparable to that of the next lower grade in the federal service.

For any grade, the required amount of experience will not, in itself, be accepted as proof of qualification for a position. The quality of experience, rather than its length, will be given primary consideration. The applicant's total education and experience must give positive evidence of ability to perform all of the duties of the position.

Substitution of Education for Experience: In addition to the basic requirements, the following amounts and levels of education are qualifying for grades GS-7 and above. This education must have been either in dietetics or nutrition, or in directly related fields such as public health nutrition.

GS-7—One full academic year of graduate education

GS-9—Completion of all requirements for a master's or equivalent degree or two full academic years of graduate education

GS-11—Completion of all requirements for a doctoral degree (Ph.D. or equivalent) or three full academic years of graduate education

Combinations of Professional Experience and Graduate Education: Equivalent combinations of professional experience and graduate education of the type described above are acceptable at each grade.

Professional experience is defined as non-routine work that required and was characterized by

- A knowledge of the principles, theories, and methods of dietetics or nutrition
- The ability to apply such knowledge in the work situation

and

- Positive and continuing development of knowledge and ability, to keep abreast of the advancing and changing discipline

Superior Academic Achievement: Superior academic achievement cannot be substituted for experience requirements of positions in this series.

Employment Interview

Applicants who meet the education, experience, and other requirements may be requested to appear for an employment interview.

Written Test

No written test is required.

Basis for Rating and Ranking Candidates

Candidates are rated on the extent, quality, and recentness of their experience and training, since a professional must keep abreast of constant changes in technology and trends. Ratings will be based upon candidates' statements in their applications and upon any additional information that may be secured, including that secured by inquiries made to supervisors, schools, and other references.

Selective Factors

For some specialized positions, only candidates who possess specific job-related knowledge, skills, and/ or abilities may be qualified. For example, if a position requires highly developed skill in research techniques or in maternal and child care, that skill or knowledge may be used as an "in-or-out" selective placement factor. Justification for selective placement factors must show:

- How the selective factor is directly related to the duties and responsibilities of the position

and

- Why possession of the knowledge, skills, and/or abilities identified as selective factors are necessary for successful performance in the position

Specialized requirements, for example, are most commonly found in the following areas:

- Research positions, some of which require advanced preparation in dietetics or nutrition as well as in research techniques, to plan, investigate, interpret, evaluate, apply, and expand knowledge in one or more phases of dietetics or nutrition, and to communicate findings through reports and publications
- Teaching positions, some of which require advanced preparation in dietetics, nutrition, and/or education, to plan, conduct, and evaluate educational programs in one or more dietetic or nutrition subject matter areas
- Professional registration (or other acceptable evidence of demonstrated ability to perform at the required level) is required for many positions of director of a dietetic or public health nutrition program in a hospital or other health care facility.

Guide for Evaluation of Candidates

Candidates for Positions at GS-5/7

Evaluation of candidates for these grades is based largely on their academic career, with consideration also being given to any experience they may have had.

Education: When evaluating a candidate's academic record, consideration should be given to the extent to which the courses successfully completed contribute to the basic knowledge required in the particular position to be filled.

Internship: In evaluating experience gained through an internship, the experience should be related to the duties to be performed.

Registration: A Registered Dietitian is a person who meets the qualifications established by the Commission on Dietetic Registration of the American Dietetic Association. Among the requirements for registration are successful completion of the examination for professional registration and the maintaining of continuing education requirements. Since the purpose of the examination and the continuing education requirements is to ensure that the Dietitian possesses and maintains the common core of knowledge of the profession, registration may be considered in the evaluation of the candidates.

Candidates for Positions at GS-9 and Above

For positions at these levels, evaluation of undergraduate college training is less important than the consideration of graduate education and professional work experience. The same factors that are used to evaluate the undergraduate academic record may also be used to evaluate the graduate record.

- The evaluation of a candidate's work experience should consider its nature and significance, its relationship to the requirements of the position, and whether it has involved the performance of professional work of increasing difficulty and complexity and has involved the assumption of more responsibility.
- Candidates qualifying on the basis of a master's degree or Ph.D. may be evaluated for completion of a clinical component.
- Registration by the Commission on Dietetic Registration of the American Dietetic Association may be considered in the evaluation of candidates for positions of Dietitian or Public Health Nutritionist.
- Candidates may also be evaluated for active membership in and presentations before professional organizations, technical publications, participation in seminars and study groups, patents, awards, and so on. Technical publications should be evaluated for their contribution to advancing knowledge in dietetics and nutrition, rather than on their quantity alone.
- Recentness of education and experience, and evidence of continuing education in dietetics, nutrition, and related fields, are important elements of full professional competence and may be considered in the evaluation of candidates.
- Candidates for positions at GS-9 and above should also be evaluated for such skills and abilities as:
  - The ability to plan work and evaluate results
  - Skill in analyzing, adapting, or developing materials, such as criteria, specifications, menus, and patient's needs and progress
  - Skill in interpersonal relationships, such as leadership, flexibility, and persuasiveness
  - Skill in oral communications for explaining nutrition to individuals or groups having a wide range of backgrounds, and for teaching students, other professionals, and communicating with groups
  - Skill in written communications for developing technical reports, informational materials, specifications, procedures, and similar tools

- The ability to stay abreast of changes and new developments within the discipline and closely related areas
- The ability to work independently, including originating workable solutions

Special Physical Requirements

Most positions involve moderate physical exertion, including moving substantial distances within hospitals or similar facilities, standing, bending, and lifting light objects such as medical or procurement records. The ability to read printed material and handwriting is required in most positions, as is the ability to communicate effectively and efficiently with patients and others. Many positions involve some amount of exposure to contagious diseases, noise, and hazards of kitchen equipment. Protective clothing is required in some situations. A few positions require travel to remote parts of the country.

DENTAL AIDE, GS-1
DENTAL ASSISTANT, GS-2/5
DENTAL ASSISTANT (EXPANDED FUNCTION), GS-5/6

Description of Work

Dental Assistants provide assistance to the dentist by receiving and preparing patients for dental treatment, preparing materials and equipment for use by the dentist, assisting the dentist at chairside or bedside in the treatment of patients, taking dental radiographs, and maintaining records related to appointments, examinations, treatment, and supplies. Dental Assistants may work in general dentistry or in a specialized field of dentistry such as prosthodontics or oral surgery.

Dental Assistants (expanded function) are primarily concerned with the performance of reversible intra-oral procedures, such as placing and finishing restorations in teeth prepared by a dentist. Dental Assistants (expanded function) also perform chairside assistance and other services typically provided by Dental Assistants.

Minimum Qualifying Experience

GS-1—No written test, experience, training, or education is required. Candidates must be willing to perform simple dental aid work and must show the ability to follow specific instructions. Evidence of this ability may be obtained from personal references, interviews, and so on.

GS-2—Six months of experience is required that has provided a knowledge of simple clinic-maintenance procedures such as clearing work areas of used materials, replacing soiled linens, storing medical and dental supplies, and filing records in alphabetic or numeric order.

GS-3—One year of experience is required that has provided all of the following knowledge:

- Knowledge of clinical routines and procedures such as receiving, routing, and scheduling patients; ordering supplies; and requesting medical or dental laboratory work
- Knowledge of the use, care, and storage of dental, medical, or laboratory instruments, materials, and equipment

- Knowledge of sterilization techniques sufficient to sterilize dental instruments and materials
  and
- Knowledge of dental or medical terminology to maintain records related to patients, supplies, and recurring medical or dental activities.

GS-4 and above—Candidates must have had one year of qualifying experience at the next lower grade in the General Schedule or equivalent experience outside the General Schedule. Qualifying experience at this level is experience in dental assistance to general or specialized dentistry, dental assistance (expanded function) work, or any combination of these appropriate to the position being filled.

Substitutions of Education and Training for Experience

GS-2—For positions at GS-2, completion of a full four-year high school curriculum or high school equivalency is qualifying.

GS-3—For positions at GS-3, the following education and training may be substituted for experience requirements:

- Successful completion of a one-year dental-assistant program or completion of one year of a dental-hygiene program accredited by the American Dental Association's Commission on Accreditation is fully qualifying.
- Successful completion of practical nurse training approved by the appropriate state or District of Columbia accrediting body is qualifying.
- Completion of education and training other than that outlined above, which is directly related to the routines, procedures, and terminology used in a medical or dental treatment situation, may be substituted on a month-for-month basis for the experience requirements. Examples of this training may include, but are not limited to, the U.S. Armed Forces, manpower development, or in-service training programs.

GS-4—For positions at GS-4, the following may be substituted:

- Successful completion of a two-year dental-assistant program or completion of a two-year dental-hygiene program accredited by the American Dental Association's Commission on Accreditation is fully qualifying.
- Other training and education that is directly applicable to the performance of dental-assistant work may be substituted on a month-for-month basis for the experience requirements. Examples of this training include the U.S. Armed Forces, manpower development, or in-service training programs.

Special Requirements for Dental Assistant (Expanded Function) Positions, GS-5 and Above:
Candidates for Dental Assistant (expanded function) positions must have completed one year of acceptable coursework, preceptorship, or other formal training and/or work assignments specifically designed to equip the candidate with the knowledge and skills required to perform intra-oral procedures involved in the position to be filled, including

- Knowledge of the methods and techniques used in dentistry to perform intra-oral procedures
- Knowledge of the characteristics of a variety of materials and instruments used in performing intra-oral procedures
  and
- The ability to recognize common dental disorders and conditions such as caries, formations of plaque and calculus, and inflammation of gums

Examples of acceptable training are

- Courses in a dental-hygiene or dental-assistant program accredited by the American Dental Association's Commission on Accreditation that are directly related to intra-oral procedures (also referred to as *expanded functions*) to be performed in the position to be filled
- The U.S. Army's Dental Therapy Assistant Training Program
- Continuing education courses in expanded functions for Dental Assistants offered by the Indian Health Service of Department of Health, Education, and Welfare
- Other training comparable to the above in private or governmental hospitals, clinics, or schools that include formal classroom instruction and clinical training in the knowledge and skills required to perform intra-oral procedures in the position to be filled

Training may be credited on a month-for-month basis for the experience requirements. Dental Assistant (expanded function) positions at GS-6 require one year of experience comparable to that of GS-5 level Dental Assistant (expanded function).

Written Test

A written test is required at grade GS-2 and is not to be waived for appointment outside the register, unless authorized by the Office of Personnel Management.

Basis for Rating and Ranking Candidates

Candidates who meet the minimum qualification requirements, including a passing score on the written test, when required, will be rated on a scale of 70 to 100 based on:

For positions at grade GS-1: An evaluation of the candidate's willingness to do simple and repetitive dental aide work, dependability, and ability to work safely

For positions at grade GS-2: The candidate's score on the written test

For positions at grades GS-3 and above: An evaluation of the quality and extent of the candidate's experience, education, training, or other achievements pertinent to the duties of the position being filled

In ranking candidates who have met the minimum experience requirements, candidates with dental-assistant training should be ranked higher based on the recognition that dental-assistant training is more specifically focused on the knowledge, skills, and abilities required by dental-assisting work.

Personal Characteristics

Dental Assistant and Dental Assistant (expanded function) positions involve significant contacts with patients. Candidates must demonstrate the ability to work with patients in a tactful and courteous manner, relieve fears, and comfort their patients.

Special Physical Requirements

Usable vision is required and, depending on the essential duties of a specific position, usable hearing and speech may be required.

DENTAL HYGIENIST, GS-4/8
COMMUNITY HEALTH DENTAL HYGIENIST, GS-5 AND ABOVE

Description of Work

Dental Hygienists work in hospitals and outpatient clinics doing the following:

- Performing oral prophylaxis
- Applying topical fluorides and desensitizing agents to the teeth
- Performing examinations of the teeth and surrounding tissues involving the use of diagnostic tests and X-rays
- Preparing treatment plans for plaque control
- Instructing individual patients, patient groups, nurses, and nursing assistants or other dental hygienists and dental assistants in the techniques and practice of maintaining oral health

Community Health Dental Hygienists work primarily in non-clinical settings on military installations or in public-health program areas planning and carrying out dental-health programs to promote public awareness, acceptance, and practice of oral health measures for groups of individuals and communities. Typically, they do the following:

- Plan and conduct oral-health instructional programs directed toward the needs of various community groups
- Provide technical advice and assistance to dental personnel on public-health matters relating to oral health
- Make on-site visits to provide policy guidance and ensure consistency among areas in accomplishing the objectives of the dental program
- Conduct surveys and special studies to evaluate the effectiveness of the oral-health program and to recommend new or improved methods of oral hygiene
- Plan and conduct dental-inspection programs
- Develop teaching aids and materials used to improve the oral health of the community
- Present lectures and demonstrations in new or improved dental techniques and developments
and
- Prepare and compile a variety of records and reports pertaining to the administration of the oral-health program

Licensure Requirements

Applicants for all grades and specifications must be currently licensed to practice as Dental Hygienists in a state or territory of the United States or the District of Columbia.

Experience Requirements for Clinical Dental Hygiene Positions

GS-4—No experience is required.

GS-5—One year of experience as a licensed Dental Hygienist. This is experience in performing routine oral prophylactic care such as

- Scaling and polishing the teeth
- Applying topical fluorides and desensitizing agents to the teeth

- Taking X-rays
- Sterilizing instruments
- Instructing patients in brushing and flossing techniques

GS-6—Two years of experience as a licensed Dental Hygienist of which at least one year included duties such as

- Examining the patient's teeth and surrounding tissues
- Cleaning, polishing, and applying topical fluorides and other anticariogenic agents to the teeth
- Treating common abnormalities such as inflammations of the gums
- Taking and interpreting X-rays for presence of caries
- Providing oral-health care instructions to individuals and groups of patients

GS-7—Three years of experience as a licensed Dental Hygienist of which at least one year included duties such as

- Performing oral prophylaxis in cases of acute gingivitis and periodontal diseases requiring the use of a variety of scalers and ultrasound equipment
- Performing deep scaling, root planing, and subgingival curettage
- Taking intra-oral impressions
- Placing temporary fillings
- Placing and removing rubber dams
- Planning dental-hygiene treatment and the series of appointments needed to complete treatment
- Providing oral-hygiene instructions to patients with special problems
- Training other hygienists and dental personnel in dental-hygiene techniques and procedures

GS-8—four years of experience as a licensed Dental Hygienist of which at least one year included advanced prophylactic and therapeutic hygiene procedures in the treatment of patients with related medical and dental problems. This includes duties such as

- Performing oral prophylaxis on ambulatory and non-ambulatory patients requiring specialized procedures for bed-ridden patients
- Preparing dental-hygiene treatment plans for patients including assessment of the oral problem, type of oral-hygiene care required, and the sequence of appointments needed to complete treatment
- Presenting lectures and demonstrations to various patient groups such as diabetics and oral-cancer patients requiring the use of motivational techniques, dental aids, and educational materials
- Performing advanced dental-hygiene procedures such as root planing and curettage under local anesthesia, polishing and finishing amalgam restorations, and inserting temporary fillings in teeth

Education and Experience Requirements for Community Health Dental Hygiene Positions

For positions at all grades, applicants must meet the basic requirements specified under paragraph A or B below:

A. Successful completion of a full four-year course of study in an accredited college or university leading to a bachelor's degree that must have included or been supplemented by successful completion of a full academic curriculum in dental hygiene accredited by the American Dental Association's Commission on Dental Accreditation.

B. Experience in an amount that, in combination with successful completion of a full academic curriculum in dental hygiene accredited by the American Dental Association's Commission on Dental Accreditation, is sufficient to total at least four years of experience and education. Appropriate experience may be equated to education on a year-for-year basis. To be appropriate, this experience must have demonstrated that the applicant possesses the following:

- The ability to plan and direct group activities
- The ability to organize, analyze, and evaluate data; to draw conclusions; and to make decisions or recommendations
- The ability to express ideas and communicate information orally and in writing in a clear, logical, and motivating manner.
- The ability to demonstrate and/or present new ideas, techniques, and procedures
- The ability to conduct meetings and present lectures
- The ability to deal effectively with individuals and with groups

For positions at GS-5, the basic requirements that apply to all grades are fully qualifying. For positions at GS-7 and above, in addition to the basic requirements, the following amounts of specialized experience are required:

Grade	Specialized Experience (Years)
GS-7	1
GS-9	2
GS-11 and above	3

Specialized experience is experience in dental hygiene or in a directly related kind of work. Examples of work that are considered specialized experience include

- Experience in preparing and conducting educational lectures and demonstrations on dental hygiene
- Experience in planning and developing public health type programs of broad scope—for example, for varying age groups and types of audiences
- Experience in supervising or instructing groups of Dental Hygienists in the performance of dental-hygiene duties
- Other experience in performing the duties of a Community Health Dental Hygienist as described in the "Description of Work" section above.

Substitution of Education and Training for Experience

For Clinical Dental Hygiene positions, successful completion of a full four-year course of study in an accredited college or university leading to a bachelor's degree in dental hygiene or in a directly related field of study such as public health, health education, or education may be substituted in full for the experience required at grade GS-5.

For Community Health Dental Hygiene Positions, successful completion of one full academic year of graduate education in dental hygiene or in a directly related field of study such as public health, health education, or education may be substituted in full for the specialized experience required at grade GS-7.

Successful completion of all requirements for a master's or equivalent degree in dental hygiene or in a directly related field of study may be substituted in full for the specialized experience requirements at grade GS-9.

Education may not be substituted for the full experience requirements above the grade GS-9.

Quality of Experience

Applicants must demonstrate progressively responsible experience of a scope, quality, and degree such as to have equipped them with the ability to perform duties at the grade level of the position for which the application is made. Typically, this is demonstrated by accomplishment of assignments of the difficulty and responsibility described in the position classification standard used to evaluate positions at the next lower grade in the normal line of promotion to the position being filled.

Employment Interview

Applicants who meet the minimum experience, training, and other requirements may be requested to appear for an employment interview.

Basis for Rating and Ranking Candidates

No written test is required. Applicants are rated on a scale of 70 to 100 based on an evaluation of the quality and extent of their experience, education, and training or other achievements pertinent to the duties of the positions to be filled. Such ratings are based upon statements of candidates in their applications, upon qualification inquiries, and upon additional information that may be secured by the examining office.

For all positions, the rating of experience and education may take into account the recentness of the experience and education. Extra credit may be given to applicants who show evidence of efforts to keep current in their field.

Accredited Schools

A listing of accredited schools of dental hygiene may be secured from the American Dental Association, Commission on Dental Accreditation, 211 East Chicago Avenue, Chicago, Illinois, 60611.

PHARMACY AIDE, GS-1/3
PHARMACY TECHNICIAN, GS-4/7

Description of Work

Pharmacy Technicians perform, under the supervision of a registered pharmacist, a variety of technical support functions in a pharmacy. Pharmacy Technicians receive, care for, store, distribute, and bulk compound pharmaceuticals; prepare sterile solutions; and set up prescriptions for a final check by a pharmacist.

Experience, Education, and Training Requirements
Grade GS-1

For grade GS-1, no written test, experience, training, or education is required. Candidates must be willing to perform simple routine pharmacy aide work and show evidence of likelihood of success on the job.

Experience Requirements: Candidates must have had experience as described below. (Education may be substituted for experience.)

Grade	General Experience (Years)	Specialized Experience (Years)	Total Experience (Years)
GS-1	None	None	None
GS-2	$1/2$	None	$1/2$
GS-3	1	None	1
GS-4	$1^1/2$	$1/2$	2
GS-5	2	1	3
GS-6	2	2	4
GS-7	2	3	5

General Experience: General experience is that which has provided a basic knowledge of laboratory procedures and equipment in chemical, biological, or medical laboratories; or background knowledge of the medical environment or hospital or pharmacy procedures.

The general experience requirements for grades GS-2 and GS-3 are broad in intent and do not require any specialized knowledge or skill in pharmacy work.

Specialized Experience: This is experience that has provided the knowledge and skills needed to perform pharmacy technician work. The specialized experience must have provided the candidate with the following:

- A basic knowledge of pharmaceutical nomenclature
- Characteristics, strengths, and dosage forms of pharmaceuticals
- Pharmaceutical systems of weights and measures
- Operation and care of a variety of pharmaceutical equipment

and

- A variety of procedures and techniques involved in the care, storage, repackaging, bulk compounding, and distribution of pharmaceuticals

The six months of specialized experience required for grade GS-4 must have been comparable in difficulty and responsibility to the GS-3 level.

At least one year of the required experience for grade GS-5 must have been comparable in difficulty and responsibility to the GS-4 level. At least six months of this experience at the GS-4 level must have been specialized experience that included duties such as the care, storage, repackaging, bulk compounding, and distribution of pharmaceuticals.

At least one year of the required specialized experience for grades GS-6 and GS-7 must have been comparable in difficulty and responsibility to the next lower grade in the federal service, or two years comparable to the second lower grade in the federal service.

Substitution of Education and Training for Experience

Successfully completed education of acceptable type and quality may be substituted for the experience requirements at the various grade levels, as specified below:

- Graduation from a full four-year or senior high school, or possession of a General Education Development High School Equivalency Certificate, may be substituted in full for the experience requirements at the GS-2 level. (High-school education, or the General Educational Development High School Equivalency Certificate, may not be substituted for any part of the experience requirements for GS-3 and above.)
- Successful completion of one academic year of post–high school education that included a course in biology, chemistry, or physics may be substituted for one year of experience and meets in full the experience requirements for GS-3.

- Successful completion of a course for medical technicians, hospital corpsmen, medical service specialists, or hospital training, obtained in a training program given by the Armed Forces or the U.S. Maritime Service under close medical and professional supervision, may be substituted on a month-for-month basis for general experience.
- Successful completion of pertinent specialized training courses in pharmaceuticals and pharmacy practices while serving in the Armed Forces or in post–high school study may be substituted on a month-for-month basis for up to a total of one year of specialized experience.
- Successful completion of two academic years of post–high school study in a resident school or institution of pharmacy or pharmacy technology that included course work in the care, storage, distribution, and preparation of pharmaceuticals, and appropriate laboratory work, may be substituted in full for two years of experience required at the GS-4 level (one and one-half years general and one-half year specialized).
- Successful completion of four years of academic study in pharmacy may be substituted for three years of experience, including one year specialized experience. This meets in full the experience requirements at the GS-5 level.

Appropriate education and training other than that outlined above, such as in "new careers" training programs, manpower development programs, and in-service training programs, will be granted credit depending upon its applicability and extent.

Post–high school education or training that is acceptable under these standards may be substituted for part of the required experience on a pro rata basis.

Written Test

Candidates for positions at GS-2 and GS-3 must pass the written test of abilities necessary to learn and perform the duties of these positions. The written test may be waived for candidates who have successfully completed the equivalent of a specialized training program in pharmacy of at least six months.

Basis for Rating and Ranking Candidates

Competitors for all positions are rated on the quality and extent of experience, education, or training in relationship to the duties of the positions. Ranking will be made on the following basis:

> **GS-1**—An evaluation of the applicant's willingness to do simple and repetitive pharmacy aide work, his dependability, and his ability to work safely

> **GS-2 and GS-3**—Written test scores, or an evaluation of experience, education, and training of candidates who attained a passing score on the written test

> **GS-4 and above**—An evaluation of experience, education, and training in relationship to the duties of the position

The information for evaluating experience, education, and training will be taken from the application form and any additional information that may be obtained through reference inquiries to supervisors, teachers, and others.

Selective Placement

Some positions may require particular knowledge and skills. For these positions, consideration may be limited to those candidates whose records show that they have the required knowledge and skills.

Basic Skills Positions

HOUSEKEEPING AIDE, GS-1
HOUSEKEEPER, GS-2/7
HOUSEMOTHER, MATRON, HOSTESS, CADET HOSTESS, GS-2/7

Applicants must have had progressively responsible experience in general housekeeping duties such as dusting, window washing, cleaning, making beds, waxing, or polishing floors; or any experience such as work involved in the care, cleaning, maintenance, and servicing of living quarters in homes, lodging houses, hospitals, or other government establishments. Alternatively, applicants must have experience in being responsible for the discipline and well-being of members of a domiciliary unit, including checking leaves and passes, receiving guests, assisting in recreational activities, orienting new members, attending members of the unit who are sick, answering the telephone, and relaying messages. The total experience must have equipped the applicant with knowledge of cleaning methods, tools, supplies, and equipment used in general housekeeping operations. For positions in grade GS-4 and below with supervisory duties, the applicant's experience must indicate that he or she possesses supervisory qualifications, preferably demonstrated by supervisory experience. Grades GS-5, 6, and 7 require supervisory experience.

Grade	Total Experience (Years)	Supervisory Experience (Years)
GS-1	$^1/_2$	None
GS-2	1	None
GS-3	$1^1/_2$	None
GS-4	2	None
GS-5	$2^1/_2$	$^1/_2$
GS-6	3	$^3/_4$
GS-7	$3^1/_2$	1

Appointment to Housekeeping Aide and to most Housekeeper positions is restricted by law to persons who are entitled to veteran preference, as long as such persons are available. There are, however, Housekeeper positions that are non-custodial in nature; for these positions, appointment is not restricted to persons who are entitled to veteran preference.

MESSENGER, GS-1/3
MESSENGER (MOTOR VEHICLE OPERATOR), GS-1/3

Appointment to these positions is restricted to persons entitled to veterans' preference as long as such persons are available.

Description of Work

Messenger work involves the receipt, individual-route sorting, collection or pick-up, and delivery of mail and a variety of other papers, documents, and administrative material processed in a mail unit or messenger room. Messenger positions may also include the performance, as required, of miscellaneous tasks such as

- Operating simple duplicating equipment in an office situation
- Light manual work such as lifting and emptying mail sacks, moving office machines and equipment, and so on
- Simple office duties such as checking outgoing material for complete addresses, noting changes on messenger routes, filing alphabetically, date-stamping material, and so on
- The operation of automotive equipment to facilitate the performance of messenger work

Requirements

For grade GS-1, no written test, experience, training, or education is required. Candidates must be interested in, and willing to perform, routine messenger work and must show likelihood of success on the job.

Experience that meets the requirements as shown below for grades GS-2 and GS-3 must have been in messenger or general clerical work.

Grade	Total Experience (Years)
GS-1	None
GS-2	$^{1}/_{2}$
GS-3	1

Substitution of Education and Training for Experience

The successful completion of a full four-year senior high school curriculum may be substituted for six months of the required experience.

Written Test

For grade GS-1, no written test is required. All candidates for competitive appointment at grades GS-2 and GS-3 are required to pass the appropriate written test.

Basis for Rating and Ranking Candidates

For GS-1—An evaluation of the candidate's interest in and willingness to perform routine and repetitive messenger work, dependability, and the ability to perform work safely.

For GS-2 and 3—The score on the written test and an evaluation of the extent and quality of experience and education.

Requirements for Motor Vehicle Operation

For those positions requiring the operation of government-owned automotive vehicles, applicants must either hold or obtain within 30 days of employment the appropriate state permit and U.S. government motor vehicle operators' identification card.

PARK AIDE, GS-1/3
PARK TECHNICIAN, GS-4/9

Description of Work

Park Aides and *Park Technicians* perform technical and practical work supporting the management, conservation, interpretation, development, and use of park areas and resources. Park Aides and Park Technicians carry out various operating tasks involved in the following:

- Law enforcement
- Traffic control
- Recreation-program operation
- Campground and picnic-area operation
- Accident prevention
- Fire control
- Plant-disease and insect control
- Fish and wildlife surveys
- Soil and water conservation
- Preservation of historical structures and objects
- Comparable aspects of park operations

The mix of duties depends on the particular needs of areas served.

Experience and Training Required

Candidates must have had experience as described as follows. (Education may be substituted for experience.)

Grade	General Experience (Years)	Specialized Experience (Years)	Total Experience (Years)
GS-1	None	None	None
GS-2	1/2	None	1/2
GS-3	1	None	1
GS-4	1 1/2	1/2	2
GS-5	2	1	3
GS-6	2	2	4
GS-7	2	3	5
GS-8 and above	2	4	6

General Experience

This is experience in park operations or in related fields that provided basic knowledge and skills applicable to general park operations and conservation work.

Specialized Experience

This is technical experience gained in actual park operations or in activities that directly support parks, fish and wildlife, recreation management, historic preservation, or conservation, or in park-related work.

Quality and Level of Experience

GS-4—For eligibility at grade GS-4, the required six months of specialized experience must have been comparable in difficulty and responsibility to the GS-3 level in the federal service.

GS-5—For eligibility at grade GS-5, at least one year of required experience, including six months of specialized experience, must have been comparable in difficulty and responsibility to the GS-4 level.

GS-6 and above—For eligibility at grades GS-6 and above, at least one year of the required specialized experience must have been comparable in difficulty and responsibility to the next lower grade in the federal service; or two years must have been comparable to the second lower grade in the federal service.

GS-9—For positions at GS-9, at least one year of the specialized experience must be directly related to the duties of the specific position to be filled. Placement of technicians in positions at GS-9 must be predicated upon a detailed analysis of the knowledge, abilities, and skills required for the work; and a sound matching of the candidate's knowledge, abilities, and skills to the requirements.

Substitution of Education and Training for Experience

Successfully completed education at the high school or higher levels may be substituted for the required experience, as indicated below:

GS-2—Completion of a senior high school curriculum or General Educational Development (GED) high school–equivalency certificate may be substituted for the general experience requirement at the GS-2 level. High-school education or a GED equivalency certificate may not be substituted for any part of the experience requirements at GS-3 and above.

GS-3—Successful completion of at least one academic year of post–high school education that included at least 12 semester hours of credit in any combination of courses listed below may be substituted for one year of experience and meets in full the experience requirements at the GS-3 level. Acceptable course work includes any field-oriented natural science, history, archaeology, police science, and park and recreation management.

GS-4—Two years of academic study as described for GS-3 above that included or was supplemented by at least 18 semester hours in any combination of the subjects shown for GS-3 above, may be substituted for two years of experience including six months of specialized experience, and meets in full the experience requirements at the GS-4 level.

GS-5—A full four-year course of study in an accredited college or university leading to a bachelor's or higher degree that includes at least 24 semester hours in any combination of the subjects described for GS-3 above may be substituted for three years of experience. Such substitution meets in full the experience requirements at the GS-5 level, including the one year of required specialized experience.

Appropriate education and training other than that outlined above, such as in manpower development programs or military training programs, will be credited depending upon their applicability and extent, generally on a month-for-month basis. Maximum substitution of education for experience is three years.

Basis for Rating and Ranking Candidates

Competitors for all positions are rated on a scale of 100. The basis for rating is as follows:

For grade GS-1—An evaluation of the candidate's willingness to do simple park aide work, his dependability, and his ability to work safely

For grades GS-2 and GS-3—Written test score

For grades GS-4 and above—An evaluation of training and experience

Ability in Working with the Public

Most of these positions require contact with the public to explain programs and procedures; give general assistance; interpret the natural, historic, scientific, and/or recreational features of park areas; and enlist the public's cooperation and support. For such positions, candidates must demonstrate that they have the required ability.

Additional Knowledge and Skills

Some Park Technician positions may require specialized technical knowledge and skills in particular phases or types of park work. These include skills in

- The use of complex audiovisual equipment
- Fire-control practices
- Wildlife-management practices
- Driving or piloting custom-built land and water conveyances
- Techniques for mountain or water rescue
- Use of special recreation equipment
- Equestrian patrolling
- Saddling horses
- Packing supplies and equipment
- Comparable activities

For such positions, candidates must show that their experience and training has given them the specific technical knowledge and skills needed to perform the duties of the position for which they are being considered.

Interview Requirements

Candidates may, at the option of the agency, be required to appear for a pre-employment interview to evaluate skill in personal relationships for the public-contact aspects of park technician work.

Requirements for Motor Vehicle Operations

The duties of these positions normally include driving an automobile or truck. The applicant must, therefore, be a capable driver and must possess at the time of appointment, or obtain within 30 days, a valid driver's permit for the state or territory in which he lives or in which he will be principally employed, and a valid U.S. government operator's permit.

Selective Placement

For positions at grades GS-4 and above that require particular knowledge and skills, consideration may be restricted to those candidates whose background indicates that they possess the required knowledge and skills.

Guide for Evaluation of Candidates in Relation to Job Requirements

In evaluating each applicant's experience and training, attention should be given to the following factors:

- Knowledge of general park operations, conservation, or outdoor recreation programs applicable to parks
- Knowledge of history or scientific fields applicable to park work
- Specialized technical knowledge and skills of the types described under the section "Additional Knowledge and Skills" (primarily for GS-5 and above)
- The ability to make constructive suggestions for the modification or improvement of methods, procedures, plans, techniques, equipment, or programs
- The ability to work independently and plan day-to-day activities
- The ability to meet and deal effectively with the park visitors

The information for evaluating experience and training will be obtained from the application form. Confidential reference inquiries may be sent to supervisors, teachers, and others who can furnish useful information about the candidate's qualifications.

Special Physical Requirements

Applicants must be physically able to perform efficiently the duties of the positions. Some of the positions require arduous physical exertion under rigorous and unusual environmental conditions, such as travel over rugged, precipitous, slippery, and extremely hazardous terrain at high elevations—while carrying packs of heavy equipment. Applicants must be proportioned as to height and weight, and gross disproportion will be cause for rejection. Amputation or serious disabilities of arm, hand, leg, or foot will disqualify an applicant for appointment; however, there may be a few positions suitable for persons with minor handicaps. Vision, with or without glasses, must test at least 20/30 (Snellen) each eye. However, applicants with vision less than 20/30 (Snellen) in one eye will receive consideration if the other eye tests 20/20 (Snellen) with or without glasses. Applicants must be able to distinguish basic colors and must be able to hear the conversational voice, in each ear, with or without the use of a hearing aid. Since the duties of the position are exacting, responsible, and require extensive oral communication with the public, applicants must possess emotional and mental stability and unimpaired speech.

Written Test

Candidates for positions at GS-2 and GS-3 must pass a written test of abilities necessary to learn and perform the duties of the positions.

The U.S. Postal Service Positions

The United States Postal Service is an independent agency of the federal government. As such, employees of the Postal Service are federal employees who enjoy the very generous benefits offered by the government. These benefits include an automatic raise at least once a year, regular cost of living adjustments, liberal paid vacation and sick leave, life insurance, hospitalization, and the opportunity to join a credit union. At the same time, the operation of the Postal Service is businesslike and independent of politics. A postal worker's job is secure even though administrations may change. An examination system is used to fill vacancies. The examination system provides opportunities for those who are able and motivated to enter the Postal Service and to move within it.

Since postal employment is so popular, entry is very competitive. In most areas, the Postal Service Entrance Exams are administered only once every three years. The resulting list is used to fill vacancies as they occur in the next three years. An individual who is already employed by the Postal Service, however, may request to take an exam during those intervening years. Any person who has satisfactorily filled a position for a year or more may ask to take the exam for any other position and, if properly qualified, may fill a vacancy ahead of a person whose name is on the regular list. It is even possible to change careers within the Postal Service. If the exam for the precise position that you want will not be administered for some time, it might be worthwhile to take the exam for another position in hopes of entering the Postal Service and then moving from within.

One very common "instant progression" within the Postal Service is that from Clerk-Carrier, a GS-5 position, to Distribution Clerk, Machine (also known as Letter Sorting Machine Operator), a GS-6 position. Anyone who qualifies as a Clerk-Carrier is automatically offered the opportunity to take the machine exam. The advantages of becoming a Letter Sorting Machine Operator include not only a higher salary, but also increased employment possibilities. Mechanization is the wave of the future. The field is expanding, and there are far more openings for Machine Operators than there are for Clerks or Carriers. Of course, the desirability of the job leads to a greater number of applicants and a still more competitive position for you. This fact should further motivate you to study hard for your exam.

Salaries, hours, and some other working conditions are subject to frequent change. The postal workers have a very effective union that bargains for them and gains increasingly better conditions. At the time of your employment, you should make your own inquiry as to salary, hours, and other conditions as they apply to you. Job descriptions and requirements are less subject to change. In the next few pages, we quote job descriptions as provided by the government.

OCCUPATIONS WITHIN THE U.S. POSTAL SERVICE

The U.S. Postal Service handles billions of pieces of mail a year, including letters, magazines, and parcels. Close to a million workers are required to process and deliver this mail. The vast majority of Postal Service jobs are open to workers with four years of high school or less. The work is steady. Some of the jobs, such as Mail Carrier, offer a good deal of personal freedom. Other jobs, however, are more closely supervised and more routine.

NATURE AND LOCATION OF THE INDUSTRY

Most people are familiar with the duties of the Mail Carrier and the Post Office Window Clerk. Yet few are aware of the many different tasks required in processing mail and of the variety of occupations in the Postal Service.

At all hours of the day and night, a steady stream of letters, packages, magazines, and papers moves through the typical large post office. Mail Carriers have collected some of this mail from neighborhood mailboxes; some has been trucked in from surrounding towns or from the airport. When a truck arrives at the post office, Mail Handlers unload the mail. Postal Clerks then sort it according to destination. After being sorted, outgoing mail is loaded into trucks for delivery to the airport or nearby towns. Local mail is left for carriers to deliver the next morning.

To keep buildings and equipment clean and in good working order, the Postal Service employs a variety of service and maintenance workers, including Janitors, Laborers, Truck Mechanics, Electricians, Carpenters, and Painters. Some workers specialize in repairing machines that process mail.

Postal Inspectors audit the operations of post offices to see that they are run efficiently, that funds are spent properly, and that postal laws and regulations are observed. They also prevent and detect crimes such as theft, forgery, and fraud involving use of the mail.

Postmasters and Supervisors are responsible for the day-to-day operation of the post office, for hiring and promoting employees, and for setting up work schedules.

The Postal Service also contracts with private businesses to transport mail. There are more than 12,500 of these "Star" route contracts. Most "Star" route carriers use trucks to haul mail, but in some remote areas, horses or boats are used instead.

Almost 85 percent of all postal workers are in jobs directly related to processing and delivering mail. This group includes Postal Clerks, Mail Carriers, Mail Handlers, and Truck Drivers. Postmasters and Supervisors make up nearly 10 percent of total employment, and maintenance workers about 4 percent. The remainder includes such workers as Postal Inspectors, Guards, Personnel Workers, and Secretaries.

The Postal Service operates more than 41,000 installations. Most are post offices, but some serve special purposes such as handling payroll records or supplying equipment.

Although every community receives mail service, employment is concentrated in large metropolitan areas. Post offices in cities such as New York, Chicago, and Los Angeles employ a great number of workers because they not only process huge amounts of mail for their own populations, but also serve as mail-processing points for the smaller communities that surround them. These large city post offices have sophisticated machines for sorting the mail. In these post offices, Distribution Clerks who have qualified as Machine Operators quickly scan addresses and send letters on their way automatically by pushing the proper button. These clerks must be able to read addresses quickly and accurately, must be able to memorize codes and sorting schemes, and must demonstrate machine aptitude by their performance on the number series part of the exam.

TRAINING, OTHER QUALIFICATIONS, AND ADVANCEMENT

An applicant for a Postal Service job must pass an examination and meet minimum age requirements. Generally, the minimum age is 18 years, but a high-school graduate may begin work at 16 years if the job is not hazardous and does not require use of a motor vehicle. Many Postal Service jobs do not require formal education or special training. Applicants for these jobs are hired on the basis of their examination scores.

Applicants should apply at the post office where they wish to work and take the entrance examination for the job they want. Examinations for most jobs include a written test. A physical examination is required as well. Applicants for jobs that require strength and stamina are sometimes given a special test. The names of applicants who pass the examinations are placed on a list in the order of their scores. Separate eligibility lists are maintained for each post office.

Every applicant must pass the exam to find a place on the eligibility list. As compensation for their service, veterans enjoy certain extra consideration in their placement on the list. Five extra points are added to the passing score of an honorably discharged veteran and 10 extra points to the score of a veteran wounded in combat or disabled. Disabled veterans who have a compensable, service-connected disability of 10 percent or more are placed at the top of the eligibility list. When a job opens, the appointing officer chooses one of the top three applicants. Others are left on the list so that they can be considered for future openings.

New employees are trained either on the job by supervisors and other experienced employees or in local training centers. Training ranges from a few days to several months, depending on the job.

Advancement opportunities are available for most postal workers because there is a management commitment to providing career development. Also, employees can get preferred assignments, such as the day shift or a more desirable delivery route, as their seniority increases. When an opening occurs, employees may submit written requests, called *bids*, for assignment to the vacancy. The bidder who meets the qualifications and has the most seniority gets the job.

In addition, postal workers can advance to better-paying positions by learning new skills. Training programs are available for low-skilled workers who wish to become technicians or mechanics.

Applicants for supervisory jobs must pass an examination. Additional requirements for promotion may include training or education, a satisfactory work record, and appropriate personal characteristics such as leadership ability. If the leading candidates are equally qualified, length of service also is considered.

Although opportunities for promotion to supervisory positions in smaller post offices are limited, workers may apply for vacancies in a larger post office and thus increase their chances.

EMPLOYMENT OUTLOOK

Employment of postal clerks is expected to grow slowly. Most openings will result from the need to replace clerks who retire, die, or transfer to other occupations.

Although the amount of mail post offices handle is expected to grow as both the population and the number of businesses grow, modernization of post offices and installation of new equipment will increase the amount of mail each clerk can handle. For example, machines that semiautomatically mark destination codes on envelopes are now being tested. These codes can be read by computer-controlled letter-sorting machines that automatically drop each letter into the proper slot for its destination. With this system, clerks read addresses only once—at the time they are coded—instead of several times, as they now do. Eventually, this equipment will be installed in all large post offices. Thus, while the total number of postal clerks may not increase, there will be greater need for Distribution Clerks who operate sorting machines, and job opportunities will open up in more and more cities.

POST OFFICE CLERK-CARRIER

The Post Office Clerk-Carrier Exam is not a regularly scheduled exam given on the same date all over the country. Rather, the Clerk-Carrier Exam is separately scheduled in each postal geographic area. An area may comprise a number of states or, in densely populated regions, may consist of only a portion of one county. The frequency of administration also varies, though generally the exam is offered every two or three years.

When an exam is about to open in a postal area, the postal examiner for the area sends notices to all the post offices serviced by that area. The examiner also places ads in local newspapers and commercials over local radio stations. State employment offices receive and post copies of the announcement, and civil service newspapers carry the information as well.

Qualification Requirements

No experience is required. All applicants are required to take a written examination designed to test aptitude for learning and performing the duties of the position. The test of literacy and basic clerical stills will consist of four parts:

- Address checking
- Memory for addresses
- Number series
- Following oral directions

The test and completion of the forms will require approximately 2 hours and 15 minutes.

Duties

Clerks work indoors and must handle sacks of mail weighing as much as 70 pounds. They sort mail and distribute it by using a complicated scheme that must be memorized. Some clerks work at a public counter or window doing such jobs as selling stamps and weighing parcels, and are personally responsible for all money and stamps. Clerks may be on their feet all day. They also have to stretch, reach, and throw mail. Assignments to preferred positions, such as window clerks, typist and stenographic positions, and so on, are filled by open bid and reassignment of the senior qualified clerk.

Carriers must collect and deliver mail. Some carriers walk; other carriers drive. Carriers must be out in all kinds of weather. Almost all carriers have to carry mailbags on their shoulders; loads weigh as much as 35 pounds. Carriers sometimes have to load and unload sacks of mail weighing as much as 70 pounds.

The duties of newly appointed clerks and carriers are at times interchangeable. As representatives of the Postal Service, they must maintain pleasant and effective public relations with patrons and others, requiring a general familiarity with postal laws, regulations, and procedures commonly used.

Employees may be assigned to work in places exposed to public view. Their appearance influences the general public's confidence and attitude toward the entire Postal Service. Employees appointed under this standard are, therefore, expected to maintain neat and proper personal attire and grooming appropriate to conducting public business, including the wearing of a uniform when required.

Carrier Positions Requiring Driving

Before eligibles may be appointed to carrier positions that require driving, they must demonstrate a safe driving record and must pass the road test to show that they can safely drive a vehicle of the type used on the job.

Eligibles who fail to qualify in the road test will not be given the test again in the same group of hires. Those who fail the test a second time will not again be considered as a result of the same examination for appointment to a position that requires driving.

A valid driver's license from the state in which this post office is located must be presented at the time of appointment. Persons who do not have the license will not be appointed, but their names will be restored to the register. They may not again be considered for carrier positions until they have obtained the required driver's license. After hire, individuals must also be able to obtain the required type of government operator's permit.

Special Physical Requirements

The distant vision for clerk and carrier positions not involving driving duties must test at least 20/30 (Snellen) in one eye, glasses permitted, and applicants generally must be able to hear ordinary conversation with or without a hearing aid, but some clerk positions may be filled by the deaf.

For carrier positions that require driving, applicants must have at least 20/30 (Snellen) in one eye and 20/50 (Snellen) in the other with or without a corrective device for unlimited operation of motor vehicles. Hearing must be at least 15/20 with or without a hearing aid.

A physical examination will be required before appointment.

MAIL HANDLER/MAIL PROCESSOR

Qualification Requirements

No experience is required. All applicants will be required to take a written examination designed to test literacy and basic clerical skills. The four-part exam includes

- Address checking
- Memory for addresses
- Number series
- Following oral directions

The test and completion of the forms will require approximately 2 hours and 15 minutes. Competitors will be rated on a scale of 100. They must score at least 70 on the examination as a whole.

Duties

Mail Handlers load, unload, and move bulk mail, and perform duties incidental to the movement and processing of mail. Duties may include

- Separating mail sacks
- Sorting letter mail
- Canceling stamps on parcel post
- Operating canceling machines, addressographs, and mimeographs
- Operating fork-lift trucks
- Rewrapping parcels

Mail Processors operate mail-processing equipment, including bar code sorters and optical bar code readers; act as minor troubleshooters for the equipment; collate and bundle processed mail and transfer it from one work area to another; hand-process mail that cannot be handled by the machines; load mail into bins and onto trucks; and perform other related tasks.

Special Physical Requirements

Persons with amputation of arm, leg, or foot should not apply. A physical examination will be required before appointment.

Strength and Stamina Test

Mail Handler

When eligibles are within reach of appointment, they will be required to pass a test of strength and stamina. In this test they will be required to lift, shoulder, and carry two 70-pound sacks—one at a time—15 feet and load them on a hand truck. They will be required to push that truck to where there are some 40-, 50-, and 60-pound sacks. They will be required to load those sacks onto the truck. They will then have to unload the truck and return the truck to its original location. Eligibles will be notified when and where to report for the test of strength and stamina.

Persons with certain physical conditions will not be permitted to take the test of strength and stamina without prior approval of a physician. These physical conditions are

- Hernia or rupture
- Back trouble
- Heart trouble
- Pregnancy
- Any other condition that makes it dangerous to the eligible to lift and carry 70-pound weights

Persons with these physical conditions will be given special instructions at the time they are notified to report for the strength and stamina test.

An eligible being considered for an appointment who fails to qualify on the test will not be tested again in the same group of hires. If he fails the test a second time, his eligibility for the position of mail handler will be cancelled.

Mail Processor

Physical requirements for mail processors are not as stringent as those for mail handlers because the work is not as strenuous.

MARK-UP CLERK, AUTOMATED

Duties

The Mark-Up Clerk, Automated operates an electro-mechanical machine to process mail that is classified as "undeliverable as addressed." In doing this, the Mark-Up Clerk operates the keyboard of a computer terminal to enter and extract data to several databases including change of address, mailer's database, and address-correction file. The Mark-Up Clerk must select the correct program and operating mode for each application, must affix labels to mail either manually or with mechanical devices, and must prepare forms for address-correction services. Other duties may include distribution of processed mark-ups to appropriate stations for further handling, operating of a photocopy machine, and other job-related tasks in support of primary duties.

Qualification Requirements

An applicant for a Mark-Up Clerk position must have had either six months of clerical or office machine–operating experience or have completed high school, or have had a full academic year (36 weeks) of business school. A Mark-Up Clerk must also demonstrate the ability to type 40 words per minute for five minutes with no more than two errors. The record of experience and training must show the following:

- The ability to use reference materials and manuals
- The ability to perform effectively under pressure
- The ability to operate any office equipment appropriate to the position
- The ability to work with others
- The ability to read, understand, and apply certain regulations and procedures commonly used in processing mail undeliverable as addressed

For appointment, a Mark-Up Clerk must be 18 years old, or 16 years old if a high-school graduate. An applicant who will reach his or her 18th birthday within two years from the date of the exam may participate. A Mark-Up Clerk must be able to read, without strain, printed material the size of typewritten characters and must have 20/40 (Snellen) vision in one eye. Glasses are permitted. In addition, the applicant must pass an examination of literacy and basic clerical skills and a computer-administered alpha-numeric typing test.

RURAL CARRIER

Duties

The work of the Rural Carrier combines the work of the Window Clerk and the Letter Carrier, but also has special characteristics of its own. The Rural Carrier's day begins with sorting and loading the mail for delivery on his or her own route. Then comes a day's drive, which may be over unpaved roads and rough terrain. The rural carrier does most deliveries and pickups of outgoing mail from the car. Occasionally, however, bulky packages must be delivered directly to the homeowner's door. Since rural postal patrons may be far from the nearest post office, the rural carrier sells stamps, weighs and charges for packages to be mailed, and performs most other services performed by window clerks in post offices. At the end of the day, the rural carrier returns to the post office with outgoing mail and money collected in various transactions. The rural carrier must be able to account for the stamps, postcards, and other supplies with which he or she left in the morning and must "balance the books" each day.

A rural carrier enjoys a great deal of independence. No supervisor looks over his or her shoulder. On the other hand, there is no supervisor to turn to for advice on how to handle a new situation that may come up.

Qualification Requirements

The qualifying exam for Rural Carrier is a four-part test of literacy and basic clerical skills that requires about 2 hours and 15 minutes to administer. The parts of the exam are

- Address checking
- Memory for addresses
- Number series
- Following oral directions

The Postal Service sends each applicant a set of sample questions along with the admission card for the exam and the detailed application form. At the test site, the applicant has a chance to try some sample questions before beginning the exam itself.

Since the rural carrier's job requires driving, the minimum age for a Rural Carrier is 18. The Rural Carrier must have a valid driver's license, good eyesight, and the ability to hear ordinary conversation (glasses and hearing aids are permitted). In addition, the Rural Carrier must demonstrate physical stamina and the ability to withstand the rigors of the job.

GARAGE MAN/DRIVER, TRACTOR/TRAILER OPERATOR, MOTOR VEHICLE OPERATOR

Duties

What all the above job titles have in common is driving various Postal Service vehicles on the highway and within the lots and properties of the Postal Service.

Garage Men are responsible for seeing that each vehicle is in the proper place at the proper time and that each vehicle is roadworthy before it is released. Garage Men must keep accurate records of all activity as it affects each vehicle and must follow through on what movement or maintenance is required.

Tractor/Trailer Operators drive the huge mail rigs from city to city along the highways, delivering large quantities of mail as quickly as possible within the bounds of safety. The work of a Postal Service Tractor/Trailer Operator is really no different from the work of a Tractor/Trailer Operator for private industry.

Motor Vehicle Operators drive the various other Postal Service vehicles as needed, both within and between towns and cities.

Qualification Requirements

The exam for all these positions is designed to test powers of observation, ability to express oneself, accuracy in record keeping, familiarity with road signs, and ability to follow instructions. The exam is in two parts of 40 questions each. Applicants have 60 minutes to answer each part. The test requires concentration and careful attention to details. The sample questions that the Postal Service sends to applicants provide a good idea of what to expect from the exam itself.

Since all these positions require driving, applicants must be licensed drivers over the age of 18. In addition, applicants must have good eyesight and hearing and be in excellent health and physical condition. A physical exam and strength and stamina tests are part of the hiring process. Candidates must also take training and qualify for federal licensing on the vehicle they are required to drive, and for a state commercial driver's license (CDL).

POSTAL POLICE OFFICER

Duties

A Postal Police Officer is essentially a security guard at post offices and at other postal installations and facilities. The Postal Police Officer may work inside postal buildings or out of doors at loading docks and in parking lots. A Postal Police Officer may be armed.

Qualification Requirements

An applicant for the position of Postal Police Officer must be at least 20 years of age, and, unless a veteran, cannot be appointed until reaching the age of 21 years. The Postal Police Officer must be physically able to perform the duties of the job, must have good weight in proportion to height, must have color vision and good distant vision (no weaker than 20/40 in one eye and 20/50 in the other eye correctable to 20/20), and must have keen hearing. Emotional and mental stability are essential for the armed officer, and a psychological interview is part of the qualification process. The candidate must demonstrate the ability to deal with the public in a courteous and tactful manner; to work in stressful situations; to collect, assemble, and act on pertinent facts; to prepare clear and accurate records; to deal effectively with individuals and groups; and to express him- or herself in both oral and written communications. A background investigation will be made on all otherwise qualified candidates. In order to be considered, each applicant must pass a written qualifying exam with a score of 70 or better out of a possible 100. The examination tests observation and memory, word knowledge, and the ability to arrange sentences in logical order.

The ACWA Groups

The acronym ACWA stands for Administrative Careers With America. The ACWA exams were introduced with great fanfare in June of 1990. There were six ACWA exams, one for each of the six ACWA occupational groups. The exams were similar in style and level of difficulty; the differences were mainly in actual subject content of the questions.

The Office of Personnel Management administered the ACWA exams and established and maintained registers of eligible job aspirants. Upon request of the various agencies, OPM made available names of eligibles in rank order. The ACWA process was meant to simplify and streamline testing and hiring for many GS-5 to GS-7 positions and to make hiring as unbiased as possible.

The decentralization movement of the mid-1990s led to reorganization of the entire hiring process. OPM remains the overseer of civil service practices, but it is no longer the testing and hiring superagency. Each department, each agency, and each bureau announces vacancies as they occur and establishes its own procedures for filling those vacancies. In some instances there is no formal written examination. Other agencies devise their own exams. Still others turn to OPM for assistance of some sort.

The current role of OPM, with respect to testing and hiring, is to serve as a consultant to individual bureaus and agencies. Upon request, OPM will still administer an exam for an individual agency, but more often OPM makes available its bank of exam questions and the agency proceeds on its own. Some agencies have simply adopted the relevant ACWA exam, dropping the ACWA designation. Others have chosen blocks of ACWA questions and merged them with questions borrowed from other OPM exams or with original questions written specifically for the exam.

ACWA no longer exists, but ACWA questions are very much alive. Many positions that fall into the "ACWA groups" test for jobs with ACWA-style questions. In addition, ACWA-style questions sometimes appear on the examinations for positions outside these groups. If your area of interest appears on the following lists, be alert to the possibility of ACWA-style questions on your exam. The name of your exam will not be ACWA, but do pay attention to the sample ACWA questions that begin on page 226.

BUSINESS, FINANCE, AND MANAGEMENT OCCUPATIONS

Agricultural Programs*: *Includes*

    Agricultural Marketing

    Agricultural Program Specialist

Business: *Includes*

    Appraising and Assessing

    Bond Sales Promotion

    Budget Analysis

    Building Management

    Communication Specialist*

    Contract Specialist*

    Financial Administration and Programs

    Financial Institution Examining*

    Food Assistance Program Specialist

    General Business and Industry

    Housing Management

    Public Utilities Specialist

    Realty

    Wage and Hour Law Administration

Finance*: *Includes*

    Financial Analysis

    Insurance Examining

    Loan Specialist

Industrial Programs*: *Includes*

    Industrial Property Management

    Industrial Specialist

    Quality Assurance Specialist

Supply: *Includes*

    Distribution Facilities and Storage Management

    General Supply

    Inventory Management

    Logistics Management

    Packaging

    Property Disposal

    Supply Cataloging

    Supply Program Management

    Trade Specialist*

Transportation*: *Includes*

    Highway Safety Management

    Traffic Management

    Transportation Industry Analysis

    Transportation Operations

    Transportation Specialist

    Unemployment Insurance*

An asterisk (*) denotes positions with specific qualification requirements.

Best Opportunities—The options offering the best opportunities for employment are Business, Contract Specialist, Industrial Programs, and Supply.

BENEFITS REVIEW, TAX, AND LEGAL OCCUPATIONS

Claims Examining: *Includes*

Civil Service Retirement Claims Examining

Contact Representative

General Claims Examining

Passport and Visa Examining

Unemployment Compensation Claims Examining

Veterans Claims Examining

Workers' Compensation Claims Examining

Land Law Examining*

Paralegal Specialist

Social Insurance Administration (Representative)* and Social Insurance Claims Examining

Social Services

Tax Law Specialist*

Tax Technician*

An asterisk (*) denotes positions with specific qualification requirements.

PERSONNEL ADMINISTRATION AND COMPUTER OCCUPATIONS

Administration: *Includes*

Administrative Officer

Miscellaneous Administration and Programs

Computer Specialists Trainee

Personnel: *Includes*

Contractor Industrial Relations

Employee Development

Employee Relations

Labor-Management Relations Examining

Labor Relations

Manpower Development

Military Personnel Management

Occupational Analysis

Personnel Management

Personnel Staffing

Position Classification

Salary and Wage Administration

Program Analysis: *Includes*

Management Analysis

Program Analysis

Vocational Rehabilitation*

An asterisk (*) denotes positions with specific qualification requirements.

HEALTH, SAFETY, AND ENVIRONMENTAL OCCUPATIONS

Environmental Protection Specialist

Hospital Housekeeping Management*

Outdoor Recreation Planning*

Public Health Program Specialist

Safety and Occupational Health Management*

An asterisk (*) denotes positions with specific qualification requirements.

LAW ENFORCEMENT AND INVESTIGATION OCCUPATIONS

Alcohol, Tobacco, and Firearms Inspection

Civil Aviation Security Specialist

Criminal Investigator

Customs Inspector

Game Law Enforcement

General Investigator

Immigration Inspector

Import Specialist and Security: *Includes*

Import Specialist

Intelligence

Security Administration

Internal Revenue Officer

Park Ranger*

Public Health Quarantine Inspection*

Securities Compliance Examining*

Wage and Hour Compliance

An asterisk (*) denotes positions with specific qualification requirements.

WRITING AND PUBLIC INFORMATION OCCUPATIONS

Agricultural Market Reporting*

Archives Specialist

General Arts and Information (excluding Fine and
Applied Arts)

Public Affairs

Technical Information Services*

Technical Writing and Editing*

Writing and Editing

An asterisk (*) denotes positions with specific qualification requirements.

THREE

Useful Information About Civil Service Tests

CONTENTS

1. Give yourself enough time to prepare for the exam. Start studying weeks ahead of time; study every day; don't cram in the last 24 hours.
2. Arrive for your exam rested and relaxed. Get a good night's sleep before the exam. Leave home early enough so that you are not flustered by traffic or transit delays.
3. Arrive a bit early so that if you are not assigned a seat you can choose one away from drafts or a flickering light.
4. Wear a watch. Bring identification and an admission ticket if one was issued to you.
5. Listen to instructions before the exam begins. Ask questions if there is anything that you do not fully understand.
6. Read directions carefully. Directions that state "Mark (D) if all three names being compared are alike" are very different from directions that state "Mark (D) if none of the three names being compared are alike." Misreading these directions will ruin your score.
7. Read every word of every question. Little words like "not," "most," "all," "every," and "except" can make a big difference.
8. Read all the answer choices before you mark your answer. Don't just choose the first answer that seems correct; read them all to find out which answer is best.
9. Mark your answers by completely blackening the space of your choice. Every answer must be recorded in a space on the answer sheet.
10. Mark only one answer for each question.
11. If you change your mind, erase completely and cleanly. Never cross out an answer.
12. Answer the questions in order. If you are not sure of an answer, eliminate those answers that are obviously wrong and guess from those remaining. Mark the question booklet so that you can return and rethink the guesses if you have time.
13. Check often to be certain that you are marking each question in the right space and that you have not skipped a space by mistake. The answer sheet is scored by a machine. Question 8 must be answered in space 8; question 52 in space 52.
14. Stay awake. Stay alert. Work steadily and carefully using all the time allowed to earn your best possible score.

OPM Examinations

The Office of Personnel Management (OPM) administers a wide range of examinations for many different positions in federal government service. Some of these exams are known by their distinctive names. Among these are the Treasury Enforcement Agent Exam (TEA), given to special agent candidates in a number of departments and to Deputy U.S. Marshal candidates; the Border Patrol Agent Exam; and Administrative Careers with America (ACWA), the entry exam for a wide variety of administrative, management, and professional careers. Other OPM exams have descriptive titles such as "The Federal Clerical Examination" or are simply known by the job titles for which they test. Some OPM-administered exams are unique to the agencies and positions for which they test. These tailor-made exams tend to draw questions from the whole gamut of OPM exams as appropriate to the specific position. Your best preparation for any unspecified exam is familiarity and competence with all exam question types represented in these pages.

The first examination that follows has no distinctive name; the Office of Personnel Management identifies it only by number, Exam 704. This examination is administered to applicants for a variety of government jobs. Among the positions to which this exam applies are Federal Protective Officer and U.S. Department of the Interior Park Police. It lends questions to other examinations as well. This exam includes five different types of questions. The first, name and number comparisons, checks for detail-mindedness and speed and accuracy of observation and discrimination. The two verbal skills question types, reading comprehension and vocabulary, seek to measure the applicant's ability to understand directions and written materials and to communicate effectively. The last two types of questions, figure analogies and number series, are measures of reasoning, analytical ability, and creative thinking.

The sample questions that follow are the official sample questions distributed by the Office of Personnel Management. Try your hand at these questions to evaluate your skill with them and your chances for success on this exam. We have supplied a full set of explanations of the correct answers to help you understand the rationale behind the questions and to lead your thinking processes so that you can answer such questions on your own.

The structure of a recent full-length exam was as follows:

Part I:	Name and Number Comparisons
	8 minutes; 50 questions
	Questions were arranged in order of increasing difficulty so that toward the end of the section, number groups consisted of 8 and 9 digits.
Part II:	Vocabulary and Reading Comprehension
	25 minutes; 30 questions
	15 vocabulary questions; 15 reading questions
Part III:	Symbol Reasoning
	20 minutes; 20 questions
	Questions were based on curves and angles, on sizes of symbols, and on location of symbols within symbols rather than on quality of lines as in the sample questions.
Part IV:	Numerical Sequence
	20 minutes; 24 questions

ANSWER SHEET: SAMPLE QUESTIONS: OPM EXAM 704

1. Ⓐ Ⓑ Ⓒ Ⓓ Ⓔ	13. Ⓐ Ⓑ Ⓒ Ⓓ Ⓔ	25. Ⓐ Ⓑ Ⓒ Ⓓ Ⓔ	37. Ⓐ Ⓑ Ⓒ Ⓓ Ⓔ
2. Ⓐ Ⓑ Ⓒ Ⓓ Ⓔ	14. Ⓐ Ⓑ Ⓒ Ⓓ Ⓔ	26. Ⓐ Ⓑ Ⓒ Ⓓ Ⓔ	38. Ⓐ Ⓑ Ⓒ Ⓓ Ⓔ
3. Ⓐ Ⓑ Ⓒ Ⓓ Ⓔ	15. Ⓐ Ⓑ Ⓒ Ⓓ Ⓔ	27. Ⓐ Ⓑ Ⓒ Ⓓ Ⓔ	39. Ⓐ Ⓑ Ⓒ Ⓓ Ⓔ
4. Ⓐ Ⓑ Ⓒ Ⓓ Ⓔ	16. Ⓐ Ⓑ Ⓒ Ⓓ Ⓔ	28. Ⓐ Ⓑ Ⓒ Ⓓ Ⓔ	40. Ⓐ Ⓑ Ⓒ Ⓓ Ⓔ
5. Ⓐ Ⓑ Ⓒ Ⓓ Ⓔ	17. Ⓐ Ⓑ Ⓒ Ⓓ Ⓔ	29. Ⓐ Ⓑ Ⓒ Ⓓ Ⓔ	41. Ⓐ Ⓑ Ⓒ Ⓓ Ⓔ
6. Ⓐ Ⓑ Ⓒ Ⓓ Ⓔ	18. Ⓐ Ⓑ Ⓒ Ⓓ Ⓔ	30. Ⓐ Ⓑ Ⓒ Ⓓ Ⓔ	42. Ⓐ Ⓑ Ⓒ Ⓓ Ⓔ
7. Ⓐ Ⓑ Ⓒ Ⓓ Ⓔ	19. Ⓐ Ⓑ Ⓒ Ⓓ Ⓔ	31. Ⓐ Ⓑ Ⓒ Ⓓ Ⓔ	43. Ⓐ Ⓑ Ⓒ Ⓓ Ⓔ
8. Ⓐ Ⓑ Ⓒ Ⓓ Ⓔ	20. Ⓐ Ⓑ Ⓒ Ⓓ Ⓔ	32. Ⓐ Ⓑ Ⓒ Ⓓ Ⓔ	44. Ⓐ Ⓑ Ⓒ Ⓓ Ⓔ
9. Ⓐ Ⓑ Ⓒ Ⓓ Ⓔ	21. Ⓐ Ⓑ Ⓒ Ⓓ Ⓔ	33. Ⓐ Ⓑ Ⓒ Ⓓ Ⓔ	45. Ⓐ Ⓑ Ⓒ Ⓓ Ⓔ
10. Ⓐ Ⓑ Ⓒ Ⓓ Ⓔ	22. Ⓐ Ⓑ Ⓒ Ⓓ Ⓔ	34. Ⓐ Ⓑ Ⓒ Ⓓ Ⓔ	46. Ⓐ Ⓑ Ⓒ Ⓓ Ⓔ
11. Ⓐ Ⓑ Ⓒ Ⓓ Ⓔ	23. Ⓐ Ⓑ Ⓒ Ⓓ Ⓔ	35. Ⓐ Ⓑ Ⓒ Ⓓ Ⓔ	47. Ⓐ Ⓑ Ⓒ Ⓓ Ⓔ
12. Ⓐ Ⓑ Ⓒ Ⓓ Ⓔ	24. Ⓐ Ⓑ Ⓒ Ⓓ Ⓔ	36. Ⓐ Ⓑ Ⓒ Ⓓ Ⓔ	48. Ⓐ Ⓑ Ⓒ Ⓓ Ⓔ

Sample Questions: OPM Exam 704

Each question has several suggested answers lettered (A), (B), (C), and so on. Decide which one is the best answer to the question. Then, on the sample answer sheet, find the answer space that is numbered the same as the number of the question and darken completely the circle that is lettered the same as the letter of your answer. Compare your answers with those given. Then study the explanations of the correct answers that follow the correct answer key.

Directions: Sample questions 1 through 20 require name and number comparisons. In each line across the page there are three names or numbers that are very similar. Compare the three names or numbers and decide which ones are exactly alike. On your sample answer sheet, mark the answer

A   if ALL THREE names or numbers are exactly ALIKE

B   if only the FIRST and SECOND names or numbers are exactly ALIKE

C   if only the FIRST and THIRD names or numbers are exactly ALIKE

D   if only the SECOND and THIRD names or numbers are exactly ALIKE

E   if ALL THREE names or numbers are DIFFERENT

1.	Davis Hazen	David Hozen	David Hazen
2.	Lois Appel	Lois Appel	Lois Apfel
3.	June Allan	Jane Allan	Jane Allan
4.	Emily Neal Rouse	Emily Neal Rowse	Emily Neal Rowse
5.	H. Merritt Audubon	H. Merriott Audubon	H. Merritt Audubon
6.	6219354	6219354	6219354
7.	2312793	2312793	2312793
8.	1065407	1065407	1065047
9.	3457988	3457986	3457986
10.	4695682	4695862	4695682
11.	Francis Ransdell	Frances Ramsdell	Francis Ramsdell
12.	Cornelius Detwiler	Cornelius Detwiler	Cornelius Detwiler
13.	Stricklund Kanedy	Stricklund Kanedy	Stricklund Kanedy
14.	Joy Harlor Witner	Joy Harloe Witner	Joy Harloe Witner
15.	R.M.O. Uberroth	R.M.O. Uberroth	R.N.O. Uberroth
16.	2395890	2395890	2395890
17.	1926341	1926347	1926314
18.	5261383	5261383	5261338
19.	8125690	8126690	8125609
20.	6177396	6177936	6177396

Sample questions 21 through 30 require verbal skills.
Directions: *Reading. In questions 21 through 25, read the paragraph carefully and base your answers on the material given.*

21. Probably few people realize, as they drive on a concrete road, that steel is used to keep the surface flat and even, in spite of the weight of buses and trucks. Steel bars, deeply embedded in the concrete, provide sinews to take the stresses so that they cannot crack the slab or make it wavy.

    The paragraph best supports the statement that a concrete road
    (A) is expensive to build.
    (B) usually cracks under heavy weights.
    (C) is used exclusively for heavy traffic.
    (D) is reinforced with other material.

22. The likelihood of America's exhausting its natural resources seems to be growing less. All kinds of waste are being reworked and new uses are constantly being found for almost everything. We are getting more use out of our goods and are making many new by-products out of what was formerly thrown away.

    The paragraph best supports the statement that we seem to be in less danger of exhausting our resources because
    (A) economy is found to lie in the use of substitutes.
    (B) more service is obtained from a given amount of material.
    (C) we are allowing time for nature to restore them.
    (D) supply and demand are better controlled.

23. Through advertising, manufacturers exercise a high degree of control over consumers' desires. However, the manufacturer assumes enormous risks in attempting to predict what consumers will want and in producing goods in quantity and distributing them in advance of final selection by the consumers.

    The paragraph best supports the statement that manufacturers
    (A) can eliminate the risk of overproduction by advertising.
    (B) distribute goods directly to the consumers.
    (C) must depend upon the final consumers for the success of their undertakings.
    (D) can predict with great accuracy the success of any product they put on the market.

24. What constitutes skill in any line of work is not always easy to determine; economy of time must be carefully distinguished from economy of energy, as the quickest method may require the greatest expenditure of muscular effort and may not be essential or at all desirable.

    The paragraph best supports the statement that
    (A) the most efficiently executed task is not always the one done in the shortest time.
    (B) energy and time cannot both be conserved in performing a single task.
    (C) a task is well done when it is performed in the shortest time.
    (D) skill in performing a task should not be acquired at the expense of time.

25. In the relations of people to nature, the procuring of food and shelter is fundamental. With the migration of people to various climates, ever new adjustments to the food supply and to the climate became necessary.

    The paragraph best supports the statement that the means by which people supply their material needs are
    (A) accidental.
    (B) varied.
    (C) limited.
    (D) inadequate.

Directions: *Vocabulary. For questions 26 through 30, choose the one of the four suggested answers that means most nearly the same as the word in italics.*

26. *Flexible* means most nearly
    (A) breakable
    (B) flammable
    (C) pliable
    (D) weak

27. *Option* means most nearly
    (A) use
    (B) choice
    (C) value
    (D) blame

28. To *verify* means most nearly to
    (A) examine
    (B) explain
    (C) confirm
    (D) guarantee

29. *Previous* means most nearly
    (A) abandoned
    (B) former
    (B) timely
    (D) younger

30. *Respiration* means most nearly
    (A) recovery
    (B) breathing
    (C) pulsation
    (D) sweating

Directions: *Each of these reasoning questions, 31 through 35, consists of two sets of symbols. Find the one rule that explains the similarity of the symbols within each set and also explains the difference between the two sets. Among the five suggested answers, find the symbol that can best be substituted for the question mark in the second set. In all these questions you will find details that have nothing to do with the principle of the question: to find the similarity between the symbols within a set and the difference between the sets.*

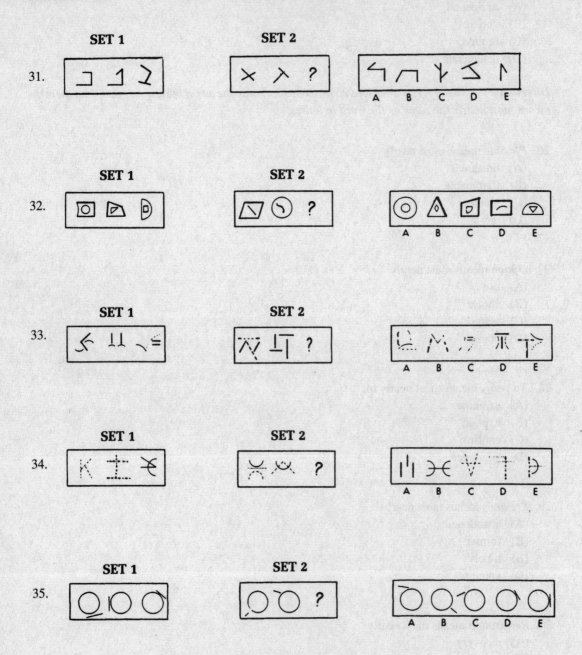

Directions: Questions 36 through 48 require number reasoning skills. In each question there is at the left a series of numbers that follow some definite order and, at the right, five sets of two numbers each. You are to look at the numbers in the series at the left and find out what order they follow. Then, from the suggested answers at the right, select the set that gives the next two numbers in the series.

36.	12 10 13 10 14 10 15	(A) 15 10	(B) 10 15	(C) 10 16	(D) 10 10	(E) 15 16
37.	9 2 9 4 9 6 9	(A) 9 9	(B) 9 8	(C) 8 10	(D) 10 8	(E) 8 9
38.	1 2 5 6 9 10 13	(A) 15 17	(B) 14 15	(C) 14 16	(D) 15 16	(E) 14 17
39.	1 2 3 2 2 3 3 2 3	(A) 2 3	(B) 3 2	(C) 3 4	(D) 4 2	(E) 4 3
40.	9 10 12 15 19 24 30	(A) 35 40	(B) 36 42	(C) 30 36	(D) 30 37	(E) 37 45
41.	35 34 31 30 27 26 23	(A) 22 19	(B) 22 20	(C) 23 22	(D) 20 19	(E) 20 17
42.	16 21 19 24 22 27 25	(A) 28 30	(B) 30 28	(C) 29 24	(D) 30 27	(E) 26 29
43.	48 44 40 36 32 28 24	(A) 22 20	(B) 24 22	(C) 23 22	(D) 20 18	(E) 20 16
44.	20 30 39 47 54 60 65	(A) 70 75	(B) 68 70	(C) 69 72	(D) 66 67	(E) 68 71
45.	10 13 13 16 16 19 19	(A) 19 19	(B) 19 22	(C) 22 22	(D) 22 25	(E) 22 24
46.	2 4 25 8 16 25 32	(A) 32 35	(B) 25 64	(C) 48 25	(D) 25 48	(E) 64 25
47.	38 15 32 17 27 19 23	(A) 20 20	(B) 21 26	(C) 20 21	(D) 21 20	(E) 21 25
48.	80 12 40 17 20 22 10	(A) 25 15	(B) 15 25	(C) 24 5	(D) 25 5	(E) 27 5

Correct Answers

1.	E	9.	D	17.	E	25.	B	33.	B	41.	A
2.	B	10.	C	18.	B	26.	C	34.	E	42.	B
3.	D	11.	E	19.	E	27.	B	35.	B	43.	E
4.	D	12.	A	20.	C	28.	C	36.	C	44.	C
5.	C	13.	A	21.	D	29.	B	37.	E	45.	C
6.	A	14.	D	22.	B	30.	B	38.	E	46.	E
7.	A	15.	B	23.	C	31.	E	39.	D	47.	D
8.	B	16.	A	24.	A	32.	D	40.	E	48.	E

Explanations

1. **(E)** In the first column, the first name differs from the first names in the other two columns. In the second column, the last name is different.

2. **(B)** In the first two columns, the two names are identical, but in the third column, the last name is different.

3. **(D)** In the second and third columns, the two names are identical, but in the first column, the first name is different.

4. **(D)** In the second and third columns, the names are identical, but in the first column, the last name is different.

5. **(C)** In all three columns, the initial and last names are identical, but in the second column, the middle name differs from the middle name in the first and third columns.

6. **(A)** All three numbers are identical.

7. **(A)** All three numbers are identical.

8. **(B)** In the first two columns, the last three digits are "407," but in the third column, they are "047."

9. **(D)** The number in the first column ends with "88," while the other two columns end with "86."

10. **(C)** Again the difference occurs in the ending of the numbers. The numbers in the first and third columns end with "682," while the number in the second column ends with "862."

11. **(E)** In the first column, the last name differs from the last name in the other two columns. In the second column, the first name differs from that in the other two.

12. **(A)** All three names are identical.

13. **(A)** All three names are identical.

14. **(D)** The only difference is that in the first column, the middle name differs from that in the other two columns.

15. **(B)** The names in the first two columns are identical, but in the third column, the second initial is different.

16. **(A)** All three numbers are identical.

17. **(E)** All the numbers differ from each other. In the first column, the last two digits are "41"; in the second column they are "47"; and in the third, "14."

18. **(B)** The first two columns end with "83," while the third ends with "38."

19. **(E)** There are differences in central digits and in final digits. The "66" in the middle of the number in the second column differs from the "56" in the middle of the other two. The "09" at the end of the number in the third column differs from the "90" at the end of the other two.

20. **(C)** The number in the second column ends with "936," while the numbers in the first and third columns end with "396."

21. **(D)** The steel bars that keep the concrete road from cracking are reinforcing it.

22. **(B)** The effect of recycling is to make greater use of resources so that we do not need to constantly deplete fresh resources.

23. **(C)** If consumers don't buy, the manufacturers are stuck with excess stock.

24. **(A)** Many considerations must enter into an assessment of efficiency. Time, effort, energy, and money are all factors.

25. **(B)** The ability of people to adjust and adapt to changing climates and to changing circumstances implies that human beings are capable of varied responses and behaviors.

26. **(C)** *Flexible*, the opposite of rigid or stiff, means *easily bent*, *adjustable*, or *pliable*.

27. **(B)** An *option* is a *choice*.

28. **(C)** To *verify* is to *check the accuracy of* or to *confirm*.

29. **(B)** *Previous* means *occurring before in time or order*, hence *former*.

30. **(B)** *Respiration* is *breathing*.

31. **(E)** The simplest general rule that guides this question is that all the symbols are made up of lines that touch each other. In the first set, each of the symbols consists of three lines that touch. The second set contains symbols consisting of two lines that touch. Only choice (E) fulfills this requirement.

32. **(D)** The general rule governing this question is that all symbols are made up to two figures, one inside the other. The first set consists of a closed figure inside the outer figure. In the second set, there is a single line inside the outer figure. Only choice (D) conforms to this rule. Note that the shapes of the figures are irrelevant to the question.

33. **(B)** The general rule is that all symbols are made up of four lines. In the first set, all symbols consist of both straight and curved lines. In the second set, the symbols are made up of straight lines only. Of the choices, only (B) is made up of only straight lines. Whether or not lines within a symbol touch is irrelevant to the question.

34. **(E)** Each symbol is made up of three lines. In set 1, the lines that compose each symbol are of like quality, that is, solid, broken, or dotted. In set 2, the lines composing each symbol are not of the same quality. Of the choices, only (E) consists of straight and dotted lines. All the other choices are of figures made up of lines of the same quality. The shapes of the lines are irrelevant.

35. **(B)** All symbols consist of a circle and a line. In the first set, the line is tangent to the circle. In the second set, the line is perpendicular or nearly perpendicular to the circle. Choice (B) best fits this requirement.

36. **(C)** The series is a simple +1 series with the number <u>10</u> inserted after each step of the series.

37. **(E)** This is a simple +2 series with the number <u>9</u> appearing before each member of the series.

38. **(E)** Read aloud (softly):   1   2 ╲   ╱5   6 ╲   ╱9   10 ╲   ╱13
    whisper   ╲3   4 ╱   ╲7   8 ╱   ╲11   12 ╱

The next number to read aloud is <u>14</u>, to be followed by a whispered <u>15</u>, <u>16</u>, and then aloud again <u>17</u>. Sometimes the ear is more perceptive than the eye.

39. **(D)** In this series a rhythm emerges when you accent the first number in each group: <u>1</u> 2 3; <u>2</u> 2 3; <u>3</u> 2 3. Try grouping and sounding out before you begin to search for more complicated patterns.

Many number series questions can be solved by writing the direction and amount of change between numbers in the space above and between each member of the series.

40. **(E)** 9^{+1} 10^{+2} 12^{+3} 15^{+4} 19^{+5} 24^{+6} 30^{+7} 37^{+8} 45

41. **(A)** 35^{-1} 34^{-3} 31^{-1} 30^{-3} 27^{-1} 26^{-3} 23^{-1} 22^{-3} 19

42. **(B)** 16^{+5} 21^{-2} 19^{+5} 24^{-2} 22^{+5} 27^{-2} 25^{+5} 30^{-2} 28

43. **(E)** 48^{-4} 44^{-4} 40^{-4} 36^{-4} 32^{-4} 28^{-4} 24^{-4} 20^{-4} 16

44. **(C)** 20^{+10} 30^{+9} 39^{+8} 47^{+7} 54^{+6} 60^{+5} 65^{+4} 69^{+3} 72

Some arithmetical series may be interrupted by a particular number that appears periodically or by a repetition of numbers according to a pattern. In marking the progression of these series, write "r" in the space between repeated numbers and circle extraneous numbers that are repeated periodically.

When choosing your answer you must be alert to the point at which the pattern was interrupted. Do not further repeat a number that has already been repeated; do not forget to repeat before continuing the arithmetical pattern if repetition is called for at this point in the series.

45. **(C)** 10^{+3} 13^r 13^{+3} 16^r 16^{+3} 19^r 19^{+3} 22^r 22

46. **(E)**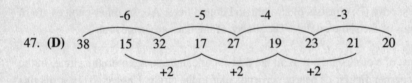

Some number series questions encompass two alternating series. Each of the two series that alternate will follow a pattern, but they may not necessarily follow the same pattern. Diagram one series above the row of numbers and the other below in order to determine the next two numbers.

47. **(D)**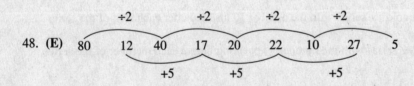

48. **(E)**

Sample Questions: The TEA Exam

The Treasury Enforcement Agent Exam (TEA) is given to candidates for the positions of Internal Security Inspector with the IRS; Secret Service Special Agent; Customs Special Agent; Bureau of Alcohol, Tobacco, and Firearms Special Agent; IRS Special Agent with the Criminal Investigation Division; Deputy U.S. Marshal; and a number of other positions as well. If you are a candidate for any of these positions, give careful attention to the official sample questions that follow. Even if you are applying for a local or state law enforcement position, you should give serious attention to all federal exam questions. Some of the same types of questions are likely to appear on whatever exam you must take.

The Treasury Enforcement Agent Exam (TEA) is divided into three parts: Part A, verbal reasoning; Part B, arithmetic reasoning; and Part C, problems for investigation. The official sample questions that follow are similar to the questions you will find in the actual test in terms of difficulty and form.

PART A—VERBAL REASONING QUESTIONS

In each of these questions you will be given a paragraph that contains all the information necessary to infer the correct answer. Use **only** the information provided in the paragraph. Do not speculate or make assumptions that go beyond this information. Also, assume that all information given in the paragraph is true, even if it conflicts with some fact known to you. Only one correct answer can be validly inferred from the information contained in the paragraph.

Pay special attention to negated verbs (for example, "are *not*") and negative prefixes (for example, "*in*complete" or "*dis*organized"). Also pay special attention to quantifiers, such as "all," "none," and "some." For example, from a paragraph in which it is stated that "it is not true that all contracts are legal," one can validly infer that "some contracts are not legal," or that "some contracts are illegal," or that "some illegal things are contracts," but one **cannot** validly infer that "no contracts are legal," or that "some contracts are legal." Similarly, from a paragraph that states "all contracts are legal" and "all contracts are two-sided agreements," one can infer that "some two-sided agreements are legal," but one **cannot** validly infer that "all two-sided agreements are legal."

Bear in mind that in some tests, universal quantifiers such as "all" and "none" often give away incorrect response choices. That is **not** the case in this test. Some correct answers will refer to "all" or "none" of the members of a group.

Be sure to distinguish between essential information and unessential, peripheral information. That is to say, in a real test question, the example above ("all contracts are legal" and "all contracts are two-sided agreements") would appear in a longer, full-fledged paragraph. It would be up to you to separate the essential information from its context and then to realize that a response choice that states "some two-sided agreements are legal" represents a valid inference and hence the correct answer.

Sample questions 1 and 2 are examples of the reading questions on the test.

1. Impressions made by the ridges on the ends of the fingers and thumbs are useful means of identification, since no two persons have the same pattern of ridges. If finger patterns from fingerprints are not decipherable, then they cannot be classified by general shape and contour or by pattern type. If they cannot be classified by these characteristics, then it is impossible to identify the person to whom the fingerprints belong.

The paragraph best supports the statement that
(A) if it is impossible to identify the person to whom fingerprints belong, then the fingerprints are not decipherable.

(B) if finger patterns from fingerprints are not decipherable, then it is impossible to identify the person to whom the fingerprints belong.

(C) if fingerprints are decipherable, then it is impossible to identify the person to whom they belong.

(D) if fingerprints can be classified by general shape and contour or by pattern type, then they are not decipherable.

(E) if it is possible to identify the person to whom fingerprints belong, then the fingerprints cannot be classified by general shape and contour or pattern.

The correct answer is response (B). The essential information from which the answer can be inferred is contained in the second and third sentences. These sentences state that "if finger patterns from fingerprints are not decipherable, then they cannot be classified by general shape and contour or by pattern type. If they cannot be classified by these characteristics, then it is impossible to identify the person to whom they belong." Since response (B) refers to a condition in which finger patterns from fingerprints are not decipherable, we know that, in that circumstance, they cannot be classified by general shape and contour or by pattern type. From the paragraph, we can infer that since they cannot be classified by these characteristics, then it is impossible to identify the person to whom the fingerprints belong.

Response (A) cannot be inferred because the paragraph does not give information about all the circumstances under which it is impossible to identify the person to whom the fingerprints belong. It may be that the person is not identifiable for reasons other than the decipherability of the person's fingerprints.

Response (C) is incorrect because the paragraph does not provide enough information to conclude whether or not it would be possible to identify the person to whom the fingerprints belong from the mere fact of the decipherability of the fingerprints.

Response (D) is wrong because it contradicts the information in the second sentence of the paragraph. From that sentence, it can be concluded that if fingerprints can be classified by general shape and contour or by pattern type, then they are decipherable.

Response (E) is incorrect for a similar reason; it contradicts the information presented in the third sentence of the paragraph.

2. Law enforcement agencies use scientific techniques to identify suspects or to establish guilt. One obvious application of such techniques is the examination of a crime scene. Some substances found at a crime scene yield valuable clues under microscopic examination. Clothing fibers, dirt particles, and even pollen grains may reveal important information to the careful investigator. Nothing can be overlooked because all substances found at a crime scene are potential sources of evidence.

The paragraph best supports the statement that

(A) all substances that yield valuable clues under microscopic examination are substances found at a crime scene.

(B) some potential sources of evidence are substances that yield valuable clues under microscopic examination.

(C) some substances found at a crime scene are not potential sources of evidence.

(D) no potential sources of evidence are substances found at a crime scene.

(E) some substances that yield valuable clues under microscopic examination are not substances found at a crime scene.

The correct answer is response (B). The essential information from which the answer can be inferred is contained in the third and fifth sentences. The third sentence tells us that "some substances found at a crime scene yield valuable clues under microscopic examination." The fifth sentence explains that "...all substances found at a crime scene are potential sources of evidence." Therefore, we can conclude that "some potential sources of evidence are substances that yield valuable clues under microscopic examination."

Response (A) cannot be inferred because the paragraph does not support the statement that all substances that yield valuable clues are found exclusively at a crime scene. It may be that valuable clues could be found elsewhere.

Responses (C) and (D) are incorrect because they contradict the fifth sentence of the paragraph, which clearly states that "all substances found at a crime scene are potential sources of evidence."

Response (E) is incorrect because the paragraph provides no information about the value of substances found somewhere other than at the crime scene.

PART B—ARITHMETIC REASONING QUESTIONS

In this part you will have to solve problems formulated in both verbal and numeric form. You will have to analyze a paragraph in order to set up the problem, and then solve it. If the exact answer is not given as one of the response choices, you should select response (E), "none of these." Sample questions 3 and 4 are examples of the arithmetic reasoning questions. The use of calculators will NOT be permitted during the actual testing; therefore, they should not be used to solve these sample questions.

3. A police department purchases badges at $16 each for all the graduates of the police training academy. The last training class graduated 10 new officers. What is the total amount of money the department will spend for badges for these new officers?
    (A) $70
    (B) $116
    (C) $160
    (D) $180
    (E) none of these

The correct response is (C). It can be obtained by computing the following:
$$16 \times 10 = 160$$

The badges are priced at $16 each. The department must purchase 10 of them for the new officers. Multiplying the price of one badge ($16) by the number of graduates (10) gives the total price for all of the badges.

Responses (A), (B), and (D) are the result of erroneous computations.

4. An investigator rented a car for six days and was charged $450. The car rental company charged $35 per day plus $.30 per mile driven. How many miles did the investigator drive the car?
    (A) 800
    (B) 900
    (C) 1,200
    (D) 1,500
    (E) none of these

The correct answer is (A). It can be obtained by computing the following:
$$6(35) + .30x = 450$$

The investigator rented the car for six days at $35 per day, which is $210; $210 subtracted from the total charge of $450 leaves $240, the portion of the total charge that was expended for the miles driven. This amount divided by the charge per mile ($240/.30) gives the number of miles (800) driven by the investigator.

Responses (B), (C), and (D) are the result of erroneous computations.

PART C—PROBLEMS FOR INVESTIGATION

In this part you will be presented with a paragraph and several related statements. Sample questions 5 through 9 are based on the following paragraph and statements. Read them carefully and then answer questions 5 through 9.

On October 30th, the Belton First National Bank discovered that the $3,000 it had received that morning from the Greenville First National Bank was in counterfeit $10, $20, and $50 bills. The genuine $3,000 had been counted by Greenville First National bank clerk, Iris Stewart, the preceding afternoon. They were packed in eight black leather satchels and stored in the bank vault overnight. Greenville First National clerk, Brian Caruthers, accompanied carriers James Clark and Howard O'Keefe to Belton in an armored truck. Belton First National clerk, Cynthia Randall, discovered the counterfeit bills when she examined the serial numbers of the bills.

During the course of the investigation, the following statements were made.

(1) Gerald Hathaway, clerk of the Greenville bank, told investigators that he had found the bank office open when he arrived to work on the morning of October 30th. The only articles that appeared to be missing were eight black leather satchels of the type used to transport large sums of money.

(2) Jon Perkins, head teller of the Greenville bank, told investigators that he did not check the contents of the black leather satchels after locking them in the vault around 4:30 p.m., on October 29th.

(3) Henry Green, janitor of the Greenville bank, said that he noticed Jon Perkins leaving the bank office around 5:30 p.m., one-half hour after the bank closed on October 29th. He said that Perkins locked the door.

(4) A scrap of cloth, identical to the material of the carriers' uniforms, was found caught in the seal of one of the black leather satchels delivered to Belton.

(5) Brian Caruthers, clerk, said he saw James Clark and Howard O'Keefe talking in a secretive manner in the armored truck.

(6) Thomas Stillman, Greenville bank executive, identified the eight black leather satchels containing the counterfeit money that arrived at the Belton First National Bank as the eight satchels that had disappeared from the bank office. He had noticed a slight difference in the linings of the satchels.

(7) Virginia Fowler, bank accountant, noticed two $10 bills with the same serial numbers as the lost bills in a bank deposit from Ferdinand's Restaurant of Greenville.

(8) Vincent Johnson, manager of Ferdinand's Restaurant, told police that Iris Stewart frequently dined there with her boyfriend.

5. Which one of the following statements best indicates that satchels containing the counterfeit bills were substituted for satchels containing genuine bills while they were being transported from Greenville to Belton?
   (A) statement (1)
   (B) statement (3)
   (C) statement (4)
   (D) statement (5)
   (E) statement (7)

The correct answer is (C). The armor carriers had the greatest opportunity to substitute counterfeit bills for real ones during the transportation procedure. The scrap of material from an armor carrier's uniform caught in the seal of one of the satchels strongly links the carriers to the crime.

6. Which one of the following statements best links the information given in statement (1) with the substitution of the counterfeit bills?
    (A) statement (2)
    (B) statement (3)
    (C) statement (4)
    (D) statement (5)
    (E) statement (6)

The correct answer is (E). Statement (1) establishes that eight satchels were missing from Greenville Bank. Statement (6) identifies the satchels that arrived at the Belton Bank as the missing satchels.

7. Which one of the following statements along with statement (7) best indicates that the substitution of the counterfeit bills casts suspicion on at least one employee of the Greenville bank?
    (A) statement (1)
    (B) statement (2)
    (C) statement (3)
    (D) statement (5)
    (E) statement (8)

The correct answer is (E). Statement (7) establishes that two stolen $10 bills were spent at Ferdinand's Restaurant. Statement (8) identifies a bank employee as a frequent diner at Ferdinand's Restaurant. This statement "casts suspicion" on the bank employee but does not prove complicity.

8. Which one of the following statements would least likely be used in proving a case?
    (A) statement (1)
    (B) statement (3)
    (C) statement (4)
    (D) statement (5)
    (E) statement (7)

The correct answer is (D). The fact that the bank clerk saw the armor carriers talking secretively may cast some suspicion but would not be useful in proving the case. Men who work together may very likely exchange private jokes or share personal information.

9. Which one of the following statements best indicates that the substitution of the counterfeit bills could have taken place before the satchels left the Greenville bank?
    (A) statement (1)
    (B) statement (2)
    (C) statement (3)
    (D) statement (4)
    (E) statement (7)

The correct answer is (B). The satchels were locked in the vault at 4:30 p.m. on one day and not delivered until the following morning. Since we learn in statement (2) that the satchels were not checked after they were locked into the vault, the exchange could have taken place in the Greenville Bank.

Sample Questions: Border Patrol Agent Exam

Applicants for the position of Border Patrol Agent must pass an OPM exam and qualify in the Spanish language. If the candidate feels comfortable speaking and understanding Spanish, he or she may choose to take an oral examination at the time of the interview for the position. If the candidate does not know any Spanish or if he or she is not certain of passing the oral exam, the candidate may elect to take a written multiple-choice test of ability to learn a foreign language. The multiple-choice language aptitude test must be requested and taken at the same time as the OPM exam. The candidate cannot choose the language aptitude exam after failing the oral Spanish exam at interview.

The following are official sample questions for the Border Patrol Agent Exam. This exam is administered by the Office of Personnel Management to candidates for other positions as well. The exam is a 65-question multiple-choice exam. It is divided into four parts, each of which is separately timed. The structure of the exam is as follows:

	Number of Questions	Timing (Minutes)
Part A		25
Vocabulary	15	
Reading Comprehension	15	
Part B		
English Usage (Grammar)	15	7
Part C		
General Knowledge and Judgement	10	10
Part D		
Logical Reasoning	10	15
Total	65	57

When the exam is scored, you will receive credit for every correct answer but suffer no penalty for a wrong answer. That means it is best to answer every question. A space left blank cannot raise your score, but even a wild guess could possibly help you. Choose the correct answer if you can. If not, eliminate obviously wrong answers and choose intelligently from the remaining choices, or make a wild stab if you must. The official instructions, which will be read to you in the examination room, state: "It will be to your advantage to answer every question in this test that you can, since your score will be number of right answers only. If you don't know the answer to a question, make the best guess you can. You may write in the test booklet if you need to."

These official sample questions are just samples. They will give you a good idea of the kinds of questions that you must answer.

Directions: *Each question has five suggested answers, lettered A, B, C, D, and E. Decide which one is the best answer to the question. Then darken completely the space corresponding to the letter that is the same as the letter of your answer. Keep your mark within the space. If you have to erase a mark, be sure to erase it completely. Mark only one answer for each question.*

Sample Answer Sheet

1. Ⓐ Ⓑ Ⓒ Ⓓ Ⓔ   4. Ⓐ Ⓑ Ⓒ Ⓓ Ⓔ   7. Ⓐ Ⓑ Ⓒ Ⓓ Ⓔ   10. Ⓐ Ⓑ Ⓒ Ⓓ Ⓔ   13. Ⓐ Ⓑ Ⓒ Ⓓ Ⓔ
2. Ⓐ Ⓑ Ⓒ Ⓓ Ⓔ   5. Ⓐ Ⓑ Ⓒ Ⓓ Ⓔ   8. Ⓐ Ⓑ Ⓒ Ⓓ Ⓔ   11. Ⓐ Ⓑ Ⓒ Ⓓ Ⓔ   14. Ⓐ Ⓑ Ⓒ Ⓓ Ⓔ
3. Ⓐ Ⓑ Ⓒ Ⓓ Ⓔ   6. Ⓐ Ⓑ Ⓒ Ⓓ Ⓔ   9. Ⓐ Ⓑ Ⓒ Ⓓ Ⓔ   12. Ⓐ Ⓑ Ⓒ Ⓓ Ⓔ   15. Ⓐ Ⓑ Ⓒ Ⓓ Ⓔ

Sample questions 1 through 3. In each of the next three sample questions, select the one of the five suggested answers that is closest in meaning to the word in italics. Then darken the proper space on the sample answer sheet.

1. The new training program is much better than any of the *previous* ones. *Previous* means most nearly
    (A) abandoned
    (B) former
    (C) unused
    (D) recent
    (E) ineffective

2. The officer made several phone calls in an attempt to *verify* the report. To *verify* means most nearly to
    (A) examine
    (B) explain
    (C) confirm
    (D) believe
    (E) improve

3. The driver's only *option* was to turn right at the intersection. *Option* means most nearly
    (A) use
    (B) direction
    (C) hope
    (D) choice
    (E) opportunity

Sample questions 4 through 6. In each of the next three sample questions, select the one of the five suggested answers that is best supported by the paragraph. Then darken the proper space on the sample answer sheet.

4. Just as the procedure of a collection department must be clear-cut and definite, the steps being taken with the sureness of a skilled chess player, so the various paragraphs of a collection letter must show clear organization, giving evidence of a mind that, from the beginning, has had a specific end in view.

    The paragraph best supports the statement that a collection letter should always
    (A) show a spirit of sportsmanship
    (B) be divided into several paragraphs
    (C) be brief, but courteous
    (D) be carefully planned
    (E) be written by the head of the collection department

5. To prevent industrial accidents it is not only necessary that safety devices be used to guard exposed machinery, but also that mechanics be instructed in safety rules that they must follow for their own protection and that the lighting in the plant be adequate.

The paragraph best supports the statement that industrial accidents
(A) may be due to ignorance
(B) are always avoidable
(C) usually result from unsafe machinery
(D) cannot be entirely overcome
(E) usually result from inadequate lighting

6. Through advertising, manufacturers exercise a high degree of control over consumers' desires. However, the manufacturer assumes enormous risks in attempting to predict what consumers will want and in producing goods in quantity and distributing them in advance of final selection by the consumers.

The paragraph best supports the statement that manufacturers
(A) can eliminate the risk of overproduction by advertising
(B) distribute goods directly to the consumers
(C) must depend on the final consumers for the success of their undertakings
(D) can predict with great accuracy the success of any product they put on the market
(E) are more concerned with advertising than with the production of goods

Sample questions 7 through 9. Each of the next three sample questions contains five sentences. Decide which one of the five sentences would be most suitable in a formal letter or report with respect to grammar and usage. Then darken the proper space on the sample answer sheet.

7. (A) The officer should of answered courteously the questions asked by the callers.
   (B) The officer must answer courteously the questions of all them callers.
   (C) The officer must answer courteously the questions what are asked by the callers.
   (D) There would have been no trouble if the officer had have always answered courteously.
   (E) The officer should answer courteously the questions of all callers.

8. (A) There are less mistakes in his work since he took the training course.
   (B) The training course being completed, he makes very few mistakes in his work.
   (C) Since he has completed the training course, he makes few mistakes in his work.
   (D) After taking the training course, his work was found to contain hardly any mistakes.
   (E) After he completed the training course, he seldom ever made any mistakes in his work.

9. (A) If properly addressed, the letter will reach my supervisor and I.
   (B) The letter had been addressed to myself and my supervisor.
   (C) I believe the letter was addressed to either my supervisor or I.
   (D) My supervisor's name, as well as mine, was on the letter.
   (E) My supervisor and me will receive the letter if it is probably addressed.

Sample questions 10 through 12. In each of these sample questions, use your judgment and general knowledge to select the best or most important answer from the five suggested answers. Then darken the proper space on the sample answer sheet.

10. From the standpoint of the prisoners, the *chief* advantage to be derived from a properly administered parole system is the
    (A) freedom from fear of being returned to prison
    (B) opportunity to adjust themselves to release from imprisonment
    (C) removal of the temptation to commit crime
    (D) reduced cost of supervising prisoners
    (E) opportunity to save whatever they are able to earn

11. An officer of the law may arrest a person without a warrant upon reasonable suspicion that the person has committed a felony. The *chief* purpose of this rule is to
    (A) prevent the person's escape while his or her guilt is being investigated
    (B) prevent the person from committing more crimes immediately
    (C) give the person a chance to confess
    (D) permit observation of the person's behavior
    (E) increase the rate of arrest in proportion to the number of crimes committed

12. Acquaintance with all types of ammunition commonly in use is extremely valuable to the worker in crime detection *chiefly* because
    (A) all criminals possess this knowledge
    (B) a broad background is desirable for success in investigative work
    (C) the worker's safety is thus insured in time of danger
    (D) the worker can thus eventually become a specialist in this line
    (E) such knowledge often simplifies the problem of investigation

Sample questions 13 through 15. Each of these sample questions consists of five related events followed by five suggested orders in which the events could have occurred. Each suggested order represents the sequence in which the five sentences should be read, i.e., 3-5-1-2-4 indicates that the third sentence should be read first, the fifth sentence second, the first sentence third, etc. Select the one of the five suggested orders, lettered A, B, C, D, and E, in which the events most probably happened. Then darken the proper space on the sample answer sheet.

13. 1. The maid discovered the body and called the police.

    2. The police found Mary at the home of her sister.

    3. A man was shot while swimming in his private pool.

    4. A gun was found in Mary's pocketbook and was identified as the murder weapon.

    5. The police questioned the maid and discovered that the victim had had a heated argument with his wife, Mary, the night before.

    (A)   1-3-5-4-2
    (B)   3-5-1-4-2
    (C)   3-1-5-2-4
    (D)   1-5-2-4-3
    (E)   3-1-2-4-5

14. 1. In addition to the paper, a printing press and a stack of freshly printed $10 bills were found in Mr. Hayes' basement.

2. A detective saw Mr. Hayes leave a printing shop with a large package.

3. Mr. Hayes was arrested for counterfeiting and taken to the station.

4. The owner of the shop said Mr. Hayes had bought very high-quality paper.

5. Mr. Hayes was under surveillance as a suspect in a counterfeiting case.

(A) 2-4-1-5-3
(B) 5-2-4-1-3
(C) 3-2-4-1-5
(D) 2-5-1-4-3
(E) 5-2-3-4-1

15. 1. The inspector realized that Ms. Smith was wearing a wig and had her searched.

2. The inspector decided to search Ms. Smith's luggage.

3. Although the inspector could not place the face, he knew that Ms. Smith looked familiar.

4. Narcotics were found sewn to the crown of Ms. Smith's wig.

5. The inspector found nothing in Ms. Smith's luggage, but her passport photograph revealed her identity as a suspected smuggler.

(A) 2-5-3-1-4
(B) 3-1-4-2-5
(C) 1-4-2-5-3
(D) 3-2-5-1-4
(E) 2-1-3-5-4

Correct Answers

1.	B	4.	D	7.	E	10.	B	13.	C
2.	C	5.	A	8.	C	11.	A	14.	B
3.	D	6.	C	9.	D	12.	E	15.	D

Explanations

1. **(B)** *Previous* means coming or occurring before something else.

2. **(C)** To *verify* means to prove or to determine the truth or correctness of something.

3. **(D)** *Option* means something that may be or is chosen.

4. **(D)** The correct answer, (D), is supported by the paragraph's statement that a collection letter should show clear organization and be written with a specific end in view. There is nothing in the paragraph to support alternatives (A) or (E). Although the paragraph does imply that collection letters may contain several paragraphs (alternative B), it does not state that they should *always* be so divided. Also, the paragraph says nothing about the length or tone of a collection letter (alternative C), but only refers to the letter's clarity of thought and organization.

5. **(A)** The correct answer, (A), is supported by the paragraph's statement that instructing mechanics in safety rules can help prevent industrial accidents, which implies that in some cases accidents may be due to ignorance of these rules. The paragraph does not support the statements that, in actual practice, industrial accidents are either *always* avoidable (alternative B) or that they cannot be entirely overcome (alternative D); it merely states the requirements of successful accident prevention. Although the paragraph does imply that industrial accidents can be caused by unsafe machinery (alternative C) and inadequate lighting (alternative E), it does not support the statements that such accidents *usually* result from these causes.

6. **(C)** The correct answer, (C), is supported by the paragraph's statement that although advertising gives manufacturers considerable control over the consumers' demands for their products, there are still big risks involved in producing and distributing their goods in advance of the consumers' final selection, which implies that manufacturers' ultimate success depends on the consumers. The paragraph's statement that there are such risks, in spite of advertising, contradicts alternatives (A) and (D); nor is there any support for the statements that manufacturers distribute goods *directly* to consumers (alternative B) or that they are more concerned with advertising than production (alternative E).

7. **(E)** Alternative (A) is incorrect because the word *have* should have been used instead of the word *of*. Alternative (B) is incorrect because the word *those* should have been used instead of the word *them*. Alternative (C) is incorrect because the word *that* should have been used instead of the word *what*. Alternative (D) is incorrect because the phrase *had have* is incorrect grammar; only the word *had* should have been used.

8. **(C)** Alternative (A) is incorrect because the word *fewer* should have been used instead of the word *less*. Alternative (B) is incorrect because poor word usage makes it seem as if *he* refers to the *training course*. Alternative (D) is incorrect because the word *few* should have been used instead of the phrase *hardly any*. Alternative (E) is incorrect because it is poor usage for the word *ever* to follow the word *seldom*.

9. **(D)** In alternative (A), "my supervisor and me" is the object of the verb. In alternative (C), "my supervisor and me" is the object of the preposition. In alternative (B), the word *myself* should be replaced with the word *me*. In alternative (E), "my supervisor and I" is the subject of the sentence.

10. **(B)** The *chief* advantage of a properly administered parole system from the prisoners' standpoint is the opportunity it provides them for information and assistance concerning their reentry into society. A parole system cannot guarantee that released prisoners will never return to prison in the future (alternative A), that they will not be tempted to commit crime (alternative C), or that they will have the opportunity to save whatever they earn (alternative E), since these possibilities are largely in the hands of the prisoners themselves. While alternative (E) may be a result of the parole system, it is not the chief advantage from the standpoint of the prisoners.

11. **(A)** The *chief* purpose of arresting a person suspected of committing a felony is to insure that the suspect does not escape while further investigation takes place. While there may be some truth in all of the other alternatives, none of them can be considered to be the primary reason for this rule.

12. **(E)** The *chief* advantage of familiarity with all types of ammunition for the worker in crime detection lies in the fact that such knowledge can be a valuable aid in discovering and following up clues during the process of investigation. Alternatives (A) and (C) are untrue, and while alternatives (B) and (D) may be true in some cases, neither one is the most important reason why acquaintance with ammunition is valuable to the worker in crime detection.

13. **(C)** The most logical order of the five events is that first the man was shot (3); second, his body was discovered by the maid and the police were called (1); third, the police questioned the maid and learned of the couple's argument of the previous night (5); fourth, the police found Mary at her sister's home (2); and fifth, a gun was found in Mary's pocketbook and identified as the murder weapon (4). The answer is not (A) because the maid could not have discovered the body (1) before the man was shot (3). The answer is not (B) because the police could not have questioned the maid (5) before she called them (1). The answer is not (D) because the first four events could not have taken place before the man was shot (3). The answer is not (E) because the police could not have looked for Mary (2) before learning from the maid that she was the victim's wife (5).

14. **(B)** The most logical order of the five events is that first Mr. Hayes was under surveillance (5); second, a detective saw him leave a printing shop with a large package (2); third, the shop owner said he had bought high-quality paper (4); fourth, a printing press and freshly printed bills were found in Mr. Hayes' basement along with the paper (1); and fifth, he was arrested for counterfeiting (3). The answer is not (A) or (D) because the detective would not have seen Mr. Hayes leave the printing shop (2) if he had not been under surveillance (5). The answer is not (C) or (E) because Mr. Hayes could not have been arrested for counterfeiting (3) before any evidence was discovered (1).

15. **(D)** The most logical order of the five events is that first the inspector saw that Ms. Smith looked familiar (3); second, he decided to search her luggage (2); third, he found nothing in her luggage but identified her from her passport photograph as a suspected smuggler (5); fourth, he realized that she was wearing a wig and had her searched (1); and fifth, narcotics were found in her wig (4). The answer is not (A) because the inspector would not have decided to search Ms. Smith's luggage (2) unless his suspicions were aroused by the fact that she looked familiar (3). The answer is not (B), (C), or (E) because the inspector would not have realized Ms. Smith was wearing a wig (1) before seeing her passport photograph (5).

THE LANGUAGE APTITUDE EXAM

If you choose to take the language aptitude exam, you will take this exam after a break on the same day as you take the OPM exam just described above. The language aptitude exam is an artificial language exam. You must demonstrate your ability to learn a foreign language by manipulating vocabulary and grammar in an artificial language.

You will be presented with a booklet describing the artificial language; the booklet will include two vocabulary lists. One list, presented alphabetically by English word, gives the English word and its artificial language equivalent (Example: alien = huskovy). The other list is alphabetized by artificial language and gives the English equivalent of each artificial language word (Example: friggar = to work).

The booklet includes a glossary of grammatical terms. Grammatical terms have the same meaning in both English and the artificial language. (Example: An adjective is a word that describes a noun.) Finally, the booklet sets out grammar rules for the artificial language. (Example: The feminine singular of a noun, pronoun, and adjective is formed by adding the suffix *ver* to the masculine singular form.)

The exam contains four different types of questions, 50 questions in all. The parts are *not* separately timed. You are allowed 1 hour and 45 minutes to study the accompanying booklet and to answer the questions. The artificial language test is a test of your ability to reason and to manipulate the vocabulary and grammar of a foreign language. It is not a memory test. It does not test your ability to remember vocabulary or language. You may keep the booklet open in front of you and refer to it frequently as you answer the questions. You do not need to memorize any information.

The Office of Personnel Management does not provide official sample questions for the artificial language test. The exam description below can give you a feeling for the phrasing and style of questions, but without a vocabulary and grammar list, you cannot even attempt to answer these unofficial sample questions.

The first part consists of questions 1 to 20. In this part you must identify correctly translated words. For example, you may be given an English sentence such as "He injured the man," followed by a sentence in the artificial language such as "Yer Zelet wir huskoy." You must then mark (A) if only #1 is translated correctly, (B) if only #2 is correct, (C) if only #3 is correct, (D) if two or more are correct, and (E) if none are correct.

The second part consists of questions 21 to 30. In this part, you must choose which of five choices correctly translates an underlined word or group of words from English into the artificial language. Example: There is the lost boy. (A) bex kapkoy, (B) wir kapvoy, (C) hex kapvoy, (D) wir kapkoy, (E) bex kapyok.

The third part, questions 31 to 42, puts a slightly different spin on translation into the artificial language. You are given an incomplete sentence in the artificial language and must complete it with the correctly translated English word, being conscious not only of the vocabulary word but also the grammatical form. Example: Synet hex avekoy (man). (A) ekapiko, (B) ekapiver, (C) kopiak, (D) ekapiak, (E) pokiver.

The fourth part, questions 43 to 50, requires you to correct a sentence in the artificial language. You must change the form of the italicized word or words in the sentence according to instructions given in parentheses. Example: Yer *bongar* wit broukon (present tense). (A) bongaro, (B) bonagar, (C) bongarara, (D) bongo, (E) bongit.

Federal Clerical Jobs

Jobs in over 60 different clerical fields are filled using the Federal Clerical Examination. These jobs, like many other jobs in the federal government, are in the General Schedule (or GS), which assigns different "grades" to jobs that have different levels of responsibility or require different levels of experience or education.

There are jobs at various grade levels in each clerical field. Generally, all you need to qualify for jobs at the entry grades is to have graduated from high school (or some previous job experience). Some of the occupations at the entry level also require specific skills, such as typing or shorthand.

As you gain experience, you become eligible for promotion to higher-level, more specialized clerical and administrative jobs. You can also enter the federal government for the first time at these higher grade levels if you already have the specialized experience or additional education these jobs require.

Except for the Clerk-Stenographer, the entry level for clerical jobs is GS-2, and initial hires are usually made at either GS-2 or GS-3. The entry level for Clerk-Stenographers is GS-3, and initial hires are usually made at GS-3 or GS-4. Appointment at the higher grade levels is made for applicants who have appropriate experience or education above the high-school level. Experience from summer jobs and part-time jobs is often appropriate. Therefore, many applicants are eligible for entry at the higher grades without additional education.

Following are descriptions of some of the jobs in the clerical field.

CLERK-TYPIST

Most hiring at the entry level in the clerical field is done for Clerk-Typist positions, which combine clerical work with typing duties. Thousands of these Clerk-Typist positions are filled each year, particularly in areas where a number of federal agencies are located. Vacancies are constantly occurring in these positions as employees are promoted to higher-graded positions, transfer to other jobs, or leave for other reasons.

CLERK-STENOGRAPHER

Clerk-Stenographer jobs combine clerical tasks with both dictation and typing duties. There are usually many job openings in areas where there are large concentrations of federal employees, and many opportunities for movement into higher grades.

OFFICE AUTOMATION CLERK

Office Automation Clerks and Assistants operate personal computers to perform word-processing tasks, desktop publishing, database management, financial spreadsheets, electronic bulletin boards, and so on. This work can also be carried out on mainframe computers through telecommunications equipment. This occupation is new, and Office Automation Clerks are taking the place of Clerk-Typists in many organizations.

DATA TRANSCRIBER

The job title *Data Transcriber* covers positions that involve the input or recording of different types of data into data-processing files. Several thousand entry-level Data Transcribers are usually hired each year, and the number of jobs in the field is increasing as more use is made of automated systems.

CLERK

The title *Clerk* covers many specific positions in which typing, stenographic, or data-entry skills either are not required or are not an important part of the job. (In a few cases, one of these skills is important, in which case it is included in the job title.) Opportunities at the entry level in these fields are more limited than for Typist, Stenographer, and Data Transcriber jobs because more of these positions require specialized experience or training. However, entry-level opportunities do exist in some fields, as described below.

There are thousands of general clerks, such as Mail and File Clerks and miscellaneous clerks, who perform a variety of typical office and record-keeping tasks. Most of these jobs are filled at the lower entry levels. There are also many entry-level openings for Sales Store Checkers. These clerks work in a variety of store-like situations, usually on military bases or in agency supply stores.

A variety of clerical jobs, such as the Calculating Machine Operator, involve the use of some type of office machine. Many of these jobs are filled at the entry level, although they often require special skills and training and have additional selection requirements specific to each job. There are several hundred of these Office Machine Operator types of jobs.

Jobs in the following fields are usually above the entry level. However, some entry-level jobs are available. There are many jobs in the personnel field, supporting the professional personnel staff. There are good opportunities for advancement to technical and administrative jobs in this field. There are opportunities in the fields of supply, transportation, and stock control. Most of these positions exist in military and supply agencies. Finally, there are clerical positions in accounting, payroll, and fiscal work. For example, Payroll Clerks keep records and do other work related to issuing paychecks, and Cash Processing Clerks handle and track cash disbursements.

SKILL REQUIREMENTS

When a job requires typing skill, you must be able to type accurately at 40 words per minute. When dictation skill is required, you must be able to transcribe dictation accurately at 80 words per minute. GS-2 Data Transcribers must be able to type accurately at 20 words per minute, and GS-3 and 4 Data Transcribers must be able to type accurately at 25 words per minute. Stenographer applicants may use any system of taking and transcribing dictation they wish.

The Federal Clerical Examination consists of two separately timed sections, a Verbal Tasks Test and a Clerical Tasks Test.

THE VERBAL TASKS TEST

What the Test Is About

The Verbal Tasks Test includes questions in such areas as spelling, meaning, and relationship of words; recognition of sentences that are grammatically correct; and reading, understanding, and using written material.

These test tasks relate to a variety of job tasks, such as proofreading and correcting typed copy, using instruction manuals, organizing new files of related materials, and carrying out written instructions.

There are 85 questions—25 on word meaning, 20 on word relationships, 20 on spelling, 10 on grammar, and 10 on reading. There are a few questions of each type on each page of the test. For each question, you will select the best answer from among a set of suggested answers.

Word meaning questions consist of one given word followed by four different words labeled (A), (B), (C), and (D). You are to select the word that has the closest meaning to the word given in the question.

It may help if you remember that you are looking for the best match among the choices given, but not necessarily a perfect match.

Answering these questions depends upon your knowledge of vocabulary, but there are some steps you can take if you do not recognize the correct answer immediately.

- If you have a general idea about what the given word means but are having trouble choosing an answer, try using the word in a short sentence. Then substitute each of the answer choices in the same sentence to see which one seems best to fit the sentence.
- Try to break the given word into parts to see if the suffix (ending) or the prefix (beginning) of the word gives a clue about its meaning.

The reading questions consist of a paragraph followed by four statements. You read the paragraph first and then select the one statement that is based on information given in the paragraph.

- Do not worry if you are unfamiliar with the subject discussed in the paragraph. You do not need to have any knowledge about the subject of the paragraph since the answer to the question is always given in the paragraph itself.
- Do not worry about whether the correct statement, or any of the incorrect statements, are true. The important thing is that the correct answer is the *only* statement that says the same thing as is said in the paragraph. Some of the other statements may be true, but they are not based on the content of the paragraph.
- To select the correct statement, first eliminate choices that clearly conflict with the paragraph. Then, if you still have two or more choices, look for the specific section of the paragraph that covers the information given in each one of the choices.
- Compare the facts given carefully, until you can eliminate the remaining incorrect choices.

Grammar questions give four versions of a single sentence. Each sentence tries to express the same thought, but only one of them is *grammatically* correct.

- Most of the incorrect sentences are obviously poorly constructed.
- Others have such errors as using singular verbs with plural nouns.
- In the more difficult questions, you must pay attention to smaller details, like the misuse of punctuation, which can make a sentence very difficult to understand.

To answer these questions, first eliminate the sentences you are sure are incorrect. Then compare the remaining ones until you can choose one as being more correct than the others.

- It is possible that one sentence will seem to be correct because it uses the same informal grammar that people often use when talking. However, this type of sentence structure is not suitable for writing.

Spelling questions give three spellings of a common word, labeled (A), (B), and (C). Each question also offers the option of "none of these" as choice (D). You must decide which one of the three given spellings is correct, or that none of them is correct.

- Sometimes it helps to answer these questions by looking away from the given choices and writing the word yourself on the margin of your test booklet. Then check to see if the spelling you believe is correct is given as one of the choices.

Word relationship questions give two words that are related in some way, and then give the first word of a second word relationship that you are to complete. You are given four choices of words to complete that relationship. The correct choice is the word that completes that relationship in the way most similar to the relationship in the first pair of words.

To answer these questions, look at the first pair of words and decide what the relationship between the words is. Then choose the answer that best completes that relationship for the second pair of words.

- Remember that the correct answer is chosen because it completes an analogous relationship, not because it is on the same subject as the first pair of words.

THE CLERICAL TASKS TEST

What the Test Is About

The Clerical Tasks Test is a test of speed and accuracy on four clerical tasks. There are 120 questions given with a short time limit. The test contains 30 questions on name and number checking, 30 on arranging names in correct alphabetical order, 30 on simple arithmetic, and 30 on inspecting groups of letters and numbers. The questions are arranged in groups or cycles of five questions of each type.

The Clerical Tasks Test is planned as a test of speed in carrying out these relatively simple clerical tasks. This means you should work quickly through the test. However, the test is also planned to measure accuracy, and there is a penalty for wrong answers in the total test score. This means that you need to be careful as you work, and that wild guessing is not a good idea. However, do not be so concerned about accuracy that you complete the test more slowly than you should. Remember that both speed and accuracy are important to achieve a good score.

The different question types in this test appear on each page of the test. You may find it easier to answer all questions of one type that appear in the test rather than switching from one question type to another. This is perfectly acceptable, but extra caution should be taken to mark your answers in the right place on the answer sheet.

Memorizing the answer choices for name and number checking questions may be helpful in increasing your speed. In these questions, you are to compare three names or numbers and decide which ones are exactly alike. You then select your answer from a set of choices that describe whether all of them, some of them, or none of them are alike. These choices are labeled (A), (B), (C), (D), and (E) and are repeated on each page of the test booklet.

- These choices remain the same for all questions of this type in the test, so if you memorize these choices, you will not have to refer constantly to them before choosing your answers.

For the alphabetizing questions, remember that the most important rule for putting the names in order is to consider each letter in the complete last name in strict alphabetical order, exactly as it appears.

- This is true even when the name includes more than one capital letter (as in DeLong), or involves prefixes that are often spelled differently in different names (as in McDuff and MacDuff).
- Ignore punctuation, such as apostrophes and hyphens, that appear in a name (as in O'Hara).

When two last names are identical in every way, then alphabetize according to the first and second names given, following the same rules.

The key to the arithmetic questions is to avoid careless errors. Remember that the correct answer may not be included as one of the given alternatives. In this case, you mark choice (E) on the answer sheet.

- Answers will always be exact (no decimal places), so if the answer you get is not exact, work the problem again.

There are several different ways of approaching the letter and number inspection questions. You should use the method that works best for you.

One method is to work from the answer choices to the questions. Look at each answer choice and, one at a time, compare each letter or number it contains with the question until you can accept or reject it. Here is how you would use this method to answer the following set of sample questions.

There is one set of suggested answers for the next group of sample questions. Do not try to memorize these answers, because there will be a different set on each page in the test.

To find the answer to a question, find which suggested answer contains numbers and letters, all of which appear in the question. If no suggested answer fits, mark (E) for that question.

1.	8 N K 9 G T 4 6	A = 7, 9, G, K
2.	T 9 7 Z 6 L 3 K	B = 8, 9, T, Z
3.	Z 7 G K 3 9 8 N	Suggested Answers C = 6, 7, K, Z
4.	3 K 9 4 6 G Z L	D = 6, 8, G, T
5.	Z N 7 3 8 K T 9	E = none of these

- Start by looking at the first number given in choice (A), which is a 7.
- Quickly scan question 1 for this number. Since it does not include a 7, choice (A) can be rejected.
- Next, consider the first number in choice (B), which is an 8. Scanning question 1 confirms that an 8 is present. Moving on to the next number in choice (B) (a 9), scanning of the question confirms its presence also, as well as the next letter in choice (B) (a T). There is no Z, however, so choice (B) is then rejected.
- Using the same process of elimination for choice (C), no number 7 is found, and this choice is rejected.
- One by one, all of the letters and numbers in choice (D) are found, so choice (D) is marked as correct on the separate answer sheet.
- If all the letters and numbers in choice (D) had not been found in question 1, then choice (E), "none of these," would have been marked as the correct answer.

You may be able to save time using this method by scanning for two of the letters or numbers given at one time.

Another method is to look at the particular question and quickly and lightly memorize all the numbers and letters it contains. Then, glance at each choice to select one that is a good possibility based on your memory.

- Carefully double-check this choice with each of the numbers and letters given in the question.
- If you use this method, be sure to spend only a few seconds memorizing the numbers and letters in the question, or you will waste too much time on one question.

Whichever method you choose, remember that any of the answer choices given may be used to answer more than one of the five questions included in the set on each page. Also, note that the letters and numbers given in the answer choices and questions do not have to be in the same order.

ANSWER SHEET FOR FEDERAL CLERICAL EXAMINATION

Verbal Tasks Test

1. Ⓐ Ⓑ Ⓒ Ⓓ Ⓔ   5. Ⓐ Ⓑ Ⓒ Ⓓ Ⓔ   9. Ⓐ Ⓑ Ⓒ Ⓓ Ⓔ   13. Ⓐ Ⓑ Ⓒ Ⓓ Ⓔ
2. Ⓐ Ⓑ Ⓒ Ⓓ Ⓔ   6. Ⓐ Ⓑ Ⓒ Ⓓ Ⓔ   10. Ⓐ Ⓑ Ⓒ Ⓓ Ⓔ   14. Ⓐ Ⓑ Ⓒ Ⓓ Ⓔ
3. Ⓐ Ⓑ Ⓒ Ⓓ Ⓔ   7. Ⓐ Ⓑ Ⓒ Ⓓ Ⓔ   11. Ⓐ Ⓑ Ⓒ Ⓓ Ⓔ   15. Ⓐ Ⓑ Ⓒ Ⓓ Ⓔ
4. Ⓐ Ⓑ Ⓒ Ⓓ Ⓔ   8. Ⓐ Ⓑ Ⓒ Ⓓ Ⓔ   12. Ⓐ Ⓑ Ⓒ Ⓓ Ⓔ   16. Ⓐ Ⓑ Ⓒ Ⓓ Ⓔ
                                                                      17. Ⓐ Ⓑ Ⓒ Ⓓ Ⓔ

The total raw score on this test consists of the total number of questions that are answered correctly. There is no penalty for wrong answers or correction made for guessing. However, no credit is given for any question with more than one answer marked.

My raw score _____

Clerical Tasks Test

1. Ⓐ Ⓑ Ⓒ Ⓓ Ⓔ   6. Ⓐ Ⓑ Ⓒ Ⓓ Ⓔ   11. Ⓐ Ⓑ Ⓒ Ⓓ Ⓔ   16. Ⓐ Ⓑ Ⓒ Ⓓ Ⓔ
2. Ⓐ Ⓑ Ⓒ Ⓓ Ⓔ   7. Ⓐ Ⓑ Ⓒ Ⓓ Ⓔ   12. Ⓐ Ⓑ Ⓒ Ⓓ Ⓔ   17. Ⓐ Ⓑ Ⓒ Ⓓ Ⓔ
3. Ⓐ Ⓑ Ⓒ Ⓓ Ⓔ   8. Ⓐ Ⓑ Ⓒ Ⓓ Ⓔ   13. Ⓐ Ⓑ Ⓒ Ⓓ Ⓔ   18. Ⓐ Ⓑ Ⓒ Ⓓ Ⓔ
4. Ⓐ Ⓑ Ⓒ Ⓓ Ⓔ   9. Ⓐ Ⓑ Ⓒ Ⓓ Ⓔ   14. Ⓐ Ⓑ Ⓒ Ⓓ Ⓔ   19. Ⓐ Ⓑ Ⓒ Ⓓ Ⓔ
5. Ⓐ Ⓑ Ⓒ Ⓓ Ⓔ   10. Ⓐ Ⓑ Ⓒ Ⓓ Ⓔ   15. Ⓐ Ⓑ Ⓒ Ⓓ Ⓔ   20. Ⓐ Ⓑ Ⓒ Ⓓ Ⓔ

On this test, there is a penalty for wrong answers. The total raw score on the test is the number of right answers minus one-fourth of the number of wrong answers. (Fractions of one-half or less are dropped.) First, count the number of correct answers you have given. Do not count as correct any questions with more than one answer marked. Then count the number of incorrect answers. Omits are not counted as wrong answers, but double responses do count as wrong. Multiply the total number of incorrect answers by one-fourth. Subtract this number from the total number correct to get the test total score.

Number right	minus	Number Wrong ($\div 4$)	equals	Raw Score
_____	–	_____	=	_____

Sample Questions: Federal Clerical Examination

VERBAL TASKS TEST

Directions: *Read each question carefully. Select the best answer and darken the proper space on the answer sheet.*

1. To *counteract* means most nearly to
    - (A) undermine
    - (B) censure
    - (C) preserve
    - (D) neutralize

2. *Deferred* means most nearly
    - (A) reversed
    - (B) delayed
    - (C) considered
    - (D) forbidden

3. *Feasible* means most nearly
    - (A) capable
    - (B) justifiable
    - (C) practicable
    - (D) beneficial

4. To *encounter* means most nearly to
    - (A) meet
    - (B) recall
    - (C) overcome
    - (D) retreat

5. *Innate* means most nearly
    - (A) eternal
    - (B) well-developed
    - (C) native
    - (D) prospective

6. STUDENT is related to TEACHER as DISCIPLE is related to
    - (A) follower
    - (B) master
    - (C) principal
    - (D) pupil

7. LECTURE is related to AUDITORIUM as EXPERIMENT is related to
    - (A) scientist
    - (B) chemistry
    - (C) laboratory
    - (D) discovery

8. BODY is related to FOOD as ENGINE is related to
    - (A) wheels
    - (B) fuel
    - (C) motion
    - (D) smoke

9. SCHOOL is related to EDUCATION as THEATER is related to
    - (A) management
    - (B) stage
    - (C) recreation
    - (D) preparation

10. (A) Most all these statements have been supported by persons who are reliable and can be depended upon.
    (B) The persons which have guaranteed these statements are reliable.
    (C) Reliable persons guarantee the facts with regards to the truth of these statements.
    (D) These statements can be depended on, for their truth has been guaranteed by reliable persons.

11. (A) The success of the book pleased both the publisher and authors.
    (B) Both the publisher and they was pleased with the success of the book.
    (C) Neither they or their publisher was disappointed with the success of the book.
    (D) Their publisher was as pleased as they with the success of the book.

12. (A) extercate   (C) extricate
    (B) extracate   (D) none of these

13. (A) hereditory   (C) hereditairy
    (B) hereditary   (D) none of these

14. (A) auspiceous   (C) auspicious
    (B) auspiseous   (D) none of these

15. (A) sequance   (C) sequense
    (B) sequence   (D) none of these

16. The prevention of accidents makes it necessary not only that safety devices be used to guard exposed machinery but also that mechanics be instructed in safety rules that they must follow for their own protection, and that the lighting in the plant be adequate.

    The paragraph best supports the statement that industrial accidents
    (A) may be due to ignorance
    (B) are always avoidable
    (C) usually result from inadequate machinery
    (D) cannot be entirely overcome

17. The English language is peculiarly rich in synonyms, and there is scarcely a language spoken that has not some representative in English speech. The spirit of the Anglo-Saxon race has subjugated these various elements to one idiom, making not a patchwork, but a composite language.

    The paragraph best supports the statement that the English language
    (A) has few idiomatic expressions
    (B) is difficult to translate
    (C) is used universally
    (D) has absorbed words from other languages

CLERICAL TASKS TEST

Directions: In questions 1 through 5, compare the three names or numbers, and mark the answer:

A   if ALL THREE names or numbers are exactly ALIKE

B   if only the FIRST and SECOND names or numbers are exactly ALIKE

C   if only the FIRST and THIRD names or numbers are exactly ALIKE

D   if only the SECOND and THIRD names or numbers are exactly ALIKE

E   if ALL THREE names or numbers are DIFFERENT

1.	5261383	5261383	5261338
2.	8125690	8126690	8125609
3.	W. E. Johnston	W. E. Johnson	W. E. Johnson
4.	Vergil L. Muller	Vergil L. Muller	Vergil L. Muller
5.	Atherton R. Warde	Asheton R. Warde	Atherton P. Warde

In questions 6 through 10, find the correct place for the name in the box.

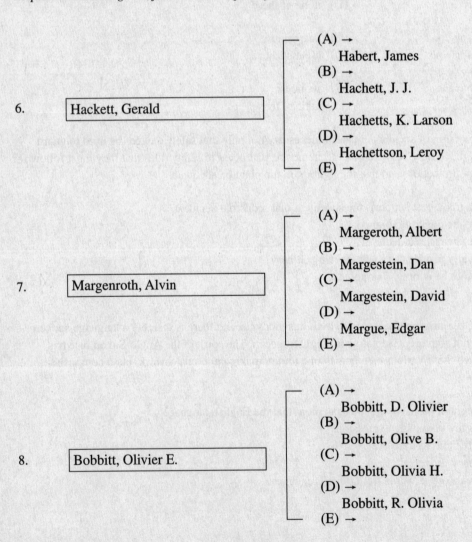

6. | Hackett, Gerald |

(A) →
    Habert, James
(B) →
    Hachett, J. J.
(C) →
    Hachetts, K. Larson
(D) →
    Hachettson, Leroy
(E) →

7. | Margenroth, Alvin |

(A) →
    Margeroth, Albert
(B) →
    Margestein, Dan
(C) →
    Margestein, David
(D) →
    Margue, Edgar
(E) →

8. | Bobbitt, Olivier E. |

(A) →
    Bobbitt, D. Olivier
(B) →
    Bobbitt, Olive B.
(C) →
    Bobbitt, Olivia H.
(D) →
    Bobbitt, R. Olivia
(E) →

9. | Mosely, Werner |

(A) →
    Mosley, Albert J.
(B) →
    Mosley, Alvin
(C) →
    Mosley, S. M.
(D) →
    Mosley, Vinson, N.
(E) →

10. | Youmuns, Frank L. |

(A) →
    Youmons, Frank G.
(B) →
    Youmons, Frank H.
(C) →
    Youmons, Frank K.
(D) →
    Youmons, Frank M.
(E) →

11. Add: 43
              + 32

(A) 55
(B) 65
(C) 66
(D) 75
(E) none of these

12. Subtract: 83
              − 4

(A) 73
(B) 79
(C) 80
(D) 89
(E) none of these

13. Multiply: 41
              × 7

(A) 281
(B) 287
(C) 291
(D) 297
(E) none of these

14. Divide: 6⟌306

    (A) 44
    (B) 51
    (C) 52
    (D) 60
    (E) none of these

15. Add:

$$37$$
$$+\ 15$$

    (A) 42
    (B) 52
    (C) 53
    (D) 62
    (E) none of these

For each question below, find which one of the suggested answers appears in that question.

16. 6 2 5 K 4 P T G
17. L 4 7 2 T 6 V K
18. 3 5 4 L 9 V T G
19. G 4 K 7 L 3 5 Z
20. 4 K 2 9 N 5 T G

Suggested Answers

A = 4, 5, K, T
B = 4, 7, G, K
C = 2, 5, G, L
D = 2, 7, L, T
E = none of these

Correct Answers

Verbal Tasks Test

1.	D	4.	A	7.	C	10.	D	13.	B	16.	A
2.	B	5.	C	8.	B	11.	D	14.	C	17.	D
3.	C	6.	B	9.	C	12.	C	15.	B		

Clerical Tasks Test

1.	B	4.	A	7.	A	10.	E	13.	B	17.	D
2.	E	5.	E	8.	D	11.	D	14.	B	18.	E
3.	D	6.	E	9.	B	12.	B	15.	B	19.	B
								16.	A	20.	A

Explanations—Verbal Tasks Test

1. **(D)** To COUNTERACT is to *act directly against* or to *neutralize*. My father's vote for the Republican candidate always counteracts my mother's vote for the Democrat.

2. **(B)** DEFERRED means *postponed* or *delayed*. Because I had no money in the bank, I deferred paying my taxes until the due date.

3. **(C)** FEASIBLE means *possible* or *practicable*. It is not feasible for the 92-year-old woman to travel abroad.

4. **(A)** To ENCOUNTER is to *come upon* or to *meet*. If you encounter my brother at the ball game, please give my regards.

5. **(C)** INNATE means *existing naturally* or *native*. Some people argue that the maternal instinct is learned rather than innate.

6.   **(B)** The DISCIPLE learns from a MASTER as a STUDENT learns from a TEACHER.

7.   **(C)** In this analogy of place, an EXPERIMENT occurs in a LABORATORY as a LECTURE occurs in an AUDITORIUM.

8.   **(B)** FUEL powers the ENGINE as FOOD powers the BODY.

9.   **(C)** RECREATION occurs in the THEATER as EDUCATION occurs in a SCHOOL.

10.   **(D)** Choice (A) might state either "most" or "all" but not both; choice (B) should read "persons who"; choice (C) should read "with regard to…"

11.   **(D)** Choice (A) is incorrect because *both* can refer to only two, but "the publisher and authors" implies at least three; choice (B) requires the plural verb "were"; choice (C) requires the correlative construction "neither…nor."

12.   **(C)** The correct spelling is *extricate*.

13.   **(B)** The correct spelling is *hereditary*.

14.   **(C)** The correct spelling is *auspicious*.

15.   **(B)** The correct spelling is *sequence*.

16.   **(A)** If instruction in safety rules will help to prevent accidents, some accidents must occur because of ignorance.

17.   **(D)** The language that has some representative in English speech has had some of its words absorbed into English.

Explanations—Clerical Tasks Test

1.   **(B)** The last two digits of the third number are reversed.

2.   **(E)** The middle digit of the second number is "6" while that of the first and third numbers is "5." The last two digits of the third number are reversed.

3.   **(D)** The surname of the second and third names is "Johnson"; the surname of the first name is "Johnston."

4.   **(A)** All three names are exactly alike.

5.   **(E)** The middle initial of the third name differs from the other two. "Asheton" of the second name differs from "Atherton" of the other two.

6.   **(E)** Hachettson; Hackett

7.   **(A)** Margenroth; Mageroth

8. **(D)** Bobbitt, Olivia H.; Bobbitt, Olivier E.; Bobbitt, R. Olivia

9. **(B)** Mosely, Albert J.; Mosely, Werner; Mosley, Alvin

10. **(E)** Youmons; Youmuns

11. **(D)**
$$\begin{array}{r} 43 \\ + 32 \\ \hline 75 \end{array}$$

12. **(B)**
$$\begin{array}{r} 83 \\ - 4 \\ \hline 79 \end{array}$$

13. **(B)**
$$\begin{array}{r} 41 \\ \times 7 \\ \hline 287 \end{array}$$

14. **(B)** $6\overline{)306} = 51$

15. **(B)**
$$\begin{array}{r} 37 \\ + 15 \\ \hline 52 \end{array}$$

16. **(A)** 6 2 **5** K **4** P T G.

17. **(D)** L **4 7 2** T 6 V K. The answer cannot be (A) because question 17 contains no 5; it cannot be (B) or (C) because question 17 contains no G.

18. **(E)** The answer cannot be (A) or (B) because question 18 contains no K; it cannot be (C) or (D) because question 18 contains no 2.

19. **(B)** G **4** K **7** L **3 5** Z. The answer cannot be (A) because question 19 contains no T.

20. **(A) 4** K **2 9** N **5** T G.

THE TYPING TEST

Assuming that you already know how to type, the best preparation for any typing test is typing. You may choose any material at all and practice copying it line for line, exactly as you see it. As on the actual typing test, spell, capitalize, punctuate, and begin and end lines exactly as they appear on the page being copied. Do NOT stop to erase or to correct. An error is an error, even if it has been corrected. And corrections take up valuable time. If you make an error, just continue, hoping to compensate for your inaccuracy with superior speed. On the actual typing exam, a basic speed is required, but then accuracy counts more than speed. Try to balance yourself so as to meet speed requirements while maintaining a very high level of accuracy.

The following is a typical test exercise, though NOT the actual test exercise that you will be given. Follow instructions exactly, and practice. Words-per-minute points are marked on the test exercise for your guidance. Try to keep your typing error-free; if you make errors, try to increase your speed. Use an accurate signal timer or have a friend or relative time you.

Space, paragraph, spell, punctuate, capitalize, and begin and end each line precisely as shown in the exercise.

You will have exactly five minutes in which to make repeated copies of the test exercise itself on the paper that will be given to you. Each time you complete the exercise, simply double-space once and begin again. If you fill up one side of the paper, turn it over and continue typing on the other side. Keep on typing until told to stop.

Keep in mind that you must meet minimum standards in both speed and accuracy and that, above these standards, accuracy is twice as important as speed. Make no erasures, insertions, or other corrections in this plain-copy test. Since errors are penalized whether or not they are erased or otherwise "corrected," it is best to keep on typing even though you detect an error.

Test Exercise	1st typing of exercise	2nd typing of exercise
Because they have often learned to know types of archi-	_____	52 wpm
tecture by decoration, casual observers sometimes fail to	_____	54
realize that the significant part of a structure is not the	_____	56
ornamentation but the body itself. Architecture, because	_____	59
of its close contact with human lives, is peculiarly and	_____	61
intimately governed by climate. For instance, a home built	_____	64
for comfort in the cold and snow of the northern areas of	_____	66
this country would be unbearably warm in a country with	_____	68
weather such as that of Cuba. A Cuban house, with its open	_____	71
court, would prove impossible to heat in a northern winter.	_____	73
Since the purpose of architecture is the construction of	_____	76
shelters in which human beings may carry on their numerous	_____	78
activities, the designer must consider not only climatic con-	_____	80
ditions, but also the function of a building. Thus, although	_____	_____
the climate of a certain locality requires that an auditorium	_____	_____
and a hospital have several features in common, the purposes	_____	_____
for which they will be used demand some difference in struc-	40 wpm	_____
ture. For centuries builders have first complied with these	42	_____
two requirements and later added whatever ornamentation they	44	_____
wished. Logically, we should see as mere additions, not as	47	_____
basic parts, the details by which we identify architecture.	49	_____

EACH TIME YOU REACH THIS POINT, DOUBLE-SPACE ONCE AND BEGIN AGAIN.

STENOGRAPHY

Only stenographer competitors take a stenography test. The sample below shows the length of material dictated. Have someone dictate the passage to you so that you can see how well prepared you are to take dictation at 80 words per minute. Take notes on your own paper.

Directions to person dictating: This practice dictation should be dictated at the rate of 80 words a minute. Do not dictate the punctuation except for periods, but dictate with the expression the punctuation indicates. Use a watch with a second hand to enable you to read the exercises at the proper speed.

Exactly on a minute start dictating	Finish reading each two lines at the number of seconds indicated below.
I realize that this practice dictation is not a part of the examination	10
proper and is not to be scored. (Period) The work of preventing and correcting	20
physical defects in children is becoming more effective as a result of change	30
in the attitude of many parents. (Period) In order to bring about this change,	40
parents have been invited to visit the schools when their children are being examined	50
and to discuss the treatment necessary for the correction of defects. (Period)	1 min.
There is a distinct value in having a parent see that his or her child is not the	10
only one who needs attention. (Period) Otherwise a few parents might feel that they	20
were being criticized by having the defects of their children singled out for medical	30
treatment. (Period) The special classes that have been set up have shown the value of	40
the scientific knowledge that has been applied in the treatment of children. (Period)	50
In these classes the children have been taught to exercise by a trained teacher	2 min.
under medical supervision. (Period) The hours of the school day have been divided	10
between school work and physical activity that helps not only to correct their defects	20
but also to improve their general physical condition. (Period) This method of treatment	30

has been found to be very effective	
except for those who have severe medical	40
defects. (Period) Most parents now see	
how desirable it is to have these classes	50
that have been set up in the regular	
school system to meet special needs. (Period)	3 min.

After dictating the practice, pause for 15 seconds to permit competitor to complete note taking.

Sample Dictation Transcript Sheet

The transcript below is part of the material that was dictated to you for practice, except that many of the words have been left out. From your notes, you are to tell what the missing words are. Proceed as follows:

Compare your notes with the transcript and, when you come to a blank in the transcript, decide what word (or words) belongs there. For example, you will find that the word "practice" belongs in blank number 1. Look at the word list to see whether you can find the same word there. Notice what letter (A, B, C, or D) is printed beside it, and write that letter in the blank. For example, the word "practice" is listed followed by the letter B. We have already written (B) in blank number 1 to show you how you are to record your choice. Now decide what belongs in each of the other blanks. (You may also write the word or words, or the shorthand for them, if you wish.) The same word may belong in more than one blank. If the exact answer is not listed, write (E) in the blank.

Alphabetic Word List

Write (E) if the answer is NOT listed.

about—B	paper—B
against—C	parents—B
attitude—A	part—C
being—D	physical—D
childhood—B	portion—D
children—A	practical—A
correcting—C	practice—B
doctors—B	preliminary—D
effective—D	preventing—B
efficient—A	procedure—A
examination—A	proper—C
examining—C	reason for—A
for—B	result—B
health—B	result of—C
mothers—C	schools—C
never—C	to be—C
not—D	to prevent—A

TRANSCRIPT

I realize that this ___B___ dictation is _____
 1 2

a ____ of the ____ ____ and is ____ ____
 3 4 5 6 7
scored.

The work ____ and ____ ____ defects
 8 9 10

in ____ is becoming more ____ as a ____
 11 12 13

a change in the ____ of many ____ .
 14 15

Alphabetic Word List

Write (E) if the answer is NOT listed.

all—A	reducing—A
at—C	satisfied—D
bring—A	say—C
collection—B	see—B
correction—C	soon—C
discuss—C	their—D
during—D	to discover—A
friend—A	to discuss—D
indicated—C	to endorse—C
insisted—D	to visit—B
is—B	treatments—A
is not—A	understand—D
know—A	undertake—B
knows—D	virtue—D
needed—B	visit—A
promote—B	volume—B
recognizing—D	young—C

TRANSCRIPT (Continued)

In order to ___ ___ this change,
  16 17

parents have been invited ___ the
                           18

schools when ___ children are being
            19

examined and ___ the ___ necessary for
           20   21

the ___ of defects. There is a distinct
   22

___ in having a parent ___ that his or her
23   24

child ___ the only one who needs
     25

attention. . . . (The rest of the sample

dictation is not transcribed here.)

(For the next sentences there would be another word list, if the entire sample dictation were transcribed.)

You will be given an answer sheet like the sample below, on which your answers can be scored by machine. Each number on the answer sheet stands for the blank with the same number in the transcript. Darken the space with the letter that is the same as the letter you wrote in the transcript. If you have not finished writing letters in the blanks in the transcript, or if you wish to make sure you have lettered them correctly, *you may continue to use your notes after you begin marking the answer sheet.*

Answer Sheet for Sample Dictation

1. Ⓐ Ⓑ Ⓒ Ⓓ Ⓔ	8. Ⓐ Ⓑ Ⓒ Ⓓ Ⓔ	14. Ⓐ Ⓑ Ⓒ Ⓓ Ⓔ	20. Ⓐ Ⓑ Ⓒ Ⓓ Ⓔ
2. Ⓐ Ⓑ Ⓒ Ⓓ Ⓔ	9. Ⓐ Ⓑ Ⓒ Ⓓ Ⓔ	15. Ⓐ Ⓑ Ⓒ Ⓓ Ⓔ	21. Ⓐ Ⓑ Ⓒ Ⓓ Ⓔ
3. Ⓐ Ⓑ Ⓒ Ⓓ Ⓔ	10. Ⓐ Ⓑ Ⓒ Ⓓ Ⓔ	16. Ⓐ Ⓑ Ⓒ Ⓓ Ⓔ	22. Ⓐ Ⓑ Ⓒ Ⓓ Ⓔ
4. Ⓐ Ⓑ Ⓒ Ⓓ Ⓔ	11. Ⓐ Ⓑ Ⓒ Ⓓ Ⓔ	17. Ⓐ Ⓑ Ⓒ Ⓓ Ⓔ	23. Ⓐ Ⓑ Ⓒ Ⓓ Ⓔ
5. Ⓐ Ⓑ Ⓒ Ⓓ Ⓔ	12. Ⓐ Ⓑ Ⓒ Ⓓ Ⓔ	18. Ⓐ Ⓑ Ⓒ Ⓓ Ⓔ	24. Ⓐ Ⓑ Ⓒ Ⓓ Ⓔ
6. Ⓐ Ⓑ Ⓒ Ⓓ Ⓔ	13. Ⓐ Ⓑ Ⓒ Ⓓ Ⓔ	19. Ⓐ Ⓑ Ⓒ Ⓓ Ⓔ	25. Ⓐ Ⓑ Ⓒ Ⓓ Ⓔ
7. Ⓐ Ⓑ Ⓒ Ⓓ Ⓔ			

The correct answers for the sample dictation are

1.	B	6.	D	11.	A	16.	A	21.	E
2.	D	7.	C	12.	D	17.	E	22.	C
3.	C	8.	B	13.	C	18.	B	23.	E
4.	A	9.	C	14.	A	19.	D	24.	B
5.	C	10.	D	15.	B	20.	D	25.	A

Compare your answers with the correct answers. If one of your answers does not agree with the correct answer, again compare your notes with the samples and make certain you understand the instructions.

Your notes should show that the word "bring" goes in blank 16, and "about" in blank 17. But "about" is *not in the list*, so (E) should be your answer for question 17.

The two words "to visit" (B) are needed for 18, and the one word "visit" (A) would be an incorrect answer.

For the actual test, you will use a separate answer sheet. As scoring will be done by an electric machine, it is important that you follow directions carefully. Make a heavy mark for each answer. If you have to change your mark for any question, be sure to erase the first mark completely (do not merely cross it out) before making another.

Correctly Filled Transcript for Sample Dictation

Check your notes against the dictation; check your notes against the alphabetic list of words and the transcript sheet; check the transcript against your answer grid. Identify your errors.

I realize that this __B__(1) dictation is __D__(2) a __C__(3) of the __A__(4) __C__(5) and is __D__(6) __C__(7) scored.

The work __B__(8) and __C__(9) __D__(10) defects in __A__(11) is becoming more __D__(12) as a __C__(13) a change in the __A__(14) of many __B__(15).

In order to __A__(16) __E__(17) this change, parents have been invited __B__(18) the schools when __D__(19) children are being examined and __D__(20) the __E__(21) necessary for the __C__(22) of defects. There is a distinct __E__(23) in having a parent __B__(24) that his or her child __A__(25) the only one who needs attention. . . . (The rest of the sample dictation is not transcribed here.)

Miscellaneous OPM Questions

The following questions represent a sample of OPM questions drawn from a variety of specialized exams.
Directions: *For each question, circle the letter of the answer you choose.*

MECHANICAL AND NON-VERBAL TESTS

Symbol Series

Questions 1 and 2 consist of a series of five symbols at the left and five other symbols labeled (A), (B), (C), (D), and (E) at the right.

In each question, first study the series of symbols at the left; then from the symbols at the right, labeled (A), (B), (C), (D), and (E), select the one that continues the series most completely.

1.

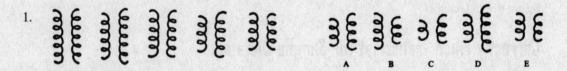

Each symbol in the series at the left has two coils. The symbols differ from one another in the number of loops that each coil has. In the first symbol, each coil has five loops; in the second, the left-hand one has four and the right-hand one has five; in the third, each coil has four. In this series, first the left-hand coil loses a loop and then the right-hand coil loses one.

Since the fifth symbol has three loops in each coil, the next symbol in this series must have two loops in the left-hand coil and three in the right-hand coil. Since symbol A is the only one that has two loops in the left-hand coil and three in the right-hand coil, (A) is the answer.

2.

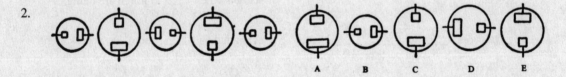

Question 2 is harder. The first five symbols show an alternation from small to large to small and a quarter-turn in a counterclockwise direction each time. The answer should be a large circle, therefore (which eliminates B from the alternatives), with the larger rectangle at the bottom of the circle (which eliminates D and E). A second look at (A) shows that the rectangles within it are larger than any of the rectangles in the other circles; this change has no basis in the series. Thus (C) is left as the correct answer.

Tools and Mechanical Principles

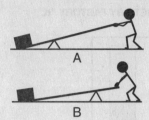

1. In which, if either, of the figures shown above can the man lift more weight?
    (A) A
    (B) B
    (C) The men in figures A and B can lift equal weights.
    (D) The man who can lift more weight cannot be determined.

The position of the fulcrum gives the man in figure A a greater mechanical advantage so answer (A) is correct.

2. In the gears shown above, as gear X turns in a counterclockwise direction, gear Y turns
    (A) clockwise at the same speed
    (B) clockwise at a faster speed
    (C) counterclockwise at a slower speed
    (D) counterclockwise at the same speed

3. In order to smooth and standardize a straight or tapered hole, the best of the following tools to use is a
    (A) reamer
    (B) drill
    (C) tap
    (D) cold chisel
    (E) compass saw

4. The tool illustrated above is a
    (A) counterbore
    (B) tap
    (C) center punch
    (D) rose countersink
    (E) pin punch

5. Which one of the following frequencies is most commonly used in the United States in alternating-current lighting circuits?
    (A) 10 cycles   (D) 60 cycles
    (B) 25 cycles   (C) 110 cycles
    (C) 40 cycles

6. The device used to mix the air and the fuel in a gasoline engine is called the
    (A) carburetor   (D) manifold
    (B) cylinder   (E) valve
    (C) distributor

7. Which one of the following would cause excessive backlash in the rear axle assembly?
    (A) bent rear axle shaft
    (B) chipped differential gears
    (C) improper lubrication
    (D) worn differential gears and thrust washers
    (E) ring gear adjusted too close to pinion

8. As a driver brought his truck into a long curve to the left at 40 miles per hour, he made a moderate application of his air brakes, and at that point he felt a pull to the right on the steering wheel. Which one of the following could *not* have caused that pull?
    (A) sudden loss of air from right front tire
    (B) lack of super-elevation on curve
    (C) lack of adequate tread on front tires
    (D) unbalanced adjustment of brakes

Answer Key

1. A   2. B   3. A   4. C   5. D   6. A   7. D   8. C

Graph and Meter Reading

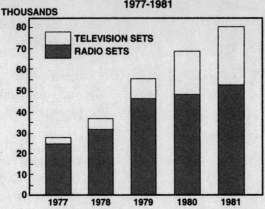

OUTPUT OF RADIO SETS AND TELEVISION SETS BY FACTORY "K"
1977-1981

THOUSANDS

TELEVISION SETS
RADIO SETS

The following questions can be answered by reading the bar graph above.

1. In the year in which the total output of the factory was the least, the percentage of that output that consisted of television sets was approximately
    (A) 10%
    (B) 20%
    (C) 25%
    (D) 30%
    (E) 40%

2. In which year did the production of television sets total approximately 20,000?
    (A) 1977
    (B) 1978
    (C) 1979
    (D) 1980
    (E) 1981

3. The position of the pointer on the meter scale is nearest to
    (A) 2.6
    (B) 3.1
    (C) 3.2
    (D) 3.3

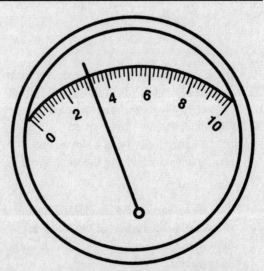

An examination of the meter scale shows, first, that only the even numbers are given on the dial. Between each pair of numbers are 10 small subdivisions. The position of the odd numbers is indicated by the slightly longer subdivision mark. Since there are five subdivisions between the positions of two successive whole numbers, each subdivision indicates $\frac{1}{5}$ or .2.

The pointer in the example is closest to one subdivision beyond 3; the correct reading of the meter would $3 + \frac{1}{5}$, or 3.2.

For a reading of 3.1, the pointer would be midway between the mark corresponding to 3 and the mark corresponding to 3.2.

Answer Key

1. A   2. D   3. C

Shop Arithmetic

1. When 100, 125, 75, and 20 are added, the answer is
   (A) 220   (D) 320
   (B) 270   (E) 420
   (C) 325

2.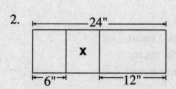

   X is what part of the whole sheet?
   (A) $\frac{1}{6}$ (D) $\frac{1}{5}$
   (B) $\frac{1}{3}$ (E) none of these
   (C) $\frac{1}{4}$

3.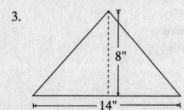

   The area of the triangle in question 3 in square inches is
   (A) 56   (D) 22
   (B) 112   (E) 448
   (C) 122

4.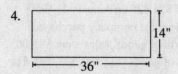

   What is the greatest number of pieces 9" × 2" that could be cut from the given sheet of metal?
   (A) 18   (D) 80
   (B) 21   (E) 28
   (C) 26

5.

   The volume of the rectangular solid in cubic inches is
   (A) 224   (D) 56
   (B) 28   (E) 32
   (C) 896

6. $\frac{1}{2}$ of $\frac{1}{4}$ is
   (A) $\frac{1}{12}$ (D) $\frac{1}{4}$
   (B) $\frac{1}{8}$ (E) 8
   (C) $\frac{1}{2}$

7. A circular saw cuts 8 boards per minute. If there are 1,440 boards to be cut, the number of *hours* required to cut these boards is
   (A) $2\frac{1}{3}$ (D) $3\frac{2}{3}$
   (B) $2\frac{2}{3}$ (E) 3
   (C) 4

8. A drawing of a certain building is 10 inches by 15 inches. On this drawing, 1 inch represents 5 feet. If the same drawing had been made 20 inches by 30 inches, 1 inch on the drawing would represent
   (A) $7\frac{1}{2}$ feet   (D) $3\frac{1}{3}$ feet
   (B) 5 feet   (E) $2\frac{1}{2}$ feet
   (C) 10 feet

9. During an 8-hour day, an apprentice earned 40 percent as much as a master mechanic. If the master mechanic earned $112.00, what was the apprentice's *hourly* earning?
   (A) $6.40   (D) $4.48
   (B) $9.60   (E) none of these
   (C) $6.72

10. An opening 6 yards long and 3 feet wide is to be covered by sheathing. Lumber is available to cover $\frac{2}{3}$ of the area of the opening. How many square feet will remain uncovered?
    (A) 2   (D) 12
    (B) 4   (E) none of these
    (C) 6

Answer Key

1. D   2. C   3. A   4. E   5. A   6. B   7. E   8. E   9. E   10. E

KNOWLEDGE TESTS FOR PROFESSIONAL AND SEMI-PROFESSIONAL POSITIONS

Statistics

1. If 4 is added to every observation in a sample, the mean is
   (A) increased by 4
   (B) increased by 4 times the number of observations
   (C) increased by 4 divided by the number of observations
   (D) decreased by 4
   (E) not affected

2. A distribution for which one of the following variables would constitute a discrete series?
   (A) weight of eighth-grade pupils
   (B) width of the visual field
   (C) "items right" score on a history test
   (D) auditory reaction time
   (E) age at marriage of 850 musicians

3. Of the following measures, which one is the most stable under conditions of random sampling?
   (A) mode
   (B) median
   (C) arithmetic mean
   (D) harmonic mean
   (E) geometric mean

4. The standard deviation is a measure of which one of the following characteristics of a population?
   (A) skewness
   (B) symmetry
   (C) normality
   (D) randomness
   (E) variability

Answer Key

1. A   2. C   3. C   4. E

Accounting

1. An operating mining company properly charged $1,200 to expense to reflect the wear and tear on its equipment. The corresponding credit should have been made to
   (A) reserve for contingent liability
   (B) reserve for depletion
   (C) reserve for depreciation
   (D) surplus reserve
   (E) earned surplus

2. The Jones Company had a merchandise inventory of $24,625 on January 1, 1950. During the year the company purchased $60,000 worth of goods, sales were $85,065, and the cost of goods sold was $28,060. The inventory on December 31,1950, was
   (A) $28,065.00
   (B) $28,500.00
   (C) $49,690.00
   (D) $57,005.00
   (E) none of these

Answer Key

1. C   2. E

Weather Forecasting

1. Particles of dust, smoke, or microbes often cause the air to be
   (A) hazy
   (B) clear
   (C) humid
   (D) dry
   (E) cold

2. Helium, neon, krypton, and xenon are
   (A) never found in the atmosphere
   (B) found in place of hydrogen in the upper atmosphere
   (C) found in the atmosphere in very small quantities
   (D) found in the Arctic region in largest proportion
   (E) found only over the ocean

3. The air warmed to the greatest extent by
   (A) the sun's rays directly
   (B) only conduction from the earth
   (C) hot vapors
   (D) dust particles
   (E) both convection and conduction from the earth

Answer Key

1. A   2. C   3. E

Safety

1. An electrical detonator is
   (A) an instrument used to measure electrical energy
   (B) a part of an electrical signaling apparatus
   (C) a device used for detecting sound
   (D) a device used to fire explosives
   (E) a part of an electric-light bulb

2. Most authorities in the field of safety planning agree that the ultimate success of any safety program depends on the
   (A) individual worker
   (B) foreman
   (C) management
   (D) state government
   (E) safety instructor

Answer Key

1. D   2. A

Mathematics

1. The product of $(3m - n)$ and $3m$ is
   (A) $9m^2 - 3mn$
   (B) $9m^2 - mn$
   (C) $9m - 3n$
   (D) $9m^2 - n^2$
   (E) $3m^2 - 3mn$

2. Find the total differential of $(x^2 + y^2)^{1/2}$.
   (A) $x(x^2 + y^2) - 1/2$
   (B) $y(x^2 + y^2) - 1/2$
   (C) $xdx + ydy$

   (D)

   (E) $xdx - ydy$

3. The length l of a spiral spring supporting a pan is increased c centimeters for x grams of weight placed on the pan. What is the length of the spring if w grams are placed on the pan?

   (A) $lc +$

   (B) $l +$

   (C) $l +$

   (D)

   (E)

Answer Key

1. A   2. D   3. C

Engineering and Other Physical Sciences

1. A plane figure consists of a square 10 inches on a side and an isosceles triangle whose base is the left edge of the square and whose altitude dropped from the vertex opposite the 10-inch base of the triangle common to the square is 6 inches. Approximately how far in inches from the left side of the square is the center of gravity of the whole figure located?
   (A) 2.92
   (B) 3.15
   (C) 3.38
   (D) 3.75
   (E) 4.28

2. The stiffness of a rectangular beam varies
   (A) as the depth
   (B) inversely as the depth
   (C) as the square of the depth
   (D) as the cube of the depth
   (E) inversely as the cube of the depth

3. At atmospheric pressure, steam at 100°C is passed into 400 grams of water at 10°C until the temperature of the water rises to 40°C. It is then found that the weight of the water has increased to 420 grams due to the condensing steam. The heat of vaporization of steam in calories per gram at 100°C is
   (A) 60
   (B) 300
   (C) 540
   (D) 600
   (E) none of these

4. The addition of HCl to a solution of sodium acetate causes
   (A) the precipitation of sodium chloride
   (B) a decrease in the concentration of acetate ion
   (C) an increase in the concentration of sodium ion
   (D) an increase in the concentration of hydroxide ion
   (E) no change in the concentration of hydroxide ion

Answer Key

1. C   2. D   3 C   4. B

Psychology

1. In experiments on the localization of sound in space, the sounds that can be most accurately located by the hearer are those sounds originating at points
   (A) in the plane equidistant from the two ears of the hearer
   (B) in front of the hearer
   (C) above and below the hearer
   (D) to the left and to the right of the hearer
   (E) behind the hearer

2. In the field of measurement of interests, the Preference Record is associated with the name of
   (A) Remmers
   (B) Kuder
   (C) Bingham
   (D) Viteles
   (E) Bell

Answer Key

1. D   2. B

Administration

1. A number of national organizations require the approval of the headquarters office on all actions originating in the field offices, instead of following the alternate procedure of delegating authority for such actions. This requirement of headquarters' review and approval is frequently unsatisfactory to the headquarters office itself. In general, the most frequent reason for the *dissatisfaction* in the headquarters office is that
   (A) headquarters may lack the information necessary for approving these cases
   (B) field offices resent the review
   (C) the review causes delay
   (D) it is felt that authority should be commensurate with responsibility
   (E) clearance through a large number of divisions is required in most headquarters offices

Answer Key

1. A

Occupational Analysis

1. In the machine shop of a manufacturing firm, a job with the title of Foreman has the following duties:

   "Installs cutting tools in various types of semiautomatic machinery. Adjusts the guides, stops, working tables of machines, and other controls to handle the size of stock to be machined. Operates and adjusts machine until accurate production (based on blueprint specifications, patterns, or templates) has been achieved. Checks production with precision gages, often to tolerances of 0.0005 inch. Turns machine over to regular operator when it is producing satisfactorily."

Which of the following would be the most descriptive title for this job?
(A) cutting-machine mechanic
(B) dimensional checker
(C) job setter
(D) machinist
(E) tool and die maker

Answer Key

1. C

Public Affairs

1. The most important way in which geographic factors influence rural community structure is by
   (A) influencing the size of the farms and thus the density of the population
   (B) influencing the birth rate
   (C) dictating the habits of the people
   (D) influencing the temperament of the people in such a way as to make them cooperative or non-cooperative
   (E) being the most important determinants of community boundaries

Answer Key

1. A

Supervision

1. In general, the most important advantage of good employee morale is that it results in
   (A) high production
   (B) decreased work for the supervisor
   (C) increased ease in rating workers' efficiency
   (D) high standing for the supervisor with management
   (E) less desire for wage increases among employees

2. Which one of the following types of information would be most useful to a supervisor in determining which employee should lose his job in case layoffs are necessary?
   (A) length of service with the supervisor
   (B) marital status
   (C) education
   (D) age
   (E) job performance rating

3. A supervisor is planning a discussion with his workers as part of a training course. To which one of the following factors should he give the most attention?
   (A) preparing in advance questions that will promote the discussion of important matters
   (B) getting as many workers as possible to attend the meeting
   (C) inviting only those workers who do not hesitate to speak in a group
   (D) making certain that the meeting will not drag out too long
   (E) selecting about six workers to make speeches that they will prepare in advance

4. A group of employees has recently been hired to perform simple, routine tasks. The use of which one of the following statements in the training of the group would be most likely, in general, to create interest in this work?
   (A) emphasis upon the pleasant working conditions and special services that the company offers its employees
   (B) explanation of the inspection system by which all work is reviewed in order to make certain that it conforms with requirements.
   (C) demonstration that the work is extremely simple and therefore there can be no excuse for failure to perform it properly
   (D) a frank statement that the work is monotonous but must be done even if it is not interesting
   (E) explanation of the relationship and the importance of the work to the total work of the organization

Answer Key

1. A   2. E   3. A   4. E

Sample Questions: ACWA

The questions selected as sample questions for the written test are similar to the questions you will find in the actual test in terms of difficulty and form. In general, the test questions deal with topics related to government business that you would be likely to encounter.

PART A—VOCABULARY AND READING

The total time allotted for Part A is 50 minutes. Part A will consist of 15 vocabulary questions and 20 reading questions. It should take you about five minutes to answer the vocabulary questions, which would leave you 45 minutes for the reading questions. Do not spend much more than five minutes on the vocabulary questions, since this would cut into the time you have for answering the reading questions. However, if you finish Part A before the allotted time is over, you should review your answers in both the Vocabulary and the Reading sections, especially any answers about which you were uncertain.

Vocabulary Questions

Federal jobs require you to communicate well both in written and spoken language. Consequently, a good vocabulary is important for successful job performance. The following questions present a key word and five suggested answers. Your task is to find the suggested answer that is closest in meaning to the key word. Wrong answers may have some connection with the word, but their meanings will be essentially different from that of the key word. Sample questions 1 and 2 are examples of the vocabulary questions in the test.

1. To *collaborate* means most nearly to work
   (A) rapidly
   (B) together
   (C) independently
   (D) overtime
   (E) carefully

The word *collaborate* means to work with another, especially on a project of mutual interest. Therefore, response (B), *together,* is the best answer. Responses (A), (D), and (E) are clearly unrelated to the meaning of *collaborate,* and response (C), *independently,* is opposite in meaning.

2. *Altruistic* means most nearly
   (A) unselfish
   (B) extended
   (C) unimaginative
   (D) organized
   (E) appealing

To be *altruistic* means to be concerned for or devoted to the welfare of others. Therefore, response (A), *unselfish,* is an excellent synonym. Response (B) could be viewed as slightly related, since *altruistic* people often extend themselves to help others. However, the basic meaning of *extended*—stretched out— is completely different from the meaning of *altruistic.* Responses (C) and (D) are clearly unrelated to the meaning of *altruistic.* A vague connection exists between *altruistic* and response (E), *appealing.*

Altruistic people often make appeals on behalf of those less fortunate than themselves. Simultaneously, the generosity of *altruistic* people often makes them very *appealing* to other people. Although this vague connection exists between *altruistic* and *appealing*, they do not share a similar meaning.

Reading Questions

In each of these questions you will be given a paragraph that contains all the information necessary to infer the correct answer. Use **only** the information provided in the paragraph. Do not speculate or make assumptions that go beyond this information. Also, assume that all information given in the paragraph is true, even if it conflicts with some fact known to you. Only one correct answer can be validly inferred from the information contained in the paragraph.

Pay special attention to negated verbs (for example, "are *not*") and negative prefixes (for example, "*in*complete" or "*dis*organized"). Also pay special attention to quantifiers, such as "all," "none," and "some." For example, from a paragraph in which it is stated that "it is not true that all contracts are legal" one can validly infer that "some contracts are not legal," or that "some contracts are illegal," or that "some illegal things are contracts," but one **cannot** validly infer that "no contracts are legal," or that "some contracts are legal." Similarly, from a paragraph that states "all contracts are legal" and "all contracts are two-sided agreements," one can infer that "some two-sided agreements are legal," but one **cannot** validly infer that "all two-sided agreements are legal."

Bear in mind that in some tests, universal quantifiers such as "all" and "none" often give away incorrect response choices. That is **not** the case in this test. Some correct answers will refer to "all" or "none" of the members of a group.

Be sure to distinguish between essential information and unessential, peripheral information. That is to say, in a real test question, the example above ("all contracts are legal" and "all contracts are two-sided agreements") would appear in a longer, full-fledged paragraph. It would be up to you to separate the essential information from its context, and then to realize that a response choice that states "some two-sided agreements are legal" represents a valid inference and hence the correct answer.

Sample questions 3 and 4 are examples of the reading questions in the text.

3. Personnel administration begins with the process of defining the quantities of people needed to do the job. Therefore, people must be recruited, selected, trained, directed, rewarded, transferred, promoted, and perhaps released or retired. However, it is not true that all organizations are structured so that workers can be dealt with as individuals. In some organizations, employees are represented by unions, and managers bargain directly only with these associations.

The paragraph best supports the statement that
(A) no organizations are structured so that workers cannot be dealt with as individuals
(B) some working environments other than organizations are structured so that workers can be dealt with as individuals
(C) all organizations are structured so that employees are represented by unions
(D) no organizations are structured so that managers bargain with unions
(E) some organizations are not structured so that workers can be dealt with as individuals

The correct answer is response (E). This conclusion can be derived from information contained in the third sentence of the paragraph, which states that "it is not true that all organizations are structured so that workers can be dealt with as individuals." From this statement, it can be inferred that *some organizations are not structured so that workers can be dealt with as individuals.*

Response (A) is incorrect because it contradicts the information in the third and fourth sentences of the paragraph. With its double negation, response (A) is in effect saying that all organizations are structured so that workers can be dealt with as individuals. This flatly contradicts the third sentence and also contradicts the fourth sentence, which says that *in some organizations, employees are represented by unions, and managers bargain with these associations.*

Response (B) is not supported by the paragraph because the paragraph gives no information about working environments other than organizations.

Response (C) is not supported by the paragraph because the paragraph says only that employees are represented by unions in *some* organizations. One cannot generalize from this to say that employees are represented by unions in *all* organizations.

Response (D) is incorrect because it contradicts the fourth sentence, which says that managers bargain with unions in some organizations.

Note that in this question, the correct answer follows basically from one sentence in the paragraph— the third sentence. The rest of the paragraph presents additional information about personnel administration that is relevant to the discussion, but not necessary to make the inference. Part of your task in the Reading section is to *understand* what you read, and then to *discern* what conclusions follow logically from statements in the paragraph. Consequently, in this test, you will find some questions in which it is necessary to use all or most of the statements presented in the paragraph, while in others, such as this one, only one statement is needed to infer the correct answer.

4. Many kinds of computer-programming languages have been developed over the years. Initially, programmers had to write instructions in machine language. If a computer-programming language is a machine language, then it is a code that can be read directly by a computer. Most high-level computer-programming languages, such as Fortran and Cobol, use strings of common English phrases that communicate with the computer only after being converted or translated into a machine code.

    The paragraph best supports the statement that
    (A) all high-level computer-programming languages use strings of common English phrases that are converted to a machine code
    (B) if a computer-programming language is a machine language, then it is not a code that can be read directly by a computer
    (C) if a computer-programming language is a code that can be read directly by a computer, then it is not a machine language
    (D) if a computer-programming language is not a code that can be read directly by a computer, then it is not a machine language
    (E) if a computer-programming language is not a machine language, then it is a code that can be read directly by a computer

The correct answer is response (D). The answer can be derived from the information presented in the third sentence. That sentence states that "if a computer-programming language is a machine language, then it is a code that can be read directly by a computer." From this statement it can be seen that all machine languages are codes that can be read directly by a computer, and that if a computer-programming language is not such a code, then it is not a machine language.

Response (A) goes beyond the information presented in the paragraph, which states only that *most* high-level computer-programming languages use strings of common English phrases.

Response (B) represents a complete contradiction of the third sentence of the paragraph.

Response (C) contradicts the paragraph. We know from the paragraph that at least some coded languages that can be read directly by a computer are machine languages.

Response (E) is incorrect because the paragraph does not say whether or not computer languages that are *not* machine languages are codes that can be read directly by a computer.

PART B—TABULAR COMPLETION AND ARITHMETIC REASONING

The total time allotted to Part B is 50 minutes. Part B will consist of 10 tabular completion questions and 15 arithmetic reasoning questions. It should take you no more than 15 minutes to answer the tabular completion questions, which would leave you 35 minutes for the arithmetic reasoning questions. Some problems in Part B may be solved by more than one method. When this is the case, use whatever method is fastest and easiest for you. Keep in mind, however, that each question has only **one** correct answer. If you finish Part B before the allotted time is over, you should review your answers in both the Tabular Completion and Arithmetic Reasoning sections, especially any answers about which you were uncertain. *The use of calculators will NOT be permitted during the actual test; therefore, they should not be used to solve these sample questions.*

Tabular Completion Questions

These questions are based on information presented in tables. Only *two* sample questions of this type appear below, although, in the actual test, you will have to find *five* unknown values in each table. You must calculate these unknown values by using the known values given in the table. In some questions, the exact answer will not be given as one of the response choices. In such cases, you should select response (E), "none of these." Sample questions 5 and 6, which are based on the accompanying table, are examples of the tabular completion questions in this test.

FEDERAL BUDGET RECEIPTS OUTLAYS, AND DEBT
FISCAL YEARS 1981-1985
(In millions of dollars)

ITEM	FISCAL YEAR				
	1981	1982	1983	1984	1985
Total Receipts	I	298,060	355,559	399,561	463,302
Federal funds	187,505	201,099	241,312	270,490	316,366
Trust funds	116,683	131,750	150,560	165,569	186,988
Interfund transactions	−25,098	−34,789	−36,313	−36,498	−40,052
Total Outlays.	324,244	364,473	400,507	448,368	490,997
Federal funds.	240,080	269,921	295,757	331,991	362,396
Trust funds	109,262	II	141,063	152,875	168,653
Interfund transactions	−25,098	−34,789	−36,313	−36,498	−40,052
Total Surplus or Deficit (−).	−45,154	−66,413	−44,948	−48,807	V
Federal funds	−52,576	−68,822	−54,444	−61,501	−40,030
Trust funds	7,422	2,409	9,496	12,694	12,336
Gross Federal Debt	544,131	631,866	III	780,425	833,751
Held by Government agencies	147,225	151,566	157,295	169,477	189,162
Held by the public.	396,906	480,300	551,843	610,948	644,589
Federal Reserve System.	84,993	94,714	105,004	IV	115,594
Other	311,913	385,586	446,839	495,468	528,995

Hypothetical data.

5. What is the value of I in millions of dollars?
   (A) 91,585
   (B) 162,407
   (C) 279,090
   (D) 304,188
   (E) none of these

The correct answer is (C). It can be calculated by adding the Receipt values for *Federal funds*, *Trust funds*, and *Interfund transactions*. Numerically, 187,505 + 116,683 + (–25,098) = 279,090.

6. What is the value of II in millions of dollars?
   (A) 329,684
   (B) 129,341
   (C) 94,552
   (D) –101,202
   (E) none of these

The correct answer is B. It can be calculated by subtracting the Outlay values for *Federal funds* and *Interfund transactions* from the value for *Total Outlays*. Numerically, 364,473 – (269,921) – (–34,789) = 129,341.

Arithmetic Reasoning Questions

In this part of the test you will have to solve problems formulated in both verbal and numeric form. You will have to analyze a paragraph in order to set up the problem, and then solve it. If the exact answer is not given as one of the response choices, you should select response (E), "none of these." Sample questions 7 and 8 are examples of the arithmetic reasoning questions in this test.

7. An interagency task force has representatives from three different agencies. Half of the task force members represent Agency A, one-third represent Agency B, and three represent Agency C. How many people are on the task force?
   (A) 12
   (B) 15
   (C) 18
   (D) 24
   (E) none of these

The correct answer is response (C). It can be obtained by computing the following:

$\frac{1}{2}x + \frac{1}{3}x + 3 = x$

x is equal to the total number of task force members; $\frac{1}{2}x$ represents the number from Agency A; $\frac{1}{3}x$ represents the number from Agency B; and 3 is the number from Agency C. The first two terms on the left side of the equation can be combined by computing their lowest common denominator, which is 6. Therefore:

$\frac{1}{2}x = \frac{3}{6}x$ and $\frac{1}{3}x = \frac{2}{6}x$

The sum of $^3/_6x$ and $^2/_6x$ is $^5/_6x$, which, when subtracted from x (or $^6/_6x$), yields the results:
$^1/_6x = 3$ and $x = 18$

Responses (A), (B), and (D) are the result of erroneous computations.

8. It has been established in recent productivity studies that, on the average, it takes a filing clerk 2 hours and 12 minutes to fill four drawers of a filing cabinet. At this rate, how long would it take two clerks to fill 16 drawers?
    (A) 4 hrs.
    (B) 4 hrs., 20 min.
    (C) 8 hrs.
    (D) 8 hrs., 40 min.
    (E) none of these

The answer is (E). The correct answer is not given as one of the response choices. The answer can be obtained by first converting 12 minutes to .2 hour, and then setting up a simple proportion:
$^{2.2}/_4 = {}^x/_{16}$

Solving this proportion, we obtain $4x = 35.2$; $x = 8.8$. This, however, is the number of hours that it would take one filing clerk to do the job. If two clerks are filling the 16 drawers, the job would be completed in half that time or in 4.4 hours, which is 4 hours, 24 minutes.

Responses (A), (B), (C), and (D) are the result of erroneous computations.

Sample Questions: Postal Exams

After many years of administering a different postal examination for each individual job title or for a small cluster of job titles, the Postal Service has determined that it is more efficient and equally effective to administer the same exam for large groups of postal occupations that require related skills and abilities.

Accordingly, the same examination is now administered for the following job titles:

Clerk-Carrier   Mark-Up Clerk

Mail Handler   Flat Sorting Machine Operator

Mail Processor   Rural Carrier

Distribution Clerk, Machine

The following are official test instructions and official sample questions distributed by the Postal Service to candidates for all of these jobs.

TEST INSTRUCTIONS

During the test session, it will be your responsibility to pay close attention to what the examiner has to say and to follow all instructions. One of the purposes of the test is to see how quickly and accurately you can work. Therefore, each part of the test will be carefully timed. You will not **START** until you are told to do so. Also, when you are told to **STOP,** you must immediately **STOP** answering the questions. When you are told to work on a particular part of the examination, regardless of which part, you are to work on that part **ONLY**. If you finish a part before time is called, you may review your answers for that part, but you will not go on or back to any other part. Failure to follow **ANY** directions given to you by the examiner may be grounds for disqualification. Instructions read by the examiner are intended to ensure that each applicant has the same fair and objective opportunity to compete in the examination.

The following questions are like the ones that will be on the test. Study these carefully. This will give you practice with the different kinds of questions and show you how to mark your answers.

PART A—ADDRESS CHECKING

In this part of the test, you will have to decide whether two addresses are alike or different. If the two addresses are exactly *alike* in every way, darken circle A for the question. If the two addresses are *different* in any way, darken circle D for the question.

Mark your answers to these sample questions on the Sample Answer Grid at the right.

1. 2134 S 20th St   2134 S 20th St

Since the two addresses are exactly alike,
mark (A) for question 1 on the Sample Answer Grid.

	Sample Answer Grid

2. 4608 N Warnock St   4806 N Warnock St
3. 1202 W Girard Dr   1202 W Girard Rd
4. Chappaqua NY 10514   Chappaqua NY 10514
5. 2207 Markland Ave   2207 Markham Av

Sample Answer Grid:
1. (A) (D)
2. (A) (D)
3. (A) (D)
4. (A) (D)
5. (A) (D)

The correct answers to questions 2 to 5 are: 2D, 3D, 4A, and 5D.

Your score on Part A of the actual test will be based on the number of wrong answers as well as on the number of right answers. Part A is scored right answers minus wrong answers. Random guessing should not help your score. For the Part A test, you will have six minutes to answer as many of the 95 questions as you can. It will be to your advantage to work as quickly and as accurately as possible. You will not be expected to be able to answer all the questions in the time allowed.

PART B—MEMORY FOR ADDRESSES

In this part of the test, you will have to memorize the locations (A, B, C, D, or E) of 25 addresses shown in five boxes, like those below. For example, "Sardis" is in Box C, "6800–6999 Table" is in Box B, etc. (The addresses in the actual test will be different.)

A	B	C	D	E
4700–5999 Table Lismore	6800–6999 Table Kelford	5600–6499 Table Joel	6500–6799 Table Tatum	4400–4699 Table Ruskin
5600–6499 West Hesper	6500–6799 West Musella	6800–6999 West Sardis	4400–4699 West Porter	4700–5599 West Nathan
4400–4699 Blake	5600–6499 Blake	6500–6799 Blake	6800–6999 Blake	

Study the locations of the addresses for five minutes. As you study, silently repeat these to yourself. Then cover the boxes and try to answer the questions below. Mark your answers for each question by darkening the circle as was done for questions 1 and 2.

1. Musella	6. Hesper	11. 4400–4699 Blake	
2. 4700–5599 Blake	7. Kelford	12. 6500–6799 West	
3. 4700–5599 Table	8. Nathan	13. Porter	
4. Tatum	9. 6500–6799 Blake	14. 6800–6999 Blake	
5. 4400–4699 Blake	10. Joel		

```
┌──────────────────────── Sample Answer Grid ────────────────────────┐
│  1. Ⓐ ● Ⓒ Ⓓ Ⓔ      5. Ⓐ Ⓑ Ⓒ Ⓓ Ⓔ      9. Ⓐ Ⓑ Ⓒ Ⓓ Ⓔ     13. Ⓐ Ⓑ Ⓒ Ⓓ Ⓔ  │
│  2. Ⓐ Ⓑ Ⓒ ● Ⓔ      6. Ⓐ Ⓑ Ⓒ Ⓓ Ⓔ     10. Ⓐ Ⓑ Ⓒ Ⓓ Ⓔ     14. Ⓐ Ⓑ Ⓒ Ⓓ Ⓔ  │
│  3. Ⓐ Ⓑ Ⓒ Ⓓ Ⓔ      7. Ⓐ Ⓑ Ⓒ Ⓓ Ⓔ     11. Ⓐ Ⓑ Ⓒ Ⓓ Ⓔ                    │
│  4. Ⓐ Ⓑ Ⓒ Ⓓ Ⓔ      8. Ⓐ Ⓑ Ⓒ Ⓓ Ⓔ     12. Ⓐ Ⓑ Ⓒ Ⓓ Ⓔ                    │
└─────────────────────────────────────────────────────────────────────┘
```

The correct answers for questions 3 to 14 are: 3A, 4D, 5A, 6A, 7B, 8E, 9C, 10C, 11A, 12B, 13D, and 14E.

During the examination, you will have three practice exercises to help you memorize the location of addresses shown in five boxes. After the practice exercises, the actual test will be given. Part B is scored right answers minus one-fourth of the wrong answers. Random guessing should not help your score. But, if you can eliminate one or more alternatives, it is to your advantage to guess. For the Part B test, you will have five minutes to answer as many of the 88 questions as you can. It will be to your advantage to work as quickly and as accurately as you can. You will not be expected to be able to answer all the questions in the time allowed.

PART C—NUMBER SERIES

For each *number series* question there is at the left a series of numbers that follow some definite order and at the right five sets of two numbers each. You are to look at the numbers in the series at the left and find out what order they follow. Then decide what the next two numbers in that series would be if the same order were continued. Mark your answers on the Sample Answer Grid.

1.   1 2 3 4 5 6 7   (A) 1 2   (B) 5 6   (C) 8 9   (D) 4 5   (E) 7 8

The numbers in this series are increasing by 1. If the series were continued for two more numbers, it would read: 1 2 3 4 5 6 7 8 9. Therefore the correct answer is 8 and 9, and you should have darkened (C) for question 1.

2.   15 14 13 12 11 10 9   (A) 2 1   (B) 17 16   (C) 8 9   (D) 8 7   (E) 9 8

The numbers in this series are decreasing by 1. If the series were continued for two more numbers, it would read: 15 14 13 12 11 10 9 8 7. Therefore the correct answer is 8 and 7, and you should have darkened (D) for question 2.

3.   20 20 21 21 22 22 23   (A) 23 23 (B) 23 24 (C) 19 19 (D) 22 23 (E) 21 22

Each number in this series is repeated and then increased by 1. If the series were continued for two more numbers, it would read: 20 20 21 21 22 22 23 23 24. Therefore the correct answer is 23 and 24, and you should have darkened (B) for question 3.

4.   17 3 17 4 17 5 17   (A) 6 17   (B) 6 7   (C) 17 6   (D) 5 6   (E) 17 7

This series is the number 17 separated by numbers increasing by 1, beginning with the number 3. If the series were continued for two more numbers, it would read: 17 3 17 4 17 5 17 6 17. Therefore the correct answer is 6 and 17, and you should have darkened (A) for question 4.

5.   1 2 4 5 7 8 10   (A) 11 12 (B) 12 14 (C) 10 13 (D) 12 13 (E) 11 13

The numbers in this series are increasing first by 1 (plus 1) and then by 2 (plus 2). If the series were continued for two more numbers, it would read: 1 2 4 5 7 8 10 (plus 1) 11 and (plus 2) 13. Therefore the correct answer is 11 and 13, and you should have darkened (E) for question 5.

Now read and work sample questions 6 through 10 and mark your answers on the Sample Answer Grid.

6.   21 21 20 20 19 19 18   (A) 18 18 (B) 18 17 (C) 17 18 (D) 17 17 (E) 18 19
7.   1 22 1 23 1 24 1   (A) 26 1   (B) 25 26 (C) 25 1   (D) 1 26   (E) 1 25
8.   1 20 3 19 5 18 7   (A) 8 9   (B) 8 17   (C) 17 10 (D) 17 9   (E) 9 18
9.   4 7 10 13 16 19 22   (A) 23 26 (B) 25 27 (C) 25 26 (D) 25 28 (E) 24 27
10.   30 2 28 4 26 6 24   (A) 23 9   (B) 26 8   (C) 8 9   (D) 26 22 (E) 8 22

Sample Answer Grid
6. Ⓐ Ⓑ Ⓒ Ⓓ Ⓔ   8. Ⓐ Ⓑ Ⓒ Ⓓ Ⓔ   9. Ⓐ Ⓑ Ⓒ Ⓓ Ⓔ   10. Ⓐ Ⓑ Ⓒ Ⓓ Ⓔ
7. Ⓐ Ⓑ Ⓒ Ⓓ Ⓔ

The correct answers to sample questions 6 to 10 are: 6B, 7C, 8D, 9D, and 10E. Explanations follow.

6. Each number in the series repeats itself and then decreases by 1 or minus 1; *21* (repeat) *21* (minus 1) *20* (repeat) *20* (minus 1) *19* (repeat) *19* (minus 1) *18* (repeat) *?* (minus 1) ?

7. The number 1 is separated by numbers that begin with 22 and increase by 1; *1 22 1* (increase 22 by 1) *23 1* (increase 23 by 1) *24 1* (increase 24 by 1) ?

8. This is best explained by two alternating series—one series starts with 1 and increases by 2 or plus 2; the other series starts with 20 and decreases by 1 or minus 1.

   1   ^   *3*   ^   *5*   ^   *7*   ^   *?*
       20   *19*   *18*   *?*

9. This series of numbers increases by 3 (plus 3) beginning with the first number—
   4 7 10 13 16 19 22 ? ?

10. Look for two alternating series—one series starts with 30 and decreases by 2 (minus 2); the other series starts with 2 and increases by 2 (plus 2).

Now try questions 11 to 15.

11.	5 6 20 7 8 19 9	(A) 10 18	(B) 18 17	(C) 10 17	(D) 18 19	(E) 10 11
12.	4 6 9 11 14 16 19	(A) 21 24	(B) 22 25	(C) 20 22	(D) 21 23	(E) 22 24
13.	8 8 1 10 10 3 12	(A) 13 13	(B) 12 5	(C) 12 4	(D) 13 5	(E) 4 12
14.	10 12 50 15 17 50 20	(A) 50 21	(B) 21 50	(C) 50 22	(D) 22 50	(E) 22 24
15.	20 21 23 24 27 28 32 33 38 39	(A) 45 46	(B) 45 52	(C) 44 45	(D) 44 49	(E) 40 46

Sample Answer Grid			
11. Ⓐ Ⓑ Ⓒ Ⓓ Ⓔ	13. Ⓐ Ⓑ Ⓒ Ⓓ Ⓔ	14. Ⓐ Ⓑ Ⓒ Ⓓ Ⓔ	15. Ⓐ Ⓑ Ⓒ Ⓓ Ⓔ
12. Ⓐ Ⓑ Ⓒ Ⓓ Ⓔ			

The correct answers to the sample questions above are: 11A, 12A, 13B, 14D, and 15A.

It will be to your advantage to answer every question in Part C that you can, since your score on this part of the test will be based on the number of questions that you answer correctly. Answer first those questions that are easiest for you. For the Part C test, you will have 20 minutes to answer as many of the 24 questions as you can.

PART D—FOLLOWING ORAL DIRECTIONS

Instructions to be read for Part D. (**The words in parentheses should NOT be read aloud.**)

You are to follow the instructions that I shall read to you. I cannot repeat them.

Look at the samples. Sample 1 has a number and a line beside it. On the line write A as in ace. (**Pause 2 seconds.**) Now on the Sample Answer Grid, find number 5 (**pause 2 seconds**) and darken the letter you just wrote on the line. (**Pause 2 seconds.**)

Look at Sample 2. (**Pause slightly.**) Draw a line under the third number. (**Pause 2 seconds.**) Now look on the Sample Answer Grid, find the number under which you just drew a line, and darken (B) as in boy. (**Pause 5 seconds.**)

Look at the letters in Sample 3. (**Pause slightly.**) Draw a line under the third letter in the line. (**Pause 2 seconds.**) Now on your Sample Answer Grid, find number 9 (**pause 2 seconds**) and darken the letter under which you drew a line. (**Pause 5 seconds.**)

Look at the five circles in Sample 4. (**Pause slightly.**) Each circle has a number and a line in it. Write (D) as in dog on the line in the last circle. (**Pause 2 seconds.**) Now on the Sample Answer Grid, darken the number-letter combination that is in the circle you just wrote in. (**Pause 5 seconds.**)

Look at Sample 5. (**Pause slightly.**) There are two circles and two boxes of different sizes with numbers in them. (**Pause slightly.**) If 4 is more than 2 and if 5 is less than 3, write A as in ace in the smaller circle. (**Pause slightly.**) Otherwise write (C) as in car in the larger box. (**Pause 2 seconds.**) Now on the Sample Answer Grid, darken the number-letter combination in the box or circle in which you just wrote. (**Pause 5 seconds.**)

Now look at the Sample Answer Grid. (**Pause slightly.**) You should have darkened 4B, 5A, 9A, 10D, and 12C on the Sample Answer Grid. (**If the person preparing to take the examination made any mistakes, try to help him or her see why he or she made wrong marks.**)

In this part of the test, you will be told to follow directions by writing in a test booklet and then on an answer sheet. The test booklet will have lines of material like the following five samples:

SAMPLE 1.   5 __

SAMPLE 2.   1   6   4   3   7

SAMPLE 3.   D   B   A   E   C

SAMPLE 4.   ⑧ __   ⑤ __   ② __   ⑨ __   ⑩ __

SAMPLE 5.   ⑦ __   ⬜6 __   ①__   ⬜12 __

To practice this part of the test, tear out the page of instructions to be read. Then have somebody read the instructions to you and you follow the instructions. When he or she tells you to darken the space on the Sample Answer Grid, use the one on this page.

Your score for Part D will be based on the number of questions that you answer correctly. Therefore, if you are not sure of an answer, it will be to your advantage to guess. Part D will take about 25 minutes.

Sample Answer Grid		
1. Ⓐ Ⓑ Ⓒ Ⓓ Ⓔ	5. Ⓐ Ⓑ Ⓒ Ⓓ Ⓔ	9. Ⓐ Ⓑ Ⓒ Ⓓ Ⓔ
2. Ⓐ Ⓑ Ⓒ Ⓓ Ⓔ	6. Ⓐ Ⓑ Ⓒ Ⓓ Ⓔ	10. Ⓐ Ⓑ Ⓒ Ⓓ Ⓔ
3. Ⓐ Ⓑ Ⓒ Ⓓ Ⓔ	7. Ⓐ Ⓑ Ⓒ Ⓓ Ⓔ	11. Ⓐ Ⓑ Ⓒ Ⓓ Ⓔ
4. Ⓐ Ⓑ Ⓒ Ⓓ Ⓔ	8. Ⓐ Ⓑ Ⓒ Ⓓ Ⓔ	12. Ⓐ Ⓑ Ⓒ Ⓓ Ⓔ

Self-Rating Questions

The self-rating sections of federal examinations are set up to look like multiple-choice tests and are timed like tests, but they are not really tests at all. There are no right or wrong answers. You cannot study for the self-rating questions; your preparation consists only of gathering statistical records from your school years and thinking about what you achieved and when. On a typical self-rating section, you will find questions about your best and worst grades in school and about your favorite and least favorite subjects; questions about your extracurricular activities in school and college (if you went to college) and about your participation in sports; and questions about attendance, part-time jobs, and leadership positions. Other questions refer to your working life or school relationships. These questions ask what you think your peers think of you; others ask similar questions with respect to your supervisors or teachers. The questions ask how you think your teachers or employers might rate you on specific traits. Similar questions ask you to suggest what your friends might say about you. Still other questions ask how you rate yourself against others.

Some of these questions offer hard choices, but you do not have time to dwell on the answers. The self-rating sections are timed in the same manner as test questions. Just answer honestly and to the best of your ability. Do not try to second-guess and give the answers you think that the examiners want. Some exams include two separate self-rating sections to check for honesty. Even where there is only one such section, it has built-in measures of general consistency.

There are no official self-rating sample questions. The following questions are representative.

1. My favorite subject in high school was
   - (A) math
   - (B) English
   - (C) physical education
   - (D) social studies
   - (E) science

2. My GPA upon graduation from high school (on a 4.0 scale) was
   - (A) lower than 2.51
   - (B) 2.51 to 2.80
   - (C) 2.81 to 3.25
   - (D) 3.26 to 3.60
   - (E) higher than 3.60

3. In my second year of high school I was absent
   - (A) never
   - (B) not more than 3 days
   - (C) 4 to 10 days
   - (D) more often than 10 days
   - (E) do not recall

4. My best grades in high school were in
   - (A) art
   - (B) math
   - (C) English
   - (D) social studies
   - (E) music

5. While in high school I participated in
   - (A) one sport
   - (B) two sports and one other extracurricular activity
   - (C) three non-athletic extracurricular activities
   - (D) no extracurricular activities
   - (E) other than the above

6. During my senior year in high school I held a paying job
   - (A) 0 hours a week
   - (B) 1 to 5 hours a week
   - (C) 6 to 10 hours a week
   - (D) 11 to 16 hours a week
   - (E) more than 16 hours a week

7. The number of semesters in which I failed a course in high school was
   (A) none
   (B) one
   (C) two or three
   (D) four or five
   (E) more than five

8. In high school I did volunteer work
   (A) more than 10 hours a week
   (B) 5 to 10 hours a week on a regular basis
   (C) sporadically
   (D) seldom
   (E) not at all

If you did not go to college, skip questions 9–20. Go to question 21.

9. My general area of concentration in college was
   (A) performing arts
   (B) humanities
   (C) social sciences
   (D) business
   (E) none of the above

10. At graduation from college, my age was
    (A) under 20
    (B) 20
    (C) 21 to 24
    (D) 25 to 29
    (E) 30 or over

11. My standing in my graduating class was in the
    (A) bottom third
    (B) middle third
    (C) top third
    (D) top quarter
    (E) top 10 percent

12. In college, I was elected to a major office in a class or in a club or organization
    (A) more than six times
    (B) four or five times
    (C) two or three times
    (D) once
    (E) never

13. In comparison to my peers, I cut classes
    (A) much less often than most
    (B) somewhat less often than most
    (C) just about the same as most
    (D) somewhat more often than most
    (E) much more often than most

14. The campus activities in which I participated most were
    (A) social service
    (B) political
    (C) literary
    (D) did not participate in campus activities
    (E) did not participate in any of these activities

15. My name appeared on the dean's list
    (A) never
    (B) once or twice
    (C) in three or more terms
    (D) in more terms than it did not appear
    (E) do not remember

16. The volunteer work I did while in college was predominantly
    (A) health-care related
    (B) religious
    (C) political
    (D) educational
    (E) did not volunteer

17. While a college student, I spent most of my summers
    (A) in summer school
    (B) earning money
    (C) traveling
    (D) in service activities
    (E) resting

18. My college education was financed
    (A) entirely by my parents
    (B) by my parents and my own earnings
    (C) by scholarships, loans, and my own earnings
    (D) by my parents and loans
    (E) by a combination of sources not listed above

19. In the college classroom I was considered
    (A) a listener
    (B) an occasional contributor
    (C) an average participant
    (D) a frequent contributor
    (E) a leader

20. The person on campus whom I most admired was
    (A) another student
    (B) an athletic coach
    (C) a teacher
    (D) an administrator
    (E) a journalist

21. My peers would probably describe me as
    (A) analytical
    (B) glib
    (C) organized
    (D) funny
    (E) helpful

22. According to my supervisors (or teachers), my greatest asset is my
    (A) ability to communicate orally
    (B) written expression
    (C) ability to motivate others
    (D) organization of time
    (E) friendly personality

23. In the past two years, I have applied for
    (A) no jobs other than this one
    (B) one other job
    (C) two to four other jobs
    (D) five to eight other jobs
    (E) more than eight jobs

24. In the past year, I read strictly for pleasure
    (A) no books
    (B) one book
    (C) two books
    (D) three to six books
    (E) more than six books

25. When I read for pleasure, I read mostly
    (A) history
    (B) fiction
    (C) poetry
    (D) biography
    (E) current events

26. My peers would say of me that, when they ask me a question, I am
    (A) helpful
    (B) brusque
    (C) condescending
    (D) generous
    (E) patient

27. My supervisors (or teachers) would say that my area of least competence is
    (A) analytical ability
    (B) written communication
    (C) attention to detail
    (D) public speaking
    (E) self-control

28. In the past two years, the number of full-time (35 hours or more) jobs I have held is
    (A) none
    (B) one
    (C) two or three
    (D) four
    (E) five or more

29. Compared to my peers, my supervisors (or teachers) would rank my dependability
    (A) much better than average
    (B) somewhat better than average
    (C) about average
    (D) somewhat less than average
    (E) much less than average

30. In my opinion, the most important of the following attributes in an employee is
    (A) discretion
    (B) loyalty
    (C) open-mindedness
    (D) courtesy
    (E) competence

31. My peers would say that the word that describes me least is
    (A) sociable
    (B) reserved
    (C) impatient
    (D) judgmental
    (E) independent

32. My attendance record over the past year has been
    (A) not as good as I would like it to be
    (B) not as good as my supervisors (or teachers) would like it to be
    (C) a source of embarrassment
    (D) satisfactory
    (E) a source of pride

There are no "right" answers to these questions, so there is no answer key.

FOUR

Appendices

CONTENTS

IMPORTANT CIVIL SERVICE EMPLOYMENT CONTACTS

Major Federal Agencies Contact Information

Central Intelligence Agency (CIA)
Washington, DC 20505
703-482-1100
www.odci.gov

Consumer Product Safety Commission
4330 East-West Highway
Bethesda, MD 20814
301-504-0580
www.cpsc.gov

Environment Protection Agency
401 M St. SW
Washington, DC 20460
202-260-2090
www.epa.gov

Federal Bureau of Investigation (FBI)
935 Pennsylvania Ave. NW
Washington, DC 20535
202-324-3000
www.fbi.gov

Federal Communications Commission
1919 M St. NW
Washington, DC 20554
202-418-0500
www.fcc.gov

Federal Deposit Insurance Corporation
(FDIC)
550 17th St. NW
Washington, DC 20429
202-393-8400
www.fdic.gov

Federal Emergency Management Agency
500 C St. SW
Washington, DC 20472
202-646-4600
www.fema.gov

Federal Highway Administration
400 7th St. SW
Washington, DC 20590
202-366-4000
www.fhwa.dot.gov

Federal Trade Commission
6th St. & Pennsylvania Ave. NW
Washington, DC 20580
202-326-2222
www.ftc.gov

Food & Drug Administration
5600 Fishers Lane
Rockville, MD 20857
301-443-1544
www.fda.gov

General Services Administration
18th St. & F St. NW
Washington, DC 20405
202-708-5082
www.gsa.gov

Health Resources & Services Administration
5600 Fishers Lane
Rockville, MD 20857
301-443-2086
www.hrsa.dhhs.gov

Immigration and Naturalization Service
425 I St. NW
Washington, DC 20530
202-514-2000
www.ins.doj.gov

Library of Congress
1st St. & Independence SE
Washington, DC 20540
202-707-5000
www.lcweb.loc.gov

National Aeronautics & Space Administration
300 E St. SW
Washington, DC 20546
202-358-2810
www.nasa.gov

National Science Foundation
4201 Wilson Blvd.
Arlington, VA 22230
703-306-1234

Securities and Exchange Commission
450 5th St. NW
Washington, DC 20549
202-942-8088
www.sec.gov

Social Security Administration
6401 Security Blvd.
Baltimore, MD 21235
410-915-8882
www.ssa.gov/ or www.nsf.gov

AUTOMATED TELEPHONE SYSTEM: LOCAL NUMBERS

ALABAMA, Huntsville	256-837-0894
CALIFORNIA, San Francisco	415-744-5627
COLORADO, Denver	303-969-7050
DISTRICT OF COLUMBIA, Washington	202-606-2700
GEORGIA, Atlanta	404-331-4315
HAWAII, Honolulu	808-541-2791
ILLINOIS, Chicago	312-353-6192
MICHIGAN, Detroit	313-226-6950
MINNESOTA, Twin Cities	612-725-3430
MISSOURI, Kansas City	816-426-5702
NORTH CAROLINA, Raleigh	919-790-2822
OHIO, Dayton	937-225-2720
PENNSYLVANIA, Philadelphia	215-861-3070
PUERTO RICO, San Juan	787-766-5242
TEXAS, San Antonio	210-805-2402
VIRGINIA, Norfolk	757-441-3355
WASHINGTON, Seattle	206-553-0888

Locations of Federal Job Information "Touch Screen" Computer Kiosks

ALABAMA:
Huntsville
520 Wynn Dr., NW

ALASKA:
Anchorage
Federal Bldg.
222 W. 7th Ave.
Rm. 156

ARIZONA:
Phoenix
VA Medical Center
650 E. Indian School Rd.
Bldg. 21, Rm. 141

ARKANSAS:

Little Rock
Federal Bldg.
700 W. Capitol
First floor lobby

CALIFORNIA:

Sacramento
801 I ("i") St.

COLORADO:

Denver
Dept. of Social Services
Employment Center
2200 W. Alameda Ave.
Ste. #5B

CONNECTICUT:

Hartford
Federal Bldg.
450 Main St.
Lobby

DISTRICT OF COLUMBIA:

Washington, DC
Theodore Roosevelt Federal Bldg.
1900 E St., NW
Rm. 1416

FLORIDA:

Miami
Downtown Jobs and Benefits Center
Florida Job Service Center
401 NW 2nd Ave.
Ste. N-214

Orlando
Florida Job Service Center
1001 Executive Center Dr.
First floor

GEORGIA:

Atlanta
Richard B. Russell Federal Bldg.
75 Spring St., SW
Main lobby, plaza level

HAWAII:

Honolulu
Federal Bldg.
300 Ala Moana Blvd.
Rm. 5316

Fort Shafter
Department of Army, Army Civilian Personnel
Office, Army Garrison
Bldg. T-1500

ILLINOIS:

Chicago
77 W. Jackson Blvd.
First floor lobby

INDIANA:

Indianapolis
Minton-Capehart Federal Bldg.,
575 N. Pennsylvania St.
Rm. 339

LOUISIANA:	New Orleans Federal Bldg. 423 Canal St. First floor lobby
MAINE:	Augusta Federal Office Bldg. 40 Western Ave.
MARYLAND:	Baltimore George H. Fallon Bldg. Lombard St. & Hopkins Plaza Lobby
MASSACHUSETTS:	Boston Thomas P. O'Neill, Jr. Federal Bldg. 10 Causeway St. First floor
MICHIGAN:	Detroit 477 Michigan Ave. Rm. 565
MINNESOTA:	Twin Cities Bishop Henry Whipple Federal Bldg. 1 Federal Dr. Rm. 501 Ft. Snelling
MISSOURI:	Kansas City Federal Bldg. 601 E. 12th St. Rm. 134
NEW HAMPSHIRE:	Portsmouth Thomas McIntyre Federal Bldg. 80 Daniel St. First floor lobby
NEW JERSEY:	Newark Peter J. Rodino Federal Bldg. 970 Broad St. Second floor, near cafeteria
NEW MEXICO:	Albuquerque New Mexico State Job Service 501 Mountain Rd. NE Lobby
NEW YORK:	Albany Leo W. O'Brian Federal Bldg. Clinton Ave. & North Pearl Basement level Buffalo Thaddeus T. Dulski Federal Bldg. 111 W. Huron St. Ninth Floor

New York City
Jacob K. Javits Federal Bldg.
26 Federal Plaza
Lobby

New York City
World Trade Center
Cafeteria

Syracuse
James M. Hanley Federal Bldg.
100 S. Clinton St.

OHIO:

Dayton
Federal Bldg.
200 W. 2nd St.
Rm. 509

OKLAHOMA:

Oklahoma City
Career Connection Center
7401 NE 23rd St.

OREGON:

Portland
Federal Bldg.
1220 SW Third Ave.
Rm. 376

Bonneville Power Admin.
905 NE 11th Ave.

Dept. of Army & Corps of Engineers
Duncan Plaza

PENNSYLVANIA:

Harrisburg
Federal Bldg.
228 Walnut St.
Rm. 168

Philadelphia
William J. Green, Jr. Federal Bldg.
600 Arch St.
Second floor

Pittsburgh
Federal Bldg.
1000 Liberty Ave.
First floor lobby

Reading
Reading Postal Service
2100 N. 13th St.

PUERTO RICO:

San Juan
U.S. Federal Bldg.
150 Carlos Chardon Ave.
Rm. 328

RHODE ISLAND:	Providence 380 Westminster Mall lobby
TENNESSEE:	Memphis Naval Air Station Transition Assistance Center 7800 3rd Ave. Bldg. South 239, Millington
TEXAS:	Dallas Federal Bldg. 1100 Commerce St. First floor lobby
	El Paso Federal Bldg. 700 E. San Antonio St. Lobby
	Houston Mickey Leland Federal Bldg. 1919 Smith St. First floor lobby
	San Antonio Federal Bldg. 727 E. Durango First floor lobby
UTAH:	Salt Lake City Utah State Job Service 720 South 2nd East Reception area
VERMONT:	Burlington Federal Bldg. 11 Elmwood Ave. First floor lobby
VIRGINIA:	Norfolk Federal Bldg. 200 Granby St.
WASHINGTON:	Seattle Federal Bldg. 915 Second Ave. Rm. 110
WASHINGTON, D.C.:	Theodore Roosevelt Federal Bldg. 1900 E St., NW Rm. 1416

WEBLIOGRAPHY OF FEDERAL EMPLOYMENT WEB SITES

Job Listings

- **Employment Index: Local and State Government Agencies' Job Listings** (www.employmentindex.com/govjob.html)—Links to the Web sites of government agencies throughout the U.S. Lists public- and private-sector jobs.
- **Federal Government Job Hotline** (www.unl.edu/careers/jobs/fedhotl.htm)—Job hot lines for various federal agencies, from the University of Nebraska–Lincoln.
- **Federal Job Opportunities Bulletin Board** (fjob.opm.gov [Telnet] or ftp.fjob.opm.gov [File Transfer Protocol])—Current worldwide federal jobs, many with full announcements, salaries and pay rates, employment information, etc.; from the U.S. Office of Personnel Management. Your name and address can be left to have applications mailed to you. Accessible via dial-up (912-757-3100).
- **Government and Law Enforcement Jobs** (jobsearch.tqn.com/msubgov.htm)—An annotated list of Web sites that list jobs with federal, state, and local governments and law enforcement agencies, from the About.com Guide to Job Searching.
- **govtjobs.com** (www.govtjobs.com)—A list of jobs in the public sector.
- **HRS Federal Job Search** (www.hrsjobs.com)—A subscription job search and e-mail delivery service, which also has a lot of free information.
- **The Internet Job Source** (www.statejobs.com/fed.htm)—The Federal Jobs section of this site links to job listings at numerous federal agencies and also to online newspapers that list federal job opportunities.
- **Jobs in State Government** (usgovinfo.about.com/blstjobs.htm)—An index of state Web sites that list government employment opportunities, with sites ranging from About.com Guide to U.S. Government Info/Resources.
- **U.S. Postal Service: Human Resources** (www.usps.gov/hrisp)—A list of vacancies in management, supervisory, administrative, professional, and technical positions only.
- **USAJOBS** (www.usajobs.opm.gov)—The official site for worldwide federal employment listings from the U.S. Office of Personnel Management, with full text job announcements, forms, and answers to frequently asked questions.

Applications and Other Forms

- **Electronic Forms** (www.opm.gov/forms/index.htm)—All forms and applications relating to federal employment, from the Office of Personnel Management.
- **The Federal Job Search and Application Form** (www.usajobs.opm.gov/bla.htm)—A description of the federal job search as a three-step process, including three downloadable versions of the OF-612 job application form.

General Information

- **Career City: Government Jobs** (www.careercity.com/content/govcareer/index.asp)—A guide to federal and local government employment, with links to job listings.
- **Federal Salaries and Wages** (www.opm.gov/oca/payrates/index.htm)—Rates from the U.S. Office of Personnel Management Web site.
- **The Federal Web Locator** (www.vcilp.org/Fed-Agency/fedwebloc.html#toc)—Links to agencies in all branches of the federal government, including federal independent establishments and government corporations.
- **Public Service Employees Network** (www.pse-net.com/)—A guide to government employment, including job listings.
- **The U.S. Office of Personnel Management Web Site** (www.opm.gov)—Tons of information on all aspects of federal employment, with an index to make navigation easier.

Online Publications

- **Federal Jobs Digest Online** (www.jobsfed.com)—An online version of this well-known publication that provides job listings, federal employment news, and advice on how to get hired.
- **FederalTimes.com** (www.federaltimes.com/)—News of interest to those in the federal government.
- **FedForce** (www.clubfed.com/fedforce/fedforce.html)—Online service for federal employees, with free registration.
- **GovExec.com** (www.govexec.com)—An online publication from *Government Executive Magazine*, bringing news to federal executives and managers.

FEDERAL OCCUPATIONS THAT REQUIRE EXAMINATIONS

Test requirements are for competitive and outside-the-register appointments only, unless otherwise specified. This list does not reflect special examining provisions.

ACWA (Administrative Careers With America) examinations refer to positions that meet the criteria for ACWA.

Series	Title/Position(s)	Grade(s)	ACWA	Written	Performance
011	Bond Sales Promotion	5/7	•		
018	Safety and Occupational Health Management	5/7	•		
019	Safety Technician	2/3		•	
023	Outdoor Recreation Planning	5/7	•		
025	Park Ranger	5/7	•		
028	Environmental Protection Specialist	5/7	•		
029	Environmental Protection Assistant	2/3/4		•	
072	Fingerprint Identification	2/3/4		•	
080	Security Administration	5/7	•		
082	United States Marshal	5/7		•	
083	Police	2		•	
083	Park Police	5		•	
083a	Police (Secret Service)	4/5		•	
085	Security Guard	2		•	
086	Security Clerical and Assistance	2/3/4		•	
105	Social Insurance Administration	5/7	•		
106	Unemployment Insurance	5/7	•		
132	Intelligence	5/7	•		
134	Intelligence Aide and Clerk	2/3/4		•	
142	Manpower Development	5/7	•		
181	Psychology Aide and Technician	2/3		•	
186	Social Services Aide and Assistant	2/3		•	
187	Social Services	5/7	•		
189	Recreation Aide and Assistant	2/3		•	
201	Personnel Management	5/7	•		
203	Personnel Clerical and Assistance	2/3/4		•	
204	Military Personnel Clerical and Technician	2/3/4		•	
205	Military Personnel Management	5/7	•		
212	Personnel Staffing	5/7	•		
221	Position Classification	5/7	•		
222	Occupational Analysis	5/7	•		
223	Salary and Wage Administration	5/7	•		
230	Employee Relations	5/7	•		
233	Labor Relations	5/7	•		

			Type of Exam		
Series	Title/Position(s)	Grade(s)	ACWA	Written	Performance
235	Employee Development	5/7	•		
244	Labor Management Relations Examining	5/7	•		
246	Contractor Industrial Relations	5/7	•		
249	Wage and Hour Compliance	5/7	•		
270	Federal Retirement Benefits	5/7	•		
301	Misc. Administration and Program	5/7	•		
302	Messenger	2/3/4		•	
303	Misc. Clerk and Assistant	2/3/4		•	
304	Information Receptionist	2/3/4		•	
305	Mail and File	2/3/4		•	
309	Correspondence Clerk	2/3/4		•	
312	Clerk-Stenographer	3/4/5		•	•
312	Reporting Stenographer	5/6			*
312	Shorthand Reporter	6/7/8/9			*
318	Secretary	3/4		•	
319	Closed Microphone Reporting	6/7/8/9			*
322	Clerk-Typist	2/3/4		•	•
326	Office Automation Clerical and Assistance	2/3/4		•	•
332	Computer Operator	2/3/4		•	
334	Computer Specialist	5/7	• (for alternative B only)		
335	Computer Clerk and Assistant	2/3/4		•	
341	Administrative Officer	5/7	•		
343	Management and Program Analysis	5/7	•		
344	Management and Program Clerical and Assistance	2/3/4		•	
346	Logistics Management	5/7	•		
350	Equipment Operator	2/3/4		•	
351	Printing Clerical	2/3/4		•	
356	Data Transcriber	2/3/4		•	•
357	Coding	2/3/4		•	
359	Electric Accounting Machine Operator	2/3/4		•	
382	Telephone Operating	2/3/4		•	
390	Telecommunications Processing	2/3/4		•	
391	Telecommunications	5/7	•		
392	General Telecommunications	2/3/4		•	
394	Communications Clerical	2/3/4		•	
404	Biological Science Technician	2/3		•	
421	Plant Protection Technician	2/3		•	
455	Range Technician	2/3		•	
458	Soil Conservation Technician	2/3		•	
459	Irrigation System Operation	2/3		•	
462	Forestry Technician	2/3		•	
501	Financial Administration and Program	5/7	•		
503	Financial Clerical and Assistance	2/3/4		•	

Series	Title/Position(s)	Grade(s)	ACWA	Written	Performance
				Type of Exam	
525	Accounting Technician	2/3/4		•	
526	Tax Technician	5/7	•		
530	Cash Processing	2/3/4		•	
540	Voucher Examining	2/3/4		•	
544	Civilian Pay	2/3/4		•	
545	Military Pay	2/3/4		•	
560	Budget Analysis	5/7	•		
561	Budget Clerical and Assistance	2/3/4		•	
570	Financial Institution Examining	5/7	•		
		(except for			
		FDIC positions)			
592	Tax Examining	2/3/4		•	
593	Insurance Accounts	2/3/4		•	
621	Nursing Assistant	2/3		•	
636	Rehabilitation Therapy Assistant	2/3		•	
640	Health Aide and Technician	2/3		•	
642	Nuclear Medicine Technician	2/3		•	
645	Medical Technician	2/3		•	
646	Pathology Technician	2/3		•	
647	Diagnostic Radiologic Technologist	2/3		•	
648	Therapeutic Radiologic Technologist	2/3		•	
649	Medical Instrument Technician	2/3		•	
651	Respiratory Therapist	2/3		•	
661	Pharmacy Technician	2/3		•	
667	Orthotist and Prosthetist	3		•	
673	Hospital Housekeeping Management	5/7	•		
675	Medical Records Technician	2/3/4		•	
679	Medical Clerk	2/3/4		•	
681	Dental Assistant	2/3		•	
683	Dental Lab Aide and Technician	2/3		•	
685	Public Health Program Specialist	5/7	•		
698	Environmental Health Technician	2/3		•	
704	Animal Health Technician	2/3		•	
802	Engineering Technician	2/3		•	
809	Construction Control	2/3		•	
817	Surveying Technician	2/3		•	
818	Engineering Drafting	2/3		•	
856	Electronics Technician	2/3		•	
895	Industrial Engineering Technician	2/3		•	
950	Paralegal Specialist	5/7	•		
958	Pension Law Specialist	5/7	•		
962	Contact Representative	3/4		•	
962	Contact Representative	5/7	•		
963	Legal Instruments Examining	2/3/4		•	
965	Land Law Examining	5/7	•		

Series	Title/Position(s)	Grade(s)	Type of Exam		
			ACWA	Written	Performance
967	Passport and Visa Examining	5/7	•		
986	Legal Clerk and Technician	2/3/4		•	
987	Tax Law Specialist	5/7	•		
990	General Claims Examining (One-grade interval)	4		•	
990	General Claims Examining (Two-grade interval)	5/7	•		
991	Workers' Comp. Claims Examining	5/7	•		
993	Social Insurance Claims Examining	4		•	
993	Railroad Retirement Claims Examining	5/7	•		
994	Unemployment Comp. Claims Examining	5/7	•		
996	Veterans Claims Examining	5/7	•		
998	Claims Clerical	2/3/4		•	
1001	General Arts and Information	2/3/4		•	
1001	General Arts and Information	5/7	•		
			(except fine arts positions)		
1016	Museum Specialist and Technician	2/3		•	
1021	Office Drafting	2/3		•	
1035	Public Affairs	5/7	•		
1046	Language Clerical	2/3/4		•	
1082	Writing and Editing	5/7	•		
1083	Technical Writing and Editing	5/7	•		
1087	Editorial Assistance	2/3/4		•	
1101	General Business and Industry	2/3/4		•	
1101	General Business and Industry	5/7	•		
1101	International Trade Analyst	5/7	•		
1102	Contracting	5/7	•		
1103	Industrial Property Management	5/7	•		
1104	Property Disposal	5/7	•		
1105	Purchasing	2/3/4		•	
1106	Procurement Clerical and Technician	2/3/4		•	
1107	Property Disposal Clerical and Technician	2/3/4		•	
1130	Public Utilities Specialist	5/7	•		
1140	Trade Specialist	5/7	•		
1140	International Trade Specialist	5/7	•		
1145	Agricultural Program Specialist	5/7	•		
1146	Agricultural Marketing	5/7	•		
1146	Grain Marketing Specialist	5/7	•		
1147	Agricultural Market Reporting	5/7	•		
1150	Industrial Specialist	5/7	•		
1152	Production Control	2/3/4		•	
1160	Financial Analysis	5/7	•		
1163	Insurance Examining	5/7	•		
1165	Loan Specialist	5/7	•		
1169	Internal Revenue Officer	5/7	•		
1170	Realty	5/7	•		

			Type of Exam		
Series	Title/Position(s)	Grade(s)	ACWA	Written	Performance
1171	Appraising and Assessing	5/7	•		
1173	Housing Management	5/7	•		
1176	Building Management	5/7	•		
1311	Physical Science Technician	2/3		•	
1316	Hydrologic Technician	2/3		•	
1341	Meteorological Technician	2/3		•	
1371	Cartographic Technician	2/3		•	
1374	Geodetic Technician	2/3		•	
1410	Librarian	7/9		• (for applicants who do not meet certain educational requirements)	
1411	Library Technician	2/3/4		•	
1412	Technical Information Services	5/7	•		
1421	Archives Specialist	5/7	•		
1421	Archives Technician	2/3/4		•	
1521	Mathematics Technician	2/3		•	
1531	Statistical Assistant	2/3/4		•	
1541	Cryptanalysis	2/3		•	
1702	Education and Training Technician	2/3		•	
1715	Vocational Rehabilitation	5/7	•		
1801	Civil Aviation Security Specialist	5/7	•		
1801	Center Adjudications Officer	5/7	•		
1801	District Adjudications Officer	5/7	•		
1802	Compliance Inspection and Support	2/3/4		• (except Detention Enforcement Officer positions)	
1810	General Investigating	5/7	•		
1811	Criminal Investigating	5/7	•		
1811	Treasury Enforcement Agent	5/7		•	
1812	Game Law Enforcement	5/7	•		
1812	Special Agent (Wildlife)	7		•	
1816	Immigration Inspection	5/7	•		
1831	Securities Compliance Examining	5/7	•		
1854	Alcohol, Tobacco, and Firearms Inspection	5/7	•		
1863	Food Inspection	5/7		•	
1864	Public Health Quarantine Inspection	5/7	•		
1884	Customs Patrol Officer	5/7		•	
1889	Import Specialist	5/7	•		
1890	Customs Inspection	5/7	•		
1896	Border Patrol Agent	5/7		• (and language proficiency)	

Series	Title/Position(s)	Grade(s)	Type of Exam		
			ACWA	Written	Performance
1897	Customs Aid	2/3/4		•	
1910	Quality Assurance	5/7	•		
1981	Agricultural Commodity Aid	2/3		•	
2001	General Supply	5/7	•		
2003	Supply Program Management	5/7	•		
2005	Supply Clerical and Technician	2/3/4		•	
2010	Inventory Management	5/7	•		
2030	Distribution Facilities and Storage Management	5/7	•		
2032	Packaging	5/7	•		
2050	Supply Cataloging	5/7	•		
2091	Sales Store Clerical	2/3/4		•	
2101	Transportation Specialist	5/7	•		
2101	Airway Transportation System Specialist (Department of Transportation Federal Aviation Administration)	5/7		•	
2102	Transportation Clerk and Assistant	2/3/4		•	
2110	Transportation Industry Analysis	5/7	•		
2125	Highway Safety	5/7	•		
2130	Traffic Management	5/7	•		
2131	Freight Rate	2/3/4		•	
2135	Transportation Loss and Damage Claims Examining	2/3/4		•	
2150	Transportation Operations	5/7	•		
2151	Dispatching	2/3/4		•	
2152	Air Traffic Control	5/7		•	
				(optional above 7)	

* Mandatory for competitive appointment and in-service placement

GLOSSARY OF CIVIL SERVICE HIRING TERMINOLOGY

When you're reading the announcement and filling out your application, you need to understand the government's hiring terminology. Take a few minutes to familiarize yourself with the words listed below. These are very common terms used repeatedly, both in the announcements and in any correspondence or conversation you may have with the federal civil service.

Career status   To be considered a *status employee*, a federal employee must have served for at least three consecutive years in a permanent position.

Certificate of Eligibles   This refers to the list of eligible candidates that results from responses to a vacancy announcement and an application process.

Competitive service   Most positions in the federal government that are subject to Title 5, U.S. Code, meaning that candidates compete for entrance with other non-status applicants.

Continuously open positions   Positions that are open for an indefinite period. These positions, however, may be closed by the agency at any time.

Eligibles   Refers to qualified employees.

Excepted service   Most positions in the legislative and judicial branches, and some in the executive branch, which are not in the *competitive service*.

Federal Wage System   The classification used for trade and labor jobs in the federal government.

FWS   See *Federal Wage System*.

General Schedule   The classification for white-collar jobs in the federal government.

Grade   Each pay category; *WG* is used to indicate pay categories for *Federal Wage System* (WS) jobs, while *GS* is used to indicated categories for *General Schedule* jobs.

GS   See *General Schedule* and also *Grade*.

High-3 average salary   Used to determine retirement benefits, this term refers to the average of your highest basic pay over any three years of consecutive service.

Job family   Grouping of occupations in the *Federal Wage System* that are related in either similarity of functions performed, transferability of knowledge and skills, or similarity of material or equipment worked on.

Merit Promotion System   This system helps determine whether current employees will be promoted within the federal government's competitive service.

Occupation   Includes all jobs at the various skill levels in a particular kind of work.

Occupational groups   Related occupations in the *General Schedule (GS)* that are grouped together within the same multiple of 100, i.e. GS-100, 200, 300, etc.

OF-612   The Optional Application for Federal Employment.

Pay comparability   Federal salaries, by law, are based on a comparison with private-sector jobs.

Probationary period   A trial period before a new employee becomes permanent.

Rating and ranking   Job candidates are evaluated and placed on a *Certificate of Eligibles* in score order.

Register   A list of qualified applicants for a specific occupation.

Reinstatement eligibility   This provision allows former federal employees to apply for jobs that are open to *status employees*.

Senior Executive Service   Top management in federal agencies.

Series   All jobs in a subgroup of an *occupational group* that are related by subject matter, basic knowledge, and skill requirements. Includes jobs at various skill levels.

SF-171   An application form used for federal employment.

Status employee   An employee with *career status* is eligible to apply for other federal jobs based on current service or reinstatement eligibility.

Temporary appointment   An appointment that lasts one year or less and has a specific expiration date.

Term appointment   An appointment that lasts for over one year and up to four years.

Veterans preference   Veterans receive preference points that are added to their scores when competing for federal jobs.

WG   See *Grade*.

Within-Grade Step Increases   Pay increases indicated by 10 steps within each *grade*. Steps are based on performance and time in grade.